THE SINGAPORE RIVER

THE SINGAPORE RIVER

A Social History 1819–2002

Stephen Dobbs

NUS PRESS
SINGAPORE

Published in 2003 by Singapore University Press.

NUS Press
National University of Singapore
AS3-01-02, 3 Arts Link
Singapore 117569
Fax: (65) 6774-0652
E-mail: nusbooks@nus.edu.sg
Website: http://nuspress.nus.edu.sg

ISBN: 978-981-4722-25-4 (Paper)

Reprint 2016
Reprint 2019

Typeset by: Scientifik Graphics (Singapore) Pte Ltd
Printed by: Markono Print Media Pte Ltd

To

Normah, Omar, Rasidah and Rafie

Contents

Maps, Plates and Figures

MAPS

PLATES

FIGURES

Abbreviations

BMA	British Military Administration
CCVS	Certificate of Coroners' Views Singapore
CO	Colonial Office Records
COBSEA	Coordinating Body on the Seas of East Asia
CSO	Colonial Secretary's Office
ENV	Ministry of the Environment
HDB	Housing Development Board
PSA	Port of Singapore Authority
PWD	Public Works Department
SSR	Straits Settlements Records
TVWA	Transport Vessel Workers Association
URA	Urban Redevelopment Authority

Acknowledgements

THIS book has been a work in 'progress' for more than a decade. Just as the Singapore River continues to evolve so has this study. It was made possible in the first instance by the grant of a Scholarship from Murdoch University. A year's fieldwork in Singapore was funded by an Australian Vice-Chancellors' Committee Award. Thanks is also due to the School of Social and Cultural Studies, at the University of Western Australia, for making available travel funds in February 2002 to enable me to visit Singapore and conduct further research toward concluding this study.

Initial field work for this study was carried out between 1993 and 1994 and I extend my thanks to the Institute of Southeast Asian Studies in Singapore for their support during this time. The 'free' office space they provided and general support in arranging visas and the like were invaluable aids in getting started on the project. Three individuals at the institute who offered friendship and support for the study deserve special mention, Patricia Lim, Diana Wong and Yao Souchou. A similar thanks goes out to a number of people who assisted me at the Singapore National Archive and Oral History Department. In particular Tan Beng Luan and Daniel Chew who made time to discuss with me various issues relative to the sources when asked. Also, David Chng for extending his friendship and opening his door at the archive to me. A special thanks is also extended to Iskander Mydin at the National Museum. Through his help I was able to gain access to materials which otherwise would have been overlooked.

There are many other individuals who have given me support and I mention only a few here. Firstly, Hau Boon Lai for assisting me to retrieve relevant material from Oral History Department interviews. Also, lighter owners Chang Ham Chwee and Ow Chin Seng, for making themselves available for exhaustive questioning and providing access to staff for similar 'encounters'. Particular thanks is extended to Ng Hwee Poh, English Secretary for the Lighter Owners Association, for his efforts in helping me to conduct interviews, often outside of his normal working hours. I thank too C. P. Wong and Ong Ah Cheng for their help and assistance — especially, with respect to working conditions for lightermen and the role played by the Transport Vessel Workers Association. A special thank you goes to Lee Kip Lin for allowing me access to his collection of historical records and photographs, a remarkable private effort which rivals that of the National Archive. Also, Professor James Warren for his unwavering support of this project over the years as well as his thoughtful and constructive commentary on all aspects of the study. A special thanks is owed to Dr Carolyn Brewer for her comments, editing skills and most importantly friendship throughout this process.

Finally, I extend my thanks and gratitude to my family. To my partner, Normah, for financial and moral support especially at those moments when it all seemed exceptionally difficult, and to our children, Omar, Rasidah and Rafic who have grown up with this project and wonder if 'school' ever comes to an end.

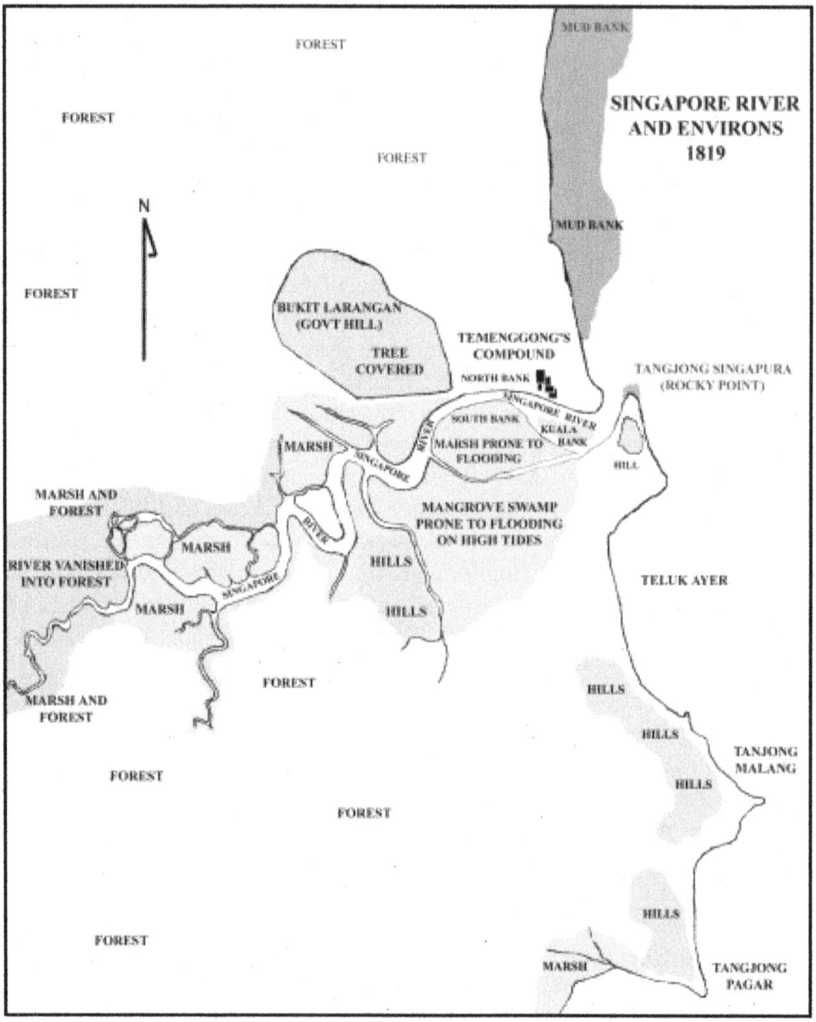

MAP 1 Singapore River and Environs 1819 (topographical details for this map were obtained by examining a number of early charts of Singapore and descriptions of the scene from various sources quoted in the text).

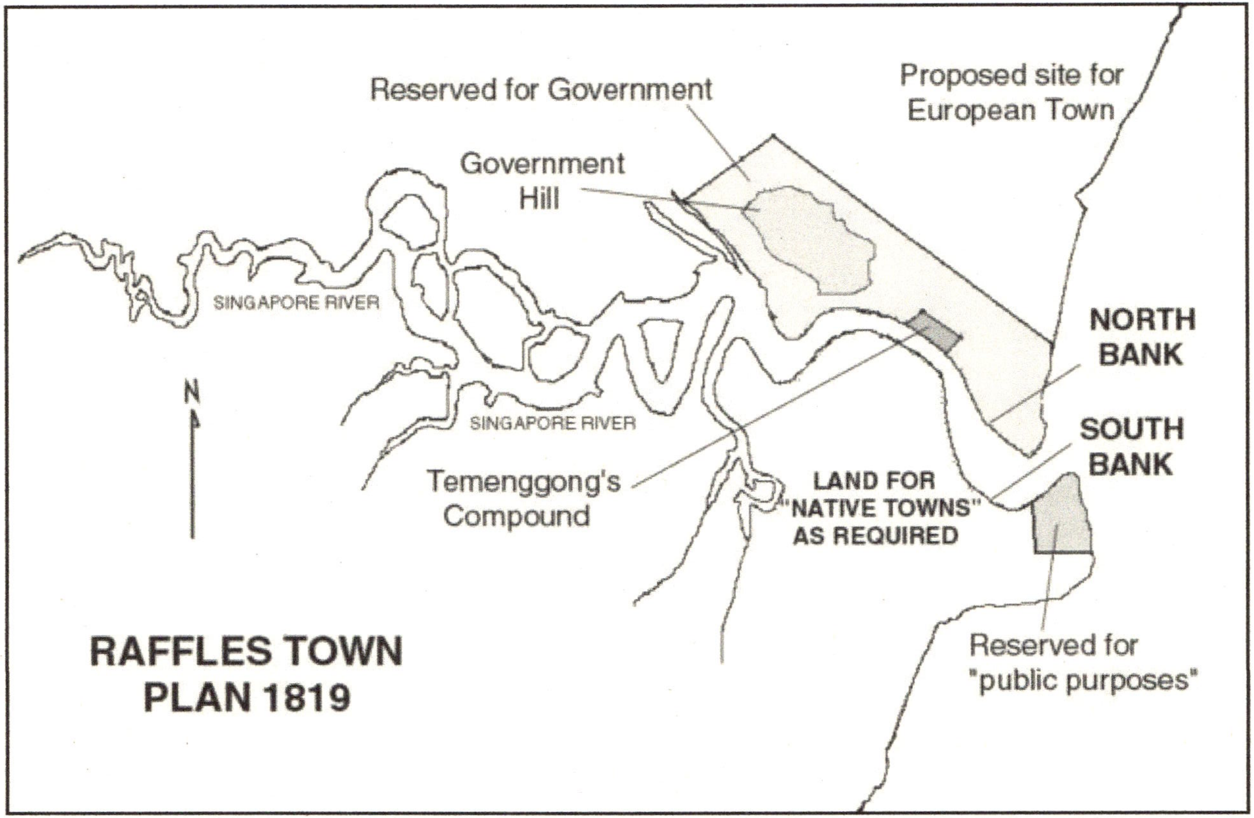

MAP 2 Raffles' Town Plan 1819 (SSR, L10, pp. 71–75; Raffles to Farquhar 25/6/1819; C Buckley, *An Anecdotal History of Old Times in Singapore 1819–1867* [Kuala Lumpur: University of Malaya Press, 1965]).

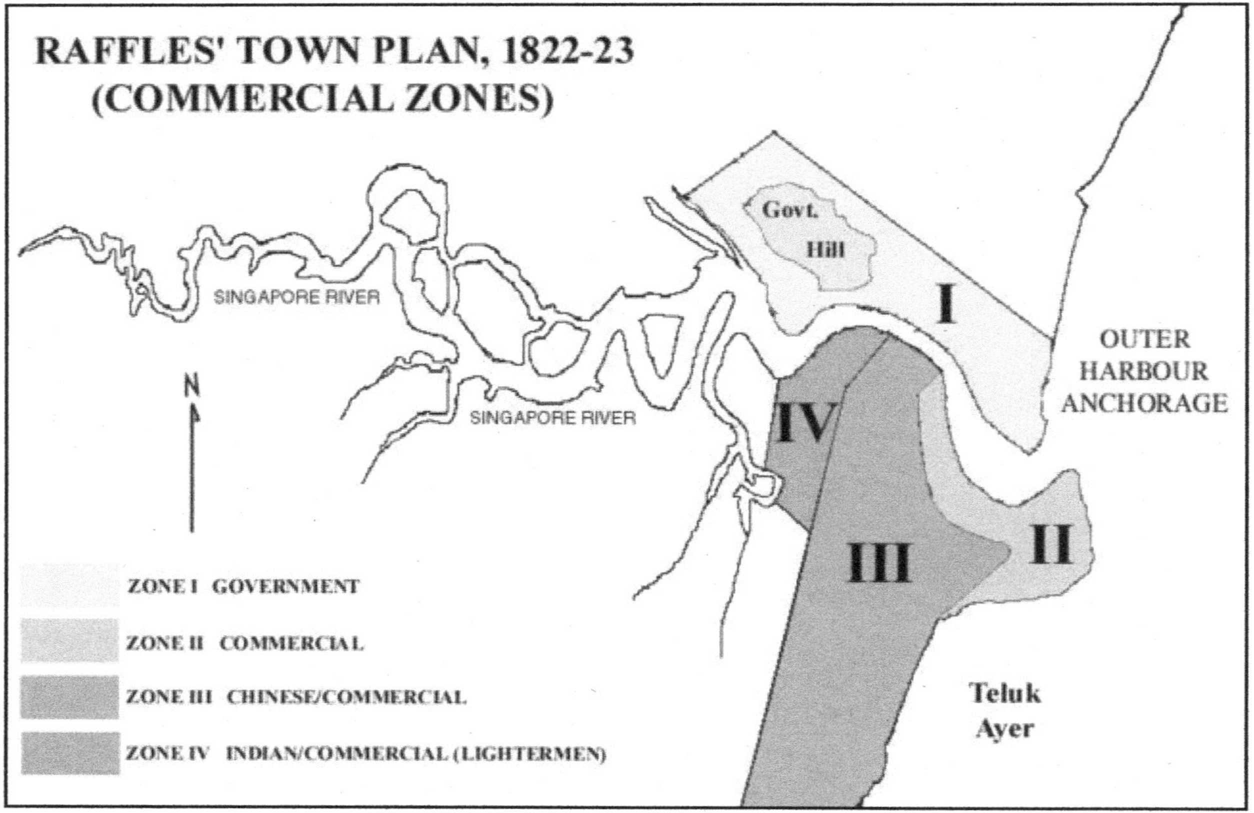

MAP 3 Raffles' Town Plan, 1822–23 (Commercial Zones); (SSR, L17, Various Correspondence, Nov. 1822 – Feb. 1823; Buckley, *An Anecdotal History of Old Times*).

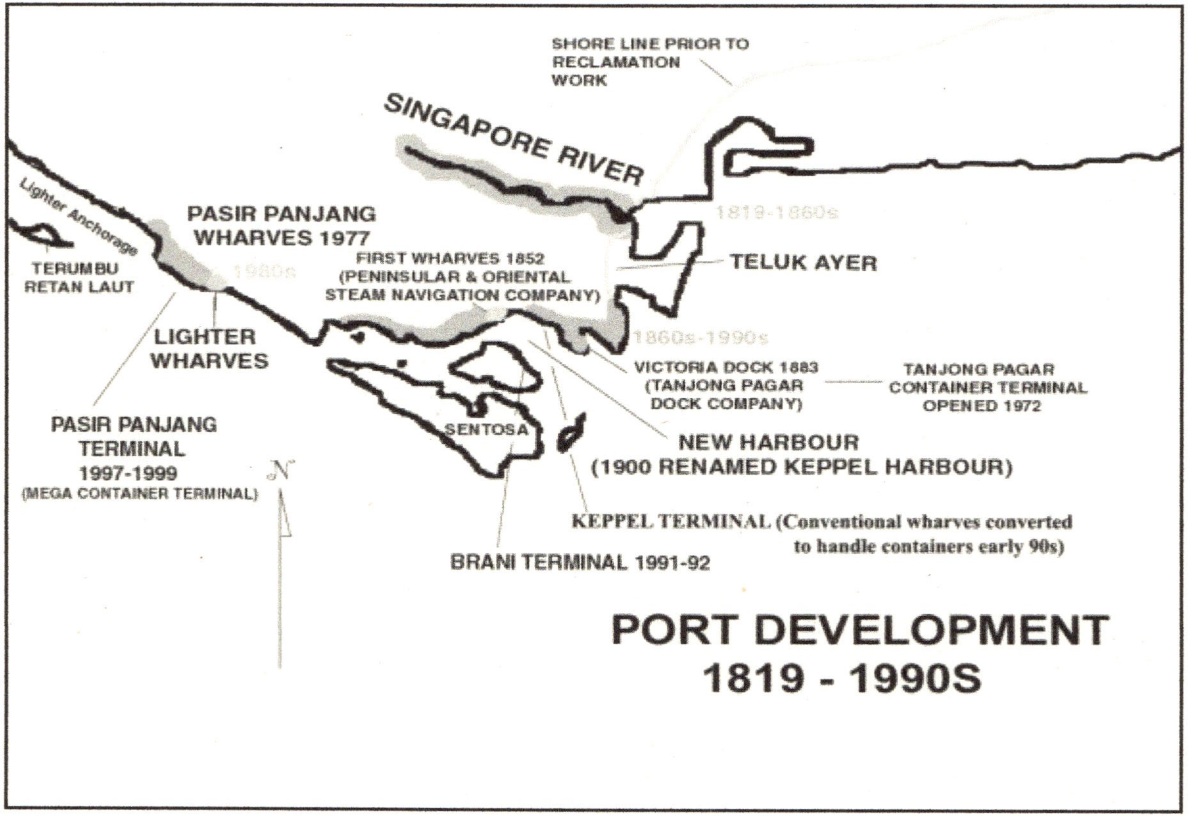

MAP 4 Port Development, 1819–1990s (map based on various sources quoted throughout the text).

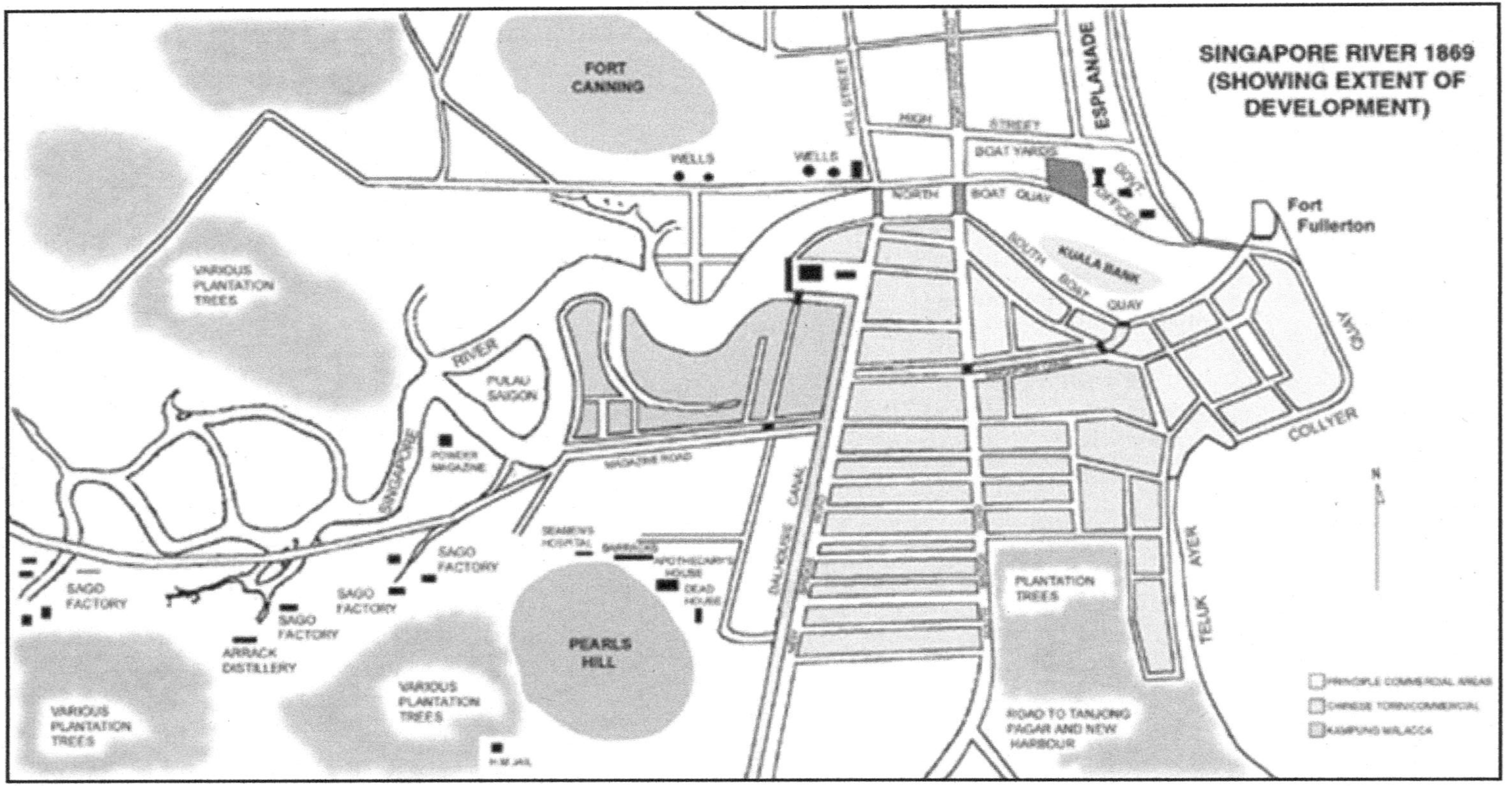

MAP 5 Singapore River 1869 (showing extent of development) ("A General Plan of the Town and Environs of Singapore", 1857; "Singapore Roads", Survey 1864, Admiralty, London, 1891).

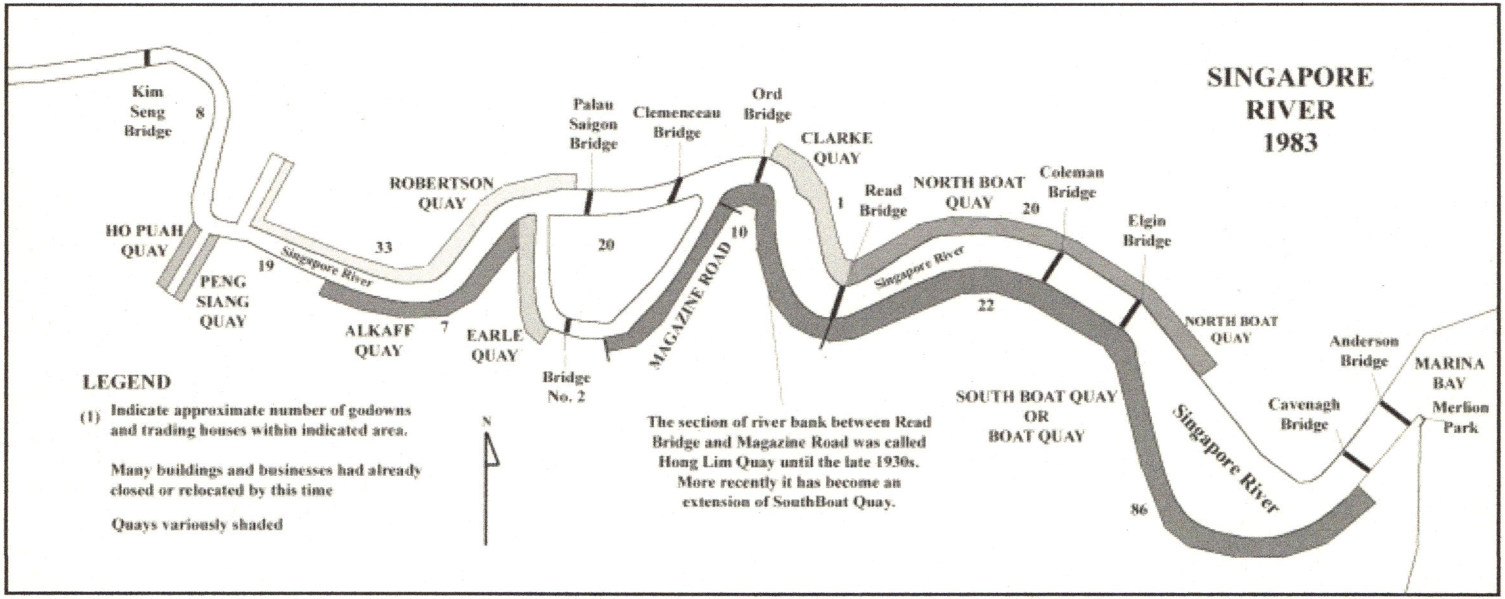

MAP 6 Singapore River 1983 (showing extent of development) (1983 Street Directory; Yap Aik Kun, *The Singapore River: Economic Landscape in Retrospect*, Academic Exercise, Department of Geography, National University of Singapore, 1983/84).

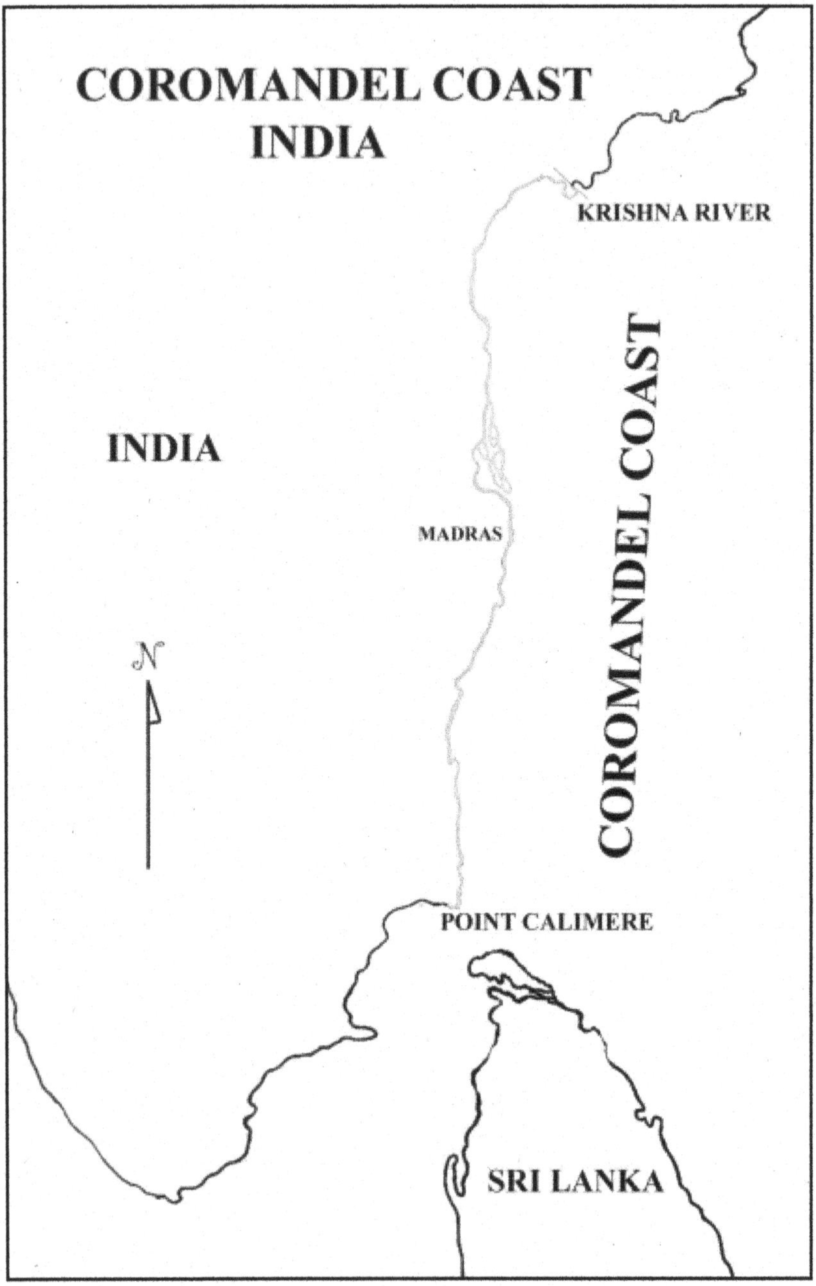

MAP 7 Coromandel Coast India.

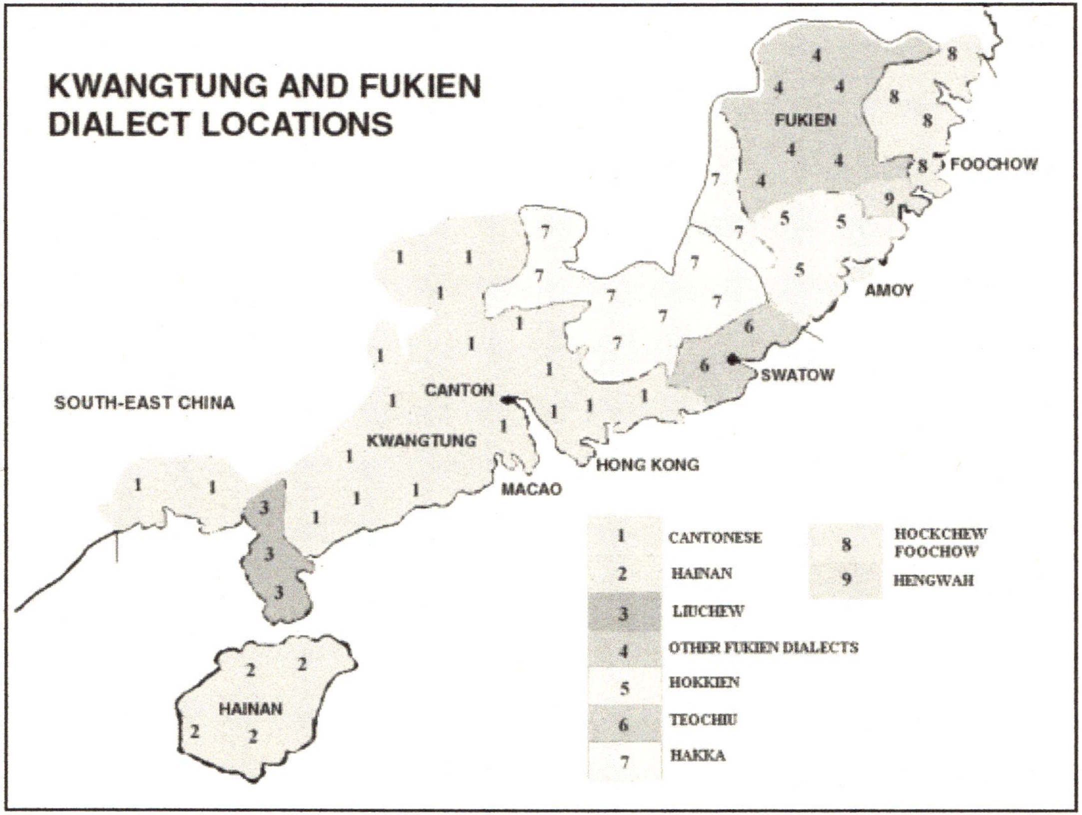

MAP 8 Kwangtung and Fukien Dialect Locations (James Warren, *Rickshaw Coolie: A People's History of Singapore 1880–1940* [Singapore: Oxford University Press, 1986]).

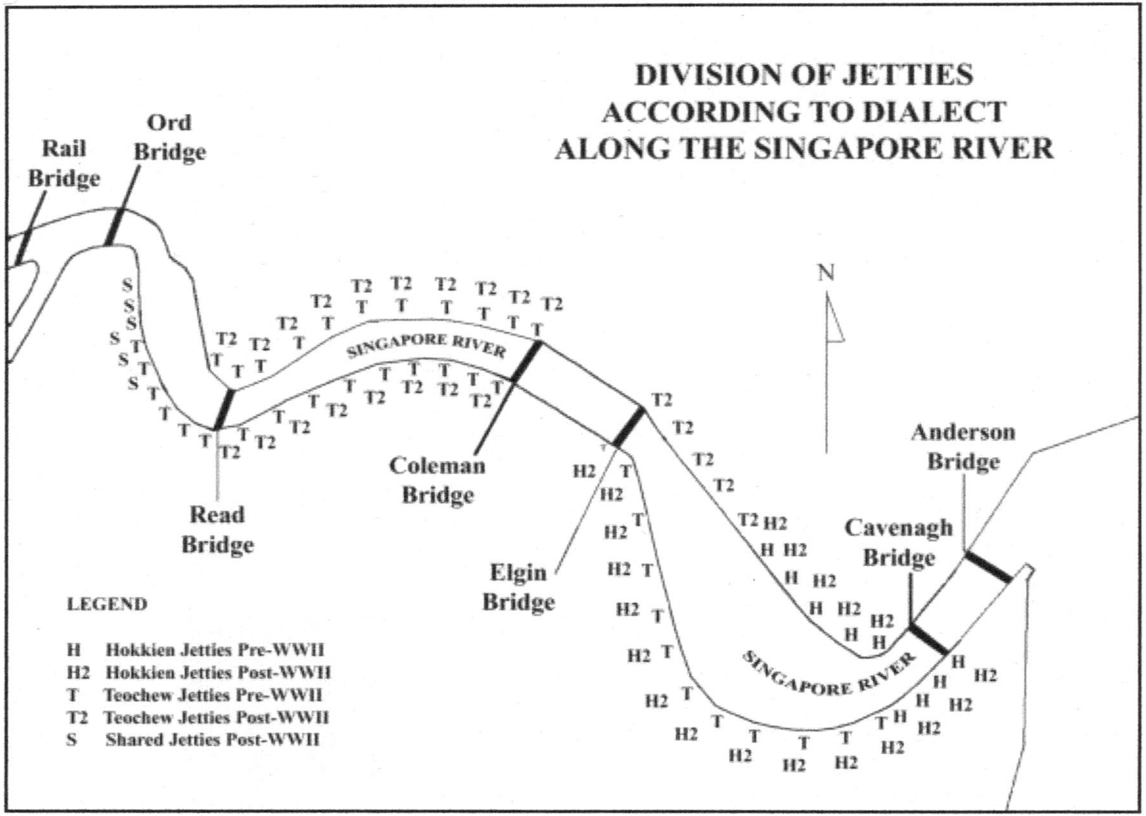

MAP 9 Dialect Distribution Along River 1900–1980s (Details based on interviews and *Singapore Lifeline: The River and Its People* [Singapore: Times Books International, 1986]).

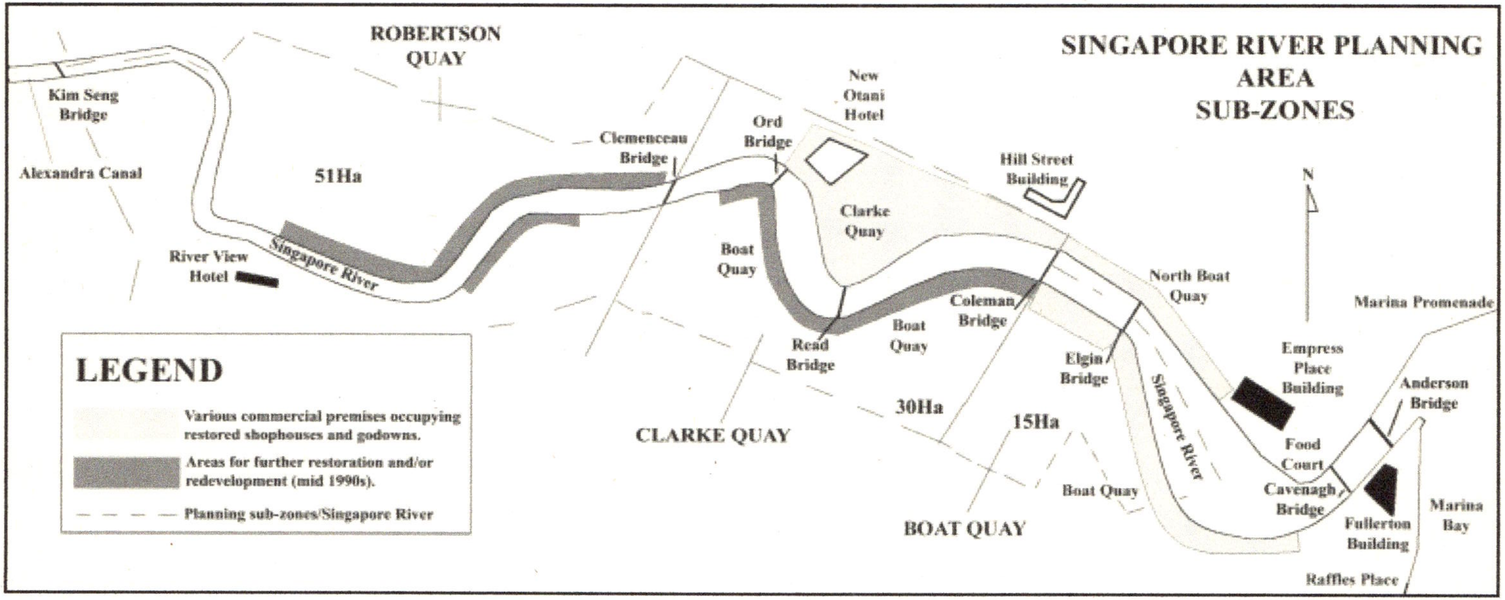

MAP 10 Singapore River Planning Area Sub-Zones (Details based on observations made in 1993–94; Singapore River Planning Report, 1994, Urban Redevelopment Authority of Singapore).

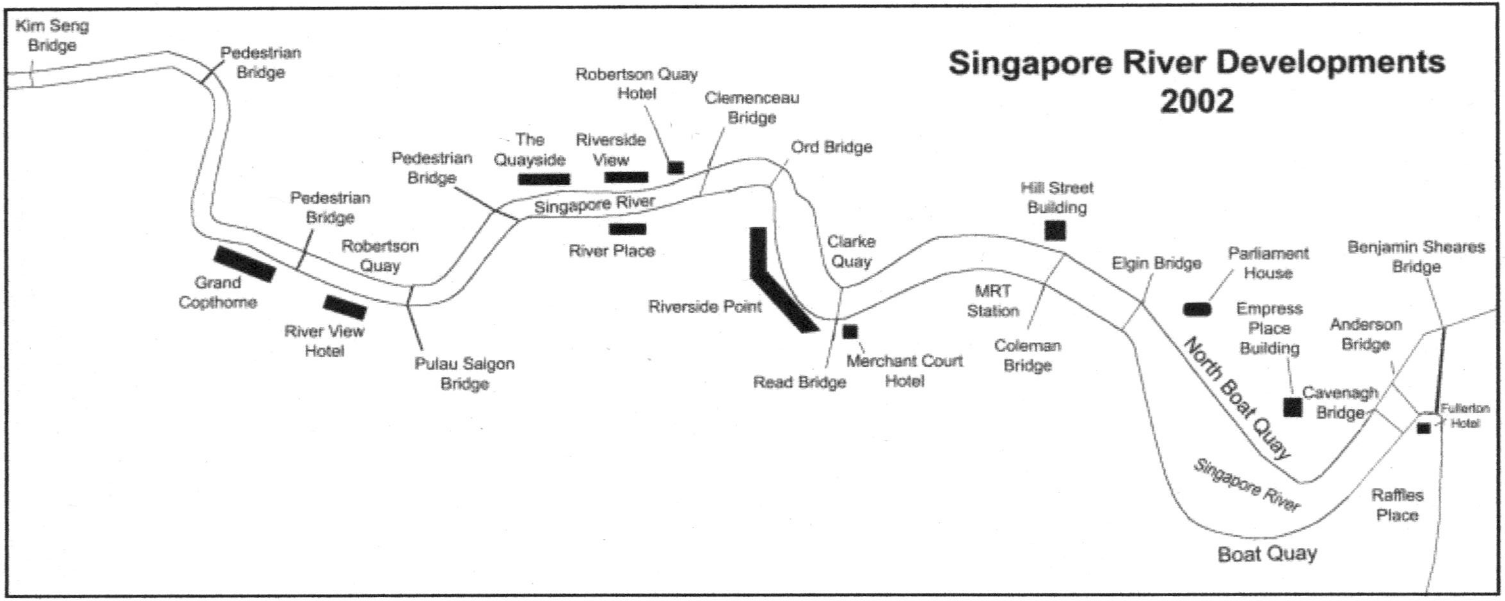

MAP 11 Singapore River Developments 2002.

PLATE 1 Draw Bridge Singapore River (John A Heraud, *Voyages and Memoirs of a Midshipman* [London: James Fraser, 1837]).

PLATE 2 1860s View of River (Albert S Bickmore, *Travels in the East Indian Archipelago* [London, 1868]).

PLATE 3 River Mouth Around 1900 (post-card).

PLATE 4 Boat Quay Around 1900 (Courtesy of National Museum, Singapore).

PLATE 5 North Boat Quay (Courtesy of National Museum, Singapore).

PLATE 6 Teluk Ayer (Courtesy of National Museum, Singapore).

PLATE 7 Clarke Quay 1920s (post-card).

PLATE 8 Bullock Carts Along South Boat Quay (post-card).

PLATE 9 River Scene Clarke Quay 1965 (Courtesy of Urban Redevelopment Authority, Singapore).

PLATE 10 River Scene Robertson Quay (Courtesy of Urban Redevelopment Authority, Singapore).

PLATE 11 View of Robertson Quay 1967 (Courtesy of Urban Redevelopment Authority, Singapore).

PLATE 12 Upper Reaches of River 1967 (Courtesy of Urban Redevelopment Authority, Singapore).

PLATE 13 Quiet Waters (Courtesy of Urban Redevelopment Authority, Singapore).

PLATE 14 Twakow near Clarke Quay (Courtesy of Urban Redevelopment Authority, Singapore).

PLATE 15 Twakow Loading 1967 (Courtesy of Urban Redevelopment Authority, Singapore).

PLATE 16 Twakow at Work near Clarke Quay 1967 (Courtesy of Urban Redevelopment Authority, Singapore).

PLATE 17 Loading Twakow North Boat Quay 1971 (Courtesy of Urban Redevelopment Authority, Singapore).

PLATE 18 Twakow Standing Off River Quay 1975 (Courtesy of Urban Redevelopment Authority, Singapore).

PLATE 19 Clarke Quay 1982 (Courtesy of Urban Redevelopment Authority, Singapore).

PLATE 20 Boat Quay 1982 (Courtesy of Urban Redevelopment Authority, Singapore).

PLATE 21 Lighters Loading Off South Boat Quay (Courtesy of Urban Redevelopment Authority, Singapore).

PLATE 22 Cluster of Lighters and Squatters along River (Courtesy of Urban Redevelopment Authority, Singapore).

PLATE 23 Heavily Laden Twakow (Courtesy of Urban Redevelopment Authority, Singapore).

PLATE 24 Twakow at Rest (Courtesy of Urban Redevelopment Authority, Singapore).

PLATE 25 Polluted Waters of River (Courtesy of Urban Redevelopment Authority, Singapore).

PLATE 26 Squatting Under Bridge (Courtesy of Urban Redevelopment Authority, Singapore).

PLATE 27 Boat Quay Restoration 1993 (Dobbs).

PLATE 28 Clarke Quay Restorations 1993 (Dobbs).

PLATE 29 Lighters Along Wharf at Pasir Panjang (Dobbs).

PLATE 30 Unloading at Pasir Panjang (Dobbs).

PLATE 31 Lighters Alongside Ship 1993 (Dobbs).

PLATE 32 Loading Rice 1993 (Dobbs).

PLATE 33 Boat Quay 2002 (Dobbs).

PLATE 34 Twakow at Clarke Quay 2002 (Dobbs).

PLATE 35 Fullerton Hotel 2002 (Dobbs).

PLATE 36 Riverside Point 2002 (Dobbs).

PLATE 37 South Boat Quay Looking to Fullerton Hotel (Dobbs).

PLATE 38 Water Taxi (Dobbs).

PLATE 39 Riverside Condominiums 2002 (Dobbs).

PLATE 40 Merchant Court Hotel 2002 (Dobbs).

PLATE 41 River Mouth — Three Bridges 1997 (Courtesy of Rahim).

PLATE 42 River End 2002 (Dobbs).

PLATE 43 Transport Vessel Workers Association — Offices (Courtesy of Ong Ah Cheng).

PLATE 44 Union Meeting 1970s (Courtesy of Ong Ah Cheng).

PART ONE

The Singapore River and City

1
Introduction: The Old and the New

THE Singapore River flowing through the administrative and business heart of the city is in many respects exemplary of the island state's rapid development and progress. In the past two decades the river has transformed from a heavily polluted industrial and port area to a fashionable neighbourhood, its banks lined with exclusive condominiums and modern commercial premises. Many of the buildings along Clarke Quay and Boat Quay are conservation properties restored to retain elements of their historical character while serving new uses. This recent transformation of the river district has introduced a new era of economic activity and marks a clear break with the past.

For many years after the establishment of the British settlement in Singapore in 1819, to speak of Singapore was to speak of the river. It was the physical center of town and the great bulk of goods traded in the settlement were handled on its banks. Even as new port facilities at Keppel Harbour came into commission in the later years of the nineteenth century, the amount of trade goods that passed through the Singapore River continued to grow until at least the late 1950s. The waters of the river were at the heart of the island's trading activities. Colourfully painted vessels called lighters, ranging in size from a few tonnes to more than 150 tonnes, crammed the confined waters of the river. They carried valuable trade goods from ships in the outer harbour to quays along the river, at times forming a virtual impenetrable blanket over its waters. A resident community of lightermen loaded a seemingly endless array of goods bound for the Southeast Asian region into these lighters of Indian and Chinese design, *tongkang* and *twakow*.

The Singapore River, cleared of these trading activities and hemmed in by office towers, condos, international restaurants, clubs and bars, now seems somewhat overshadowed. The waters of the river are today only disturbed by occasional water taxi, and the sounds of urban traffic and high rise construction on nearby building sites. Yet the role of this tranquil waterway in the history of modern Singapore is comparable, in many respects, to that of other great rivers in lands around the globe. The Singapore River is no Amazon, Mississippi or Mekong. It does not link a vast hinterland area with the coast and its maximum navigable length is only some three kilometres. Its shallow depth and narrow breadth have never permitted the entry of large vessels, however, its importance to Singapore equals that of the great rivers of the world to the countries through which they flow. From the foundation of the colonial port city in 1819 until the removal of the last twakow in 1983, the river was a focal point for regional and international trade, and its history is inextricably bound to that of the island of Singapore and the evolution of this modern city state.

There is considerable evidence that the river played an important role in the history of pre-modern Singapore as well. Ancient fortifications described by Dr John Crawfurd in the 1820s are clear evidence of the island's political and economic significance at an earlier time. Crawfurd describes a fortification embankment with a breadth of five metres at its base and some eight to nine feet high running for a distance of 1.6 kilometres from the beach to Government Hill near the Singapore River. Centuries before the British East India Company established a trading factory at Singapore these fortifications were protecting a thriving community and port along the river.[1]

The history of the river and the lightermen, the men who crewed the vessels that plied its waters, are the primary focus of this study. The study highlights the critical role played by the river and lightermen in the development of Singapore as an entrepôt port and city, and encompasses the period from 1819, the founding of 'modern' Singapore, to the present. This time span marks a meaningful way of locating the river and the lightermen in the historical development of the present day city state of Singapore. The year 1819 marked a real break with the past for the island. Following Singapore's incorporation into the holdings of the East India Company, it was increasingly integrated into an expanding global and regional network of commerce with the river as its port centre. The river from 1819 until the early 1980s played an important part in Singapore's economic development. Now the lighters are gone and the maritime trade of Singapore is serviced by one of the world's most modern and efficient ports. The river continues, though, to be of economic importance, and a new trade has burgeoned along its banks. It has become the focal point of 'modern' recreational industries. Hotels, restaurants and theme park-like historical restorations now adorn the riverbanks, attracting a new commerce.

The river is not a mere physical entity, but constitutes an interdependent social, political and economic landscape and environment. It helped determine the location of the settlement of 1819, by providing a convenient, natural entry into the island. Over the years it was channelled and contained, its appearance inextricably altered. The men of the river were the essential labour force that tapped its potential and played a significant role in bringing to fruition Raffles' vision of Singapore. Along its oily surface generations of men from India and China plied craft laden with the goods that built and sustained an empire and established the foundations of a modern city state.

Like many other occupational groups, the boatmen have been all but ignored by historians interested in the development of Singapore. Because of a historical preoccupation with elites during the island's colonial and post colonial eras, the working lives of ordinary individuals in Singapore have generally been overlooked.[2] Much of the historiographical work on

Singapore, and other parts of Southeast Asia, has tended to focus on colonial administration, economic development and the role of indigenous elites. This 'big picture' bias is only partly a consequence of scarce source materials pertaining to the lives of ordinary people. Just as important are notions of the meaning of history, and what constitutes 'proper' history. Occupational groups such as boatmen, coolies, rickshaw pullers and prostitutes, to mention a few, by virtue of their low socio-economic status have been neglected in the historiography of Singapore. Their contribution to the process of constructing the modern city state, and their own daily struggles with the social, political and economic environment of Singapore have been ignored by elite histories focused on macro-historical events deemed to be of greater importance than the individual or group efforts of workers like lightermen.

The labouring masses of Singapore did more than just passively react to the world they inhabited. They also shaped their world. Their very presence and their activities sustained Singapore and helped make it what it is. Arriving in Singapore from India and China they adapted to the situation they found themselves in and forged a society distinct from the world they left behind.

The Establishment Years of the River Port, 1819–69

The more than 180 years covered by this book can be divided up into shorter periods to highlight changes along the river in relation to Singapore's role as a port, mercantile centre, colonial settlement and, most recently, independent 'showcase' state. The first of these eras, what might be termed the establishment period, encompasses the 50 years between the founding of a British settlement on the island of Singapore to the opening of the Suez Canal in 1869. During this period, the economic, political and even social life of the young community literally developed on and along the river foreshore.

Trade was the *raison d'être* for British colonisation of Singapore and the river was the focal point of all regional and global trade passing through the island. From its founding Singapore became a central port of call in Southeast Asia for sailing vessels of all nationalities. It was a vital link in the trade route between Europe and China and a sorting house for the trade of the archipelago. Its free port status and central location in the region attracted junks from China, Cochin China and Siam, with annual voyages being made to the island. Similarly, prows and other craft from the Eastern Archipelago increasingly traded in the harbour. In a comparatively short space of time the flags of most European and Asian nations were seen flying over the harbour filled with square rigged vessels and prows.[3] Throughout the 1830s and 1840s visitors to Singapore seldom failed to mention the large number of craft in the harbour or the amount of commercial activity being carried out along the river as 'native vessels of all classes' moved to and fro between the anchorage and river quays.[4] In 1819 Farquhar told the government at Fort Williams, Calcutta, that the settlement had been well received by neighbouring merchants and traders. In a report brimming with optimism, he declared, that in spite of Dutch attempts to hamper the progress of the British factory, including the cutting off of fresh food supplies from nearby islands, 'everything has gone on in the most prosperous manner inhabitants are flocking in from every quarter'.[5] Over the next decade various officials made similar statements of confidence in the port's growth and emerging role in regional trade.[6] The burgeoning cross-cultural commerce passing through Singapore and the general feeling of optimism continued, almost unabated, in the decades that followed.

While the commercial importance of Singapore as an entrepôt port grew, and the population increased beyond the expectations of its founder, this early period was not without serious difficulties. Dutch opposition to an English presence in the eastern seas, beyond Penang, was considerable. Their first protests were lodged with the Governor at Fort Cornwallis within two weeks of the agreement signed between Raffles, Sultan Hussein and Temenggong Abdul Rahman of Singapore.[7] For some time, there was a fear that the Netherlands might resort to force to dislodge the British from their strategic settlement at the entrance to the Straits of Malacca. This tension was further heightened by the fact that the Government in India seemed indecisive and Governor Bannerman, in Penang, did not support the new trading factory because of personal feelings of jealousy towards Raffles.[8] The initial optimism displayed by Raffles regarding Singapore's future as a British port was not shared by all of his peers, and even Farquhar, writing to him in 1822, spoke of the uncertain status of the settlement since its establishment. Farquhar states in a lengthy letter to Raffles that his orders in regards to the status of the settlement had changed a number of times, at one point he was ordered to view it merely as a military establishment and then later asked to view it as a mercantile establishment.[9] It was not until late the following year that the Advocate General felt confident enough to state that 'Singapore may now be fairly considered as a British Settlement'.[10] For a brief time, official equivocation and the general sense of uncertainty it engendered brought to a halt the construction of houses and *godowns* (warehouses) by merchants fearful that Britain might yet withdraw.[11] The ambiguity surrounding Singapore's political situation with respect to trade rivalry was resolved in 1824 with the signing of the Anglo-Dutch treaty. This agreement effectively demarcated the relative spheres of interest in the archipelago to be controlled by each power. From this point on British interests in Malaya were recognised by the Dutch, and Britain for its part acknowledged the Netherlands' interests in the island world of the archipelago. This March treaty was followed by a new agreement between the local Malay authorities and the East India Company, in August the same year, which effectively signed over Singapore and the surrounding islands to the company.[12]

The political administrative structure under which Singapore was governed, during this foundation period, changed several times. At first it was linked to Bencoolen and hence fell under the direct control of

Lieutenant Governor Raffles. This changed though upon his retirement, with Raffles issuing a Proclamation on the day of his final departure from Singapore announcing the company's decision to place the colony directly under the authority of India.[13] In 1826, a further administrative change took place with the linking of Singapore, Penang and Malacca (the Straits Settlements) to form the fourth Presidency of India. Due to financial pressures this regional administrative arrangement only lasted four years and in 1830 the three settlements were reduced to a residency dependent on Bengal.[14] In April 1867 the Straits Settlements, including Singapore, became a Crown Colony governed by the Colonial Office.

The river and settlement of Singapore are largely inseparable throughout this early period of the island's development. From a small green patch of clear ground near the shore line, barely sufficient for the tents of the contingent left by Raffles,[15] Singapore began to grow and prosper (see Map 1). Raffles, on his second visit to Singapore, in May–June 1819, set out the way he wanted the town laid out, a task he undertook with relish. His plan proved though in some important respects to be impractical.[16] Remarkably, the central place of the river as a port was not fully recognised by Raffles in the allocation of space for the different communities, and for government and business activities, at least not in his early plans for the town. He seems to have seen the river only as a useful natural feature for dividing various ethnic groups and the European town. Most of the 'native' population were to move to the south bank of the river, with the Malays forming their *kampungs*[17] above the present-day Elgin Bridge, in the direction of the river's source, and the Chinese occupying ground below the bridge towards the river's mouth. The Singapore River flows, with a number of sharp twists and turns, in what is essentially an easterly direction. For the purposes of this study the south bank refers to that side of the river where the business heart of the city is located around Raffles Place. The north bank is where Parliament stands (see Map 6).[18] The north bank of the river near its entrance was to be cleared and reserved for government purposes with the European town running eastward from this official allotment along the beach.[19] Raffles anticipated, incorrectly, that Europeans would build their godowns and landing sites along the beach front east of the river, approximately along the site of the present-day *padang* (see Map 2).

Some of the obvious functional benefits of the river that Raffles overlooked were quickly recognised by others. For example, the river provided a safe place to land cargo as well as a sheltered mooring for small craft. Soon after arriving in 1819 the brig *Ganges*, one of the vessels of Raffles' small fleet, was winched into the river to act as a store for the company's goods, a role it filled for five months.[20] In fact, the river really provided the only wharf site. It was particularly suited to the kind of commercial activity prevalent in Singapore, which consisted of much bulky, low value produce being imported, repackaged and then shipped on to other destinations. Such goods were more easily handled in the sheltered waters of the river than along the exposed foreshore.[21]

Any thoughts of utilising the beach as a landing stage were frustrated by the shallowness of the water and the size of the swell especially during the northeast monsoon, which made the handling of cargo dangerous and increased the risk of loss and damage to goods. The merchants who made their way to the settlement in the early years were unanimous in voicing approval of the river as the principle point of entry for their merchandise.[22]

The river then had a very different shape and appearance to what it would have later. Even if the modern city towers were to be erased from the landscape it would be difficult to associate the snake-like symmetry of its current course with the river's appearance in those early years (see Map 1). As a natural geographical feature its shape and size have been radically transformed and this early period of development between 1819 and 1867 was quite significant in this respect. To facilitate trade the river had to be contained and controlled. The north bank and a small hill, near the present-day Fullerton Hotel, on the south bank were the only locations suitable for the construction of buildings and landing platforms. The south bank beyond the rise at the river entrance was some nine feet lower than the opposite shore creating, at high tide, a vast inland lake up to 12 feet deep that engulfed the entire Chinatown area to Pearl's Hill, and at low tide a marshy bog.[23]

Accordingly, the settlement took shape on the north bank. With Farquhar in charge and under strict orders to keep expenses to a bare minimum,[24] Raffles' town plan proved unworkable. Some enterprising Chinese quickly established themselves on the only dry ground near the river mouth on the south side of the river, but most other commercial activity was conducted on the land set aside by Raffles for government buildings. This deviation from the original plan was a major cause of the much written about falling out between Raffles and Farquhar in late 1822.[25] A serious difference of opinion about the role of the river transpired, and while Raffles publicly castigated Farquhar for ignoring his instructions, he privately revised his earlier town plan to give the river an important place in the future development of Singapore. It is clear from the report of a committee set up to investigate the feasibility of utilising the south bank that Farquhar was not wholly wrong, and that the south bank would be suited to commerce and building only after a considerable investment on embanking and back filling,[26] a luxury not afforded by Farquhar. The major changes made to the original plan involved the transfer of the business sector, including the Europeans, to the south bank close to the river mouth (see Map 3). The approximate location of what became Raffles Place was to be the commercial heart of the town, with European and 'respectable' Chinese allocated lots there. The Chinese kampung was moved up the river in order to make room for the new commercial zone. The revised plan also reserved land for south Asian settlers adjoining the Chinese section of the town, with the explicit intention of giving them access to the river in order to carry out one of their principal occupations, which was lighterage.[27] The problem of tidal overflow and flooding was overcome by raising the south bank of the river and filling in the marsh behind it. This reclaimed land would be used for the envisaged kampungs. Raffles initiated this project by employing migrant labour to level the hill near the river mouth to obtain earth for filling in the commercial area. Vestiges of Raffles' master plan are still evident in Singapore today; Chinatown, Kampung Malacca, Empress Place and of course Raffles Place are all still situated in accordance with his original design.

As the town and population grew in response to the demands of regional and global trade, so the river was contained and transformed to accommodate this growth. All manner of businesses and housing spread along its banks. The importance of the river as the commercial lifeline of the settlement continued unchallenged over the next several decades. The work of embankment and reclamation during this establishment period shaped the lower reaches of the river, producing the present watercourse. This was a process fraught with difficulties and controversy as the forces of nature proved more difficult to overcome than expected, especially with much needed funds for major public works always in short supply. Nevertheless, improvements to the settlement continued gradually, with the construction of bridges and access roads, and other public works. By the 1860s the business sector was housed around Commercial Square in multi-storeyed buildings, with adjoining Chinese enterprises along the river bank (South Boat Quay) in the direction of the new Elgin Bridge. Across the river stood the government offices, with the Town Hall, St. Andrew's Cathedral and the Singapore Institution clearly visible behind them. In appearance, the town was a model colonial establishment, highly praised by Europeans who passed through during the establishment years.[28] The town was still relatively small, while roads linked it with virtually all parts of the island, the town itself barely stretched more than a mile or two from its commercial and port centre, the river.[29]

From Steamships to Containerisation 1869–1972

The opening of the Suez Canal on 17 November 1869 marked the beginning of a new phase in the history of the river as the settlement's port, as well as in the relationship between the river and town, which would last for more than a century. During the decades that followed, the river and New Harbour (Keppel Harbour) built to the west of the river on the coast would function in an interdependent relationship as steamships began to introduce fundamental changes in trading arrangements. New technologies in communications, power and transport would bring about rapid social and economic change across the globe, and allow Singapore to consolidate its position as a regional entrepôt on a global scale.[30] As the island's reputation as a booming free port grew, the inflow of migrants increased. Chinese, Indian, as well as people from the archipelago world of Southeast Asia, all sought their fortunes in what they hoped was to be a land of opportunity. Often driven by poverty from their homelands, these migrants provided cheap labour for empire building. In the 1860s and 1870s, the town grew beyond its previous municipal limits, further changing the face of the landscape. New demands on the port's facilities resulted in a massive reclamation project as the foreshore and river were further altered to increase their economic potential. Use of the river was pushed to its maximum between the opening of the Suez Canal in 1869 and development of containerisation in the 1970s. The town spread rapidly along its banks, spewing its waste into an ever more altered and contained waterway, and this, coupled with the island's importance as a port, caused the river to become extremely congested and polluted.

Steam power increasingly reigned supreme in ocean trading from the late 1860s, and the Suez Canal exposed Asia to steam far more quickly than would otherwise have been the case. The canal facilitated a speedy increase in the number of steamships operating in Southeast Asia, rapidly ushering in a new mechanised age of sea transportation to the region.[31] No longer was it necessary for steamships from Europe to make the long expensive journey around the African Cape. This new route, linking the Mediterranean and Indian Ocean via the Red Sea, reduced the length of time it took for steam vessels from Europe to reach Asia by one-third. This time-saving, coupled with improvements in marine engines, resulted in larger and more efficient craft being built that could carry increased cargoes which greatly reduced freight costs. Bogaars suggests the opening of the Suez Canal resulted in a doubling of the Singapore merchants' capital through savings in transport costs and speed of delivery.[32] The benefits were immediately felt in Singapore as its 'trade figures jumped from just over £58 million in 1868 to nearly £90 million in 1873'.[33] However, the Suez route was not practical for sailing vessels as adverse winds and currents in the canal made it far too dangerous for them and its opening hastened the end of the age of clipper ships.[34]

By 1870, the Singapore press was heralding a new age of trans-global trade and communication. The editor of *The Straits Times* wrote of this new era, 'it is to the Suez Canal ... we look as the agency which is to quicken trade, and ... increase the importance of Singapore as a commercial centre and port of call'.[35] Readers of the *Singapore Daily Times* were told in the same year how cotton from Bombay was shipped to Liverpool, spun into yarn and seven days later returned to Asia on the very same vessel. The turnaround time for this particular venture was only 53 days.[36] The single round trip a year of the best clippers was snail-like when compared to the possibility of making two to three trips a year by steamer. Proof of the advantages of the Suez Canal in collapsing space and time was also seen in the steamer *Shantung*'s 42-day record trip between Glasgow and Singapore.[37] For several years after the canal's opening the press of Singapore reported enthusiastically each new record breaking journey and already by 1872 the number of steam vessels calling at the port overtook sailing craft.[38] Small steam ships from the 1880s also began to displace sailing vessels on coastal shipping routes in the region.[39]

While steamships had been calling at Singapore for many years, their sudden growth in numbers after 1869, and the new bunkering demands of these vessels, caused the river to be eclipsed as the central port. New

Harbour, or Keppel Harbour, first used from 1852,[40] offered deep water berthing and better servicing facilities for larger vessels. The first regular steamship service to pass through Singapore began operations in 1845 and was operated by the Eastern Steam Navigation Company and the Peninsular & Oriental Steam Navigation Company (P & O). By 1852, P & O had built wharves and bunkering facilities at Keppel Harbour to take advantage of the deeper waters. The wharves at Keppel Harbour allowed bunkering, as well as loading and unloading cargo, to be carried on at any phase of the tide. By the turn of the century, new technologies such as electric lighting and improved winches on the docks at the harbour produced a doubling of working hours and a consequent massive increase in cargo handling capability. By comparison vessels serviced from the river faced serious delays due to tide times and bad weather, and coal stores along the river and its branches could only be accessed at high water. Moreover, the coal itself had to be handled twice first when it was loaded onto a lighter and again when it was transferred to the waiting ship. It was a dirty, time-consuming and back breaking task often fraught with danger as unstable lighters could be swamped in heavy swells or battered against the hulls of the vessels they were servicing, causing loss of life and cargo. These factors, coupled with the dramatic increase in shipping that took place following the opening of the Suez Canal, caused a shift of activity to Keppel Harbour.

The Singapore River continued to play an important role in the trade of Singapore. While Keppel Harbour attracted ocean-going vessels, smaller coastal ships and various other craft such as large prows and junks preferred to anchor near the river. The demand for regional produce generated by the port's expanding role in the global trading network caused a significant increase in the number of these craft calling at Singapore. Marine department reports between the 1880s and 1920s show a fourfold increase in the number of 'native' and small coastal steamers arriving at the port. In 1880, 4,657 such vessels entered the port and by 1920 this figure had risen to 17,167. The increase in tonnage of goods handled was more than sevenfold during this period reaching more than one million tonnes annually. There were of course years in which dips occurred owing to local and global recessionary pressures, but the overall trend was a steady rise in the number of small trading craft calling at Singapore and in the gross tonnage of goods handled. Between 1929 and 1939 a severely depressed world economy caused a fall in the volume of goods carried on regional vessels.[41] In the post World War II era, trade in the river would pick up substantially, so much so that by 1959 Goh Keng Swee, the then Minister for Finance, could tell parliament that more goods were handled in the river than at the wharves of the Singapore Harbour Board.[42]

There was a huge amount of traffic and transhipment between the two port areas, with much of the merchandise that entered the river leaving the island via Keppel Harbour and vice versa. In the years immediately following the opening of facilities at Keppel Harbour goods were moved between the river and Keppel facilities by bullock cart. These carts were phased out of use as more efficient methods of transport were introduced during the first decades of the twentieth century. Large scale reclamation of the foreshore between the town and Keppel Harbour provided ground for better road transport and eventually a rail link. The first phase of this work, completed in 1887, altered the shoreline between the river and Keppel Harbour, filling in a stretch of sea from Teluk Ayer Street to present-day Raffles' Quay. The soil for this reclamation work came in part from several small hills which stood between the town and Keppel Harbour. With these hills levelled to extend the foreshore, space became available to build new roads between the river and Keppel Habour. Transportation links were further improved with the laying of tramlines between the town and wharves and in 1907 the extension of the Tank Road–Kranji railway to the harbour. Further reclamation work in Teluk Ayer and the construction of a protective mole allowed the building of more wharves along this stretch of the shore. By 1932, the year in which Teluk Ayer Basin was formerly opened, the port stretched almost continuously from the Singapore River in a westerly direction to Keppel Harbour.

At the turn of the century, Singapore was becoming a sprawling metropolis (see Map 5), and the river had ceased to be the physical heart of the city or of the port. During this phase of Singapore's history the full length of the river was finally contained within the banks of its present course. Above Coleman Bridge extensive earthworks were carried out to fill what remained of the swamps further up the river. This process finally subordinated the river totally to the trade and development demands of the new Singapore. As marsh land in the river's upper reaches was filled beyond the level of the tide, more land was opened for construction as its newly-formed banks extended further inland allowing additional space for godowns and other types of riverside businesses to be established.

Increased international trade meant greater wealth for Singapore, but it also brought new problems with respect to the river. Constrained by its new banks, the river became more polluted, and for those trying to navigate its course, presented ever more difficulties. Between 1870 and 1970 numerous reports and inquiries were held to find ways of 'fixing' the navigational and pollution problems of the river. While various ecological issues had been raised as early as 1829 following the collapse of a section of river embankment,[43] and attempts had been made to dredge the river and its mouth, the years following 1870 brought concerns over silting and pollution. Administration Reports of the Singapore Municipality for the 1890s provide a considerable amount of detail on the extent of pollution in the river and consequent health problems. For example, the report for 1896 states that outbreaks of cholera and diarrhoea in the settlement could be directly attributed to the 'insanitary state of the Singapore River'. The first serious attempt to deal squarely with these matters came with the establishment of the Singapore River Commission in 1898.[44] The Commission's report was the most wide ranging ever compiled on the river and questions of pollution, trade and how best to utilise the waterway as part of the total port scheme. The Commission took evidence from a wide range of interested parties including businessmen, government officials, boat owners, police and boatmen.

Although the commissioners were well aware of the river's vital role in the commerce of the port, they were stunned by the results of their inquiries which highlighted the extraordinary number of craft plying its waters and the huge quantity of goods moved along it. They found that more than 1.3 million tons of goods per annum were handled in the river bound for Europe and the United States alone![45] In one three-day period in 1899 more than 6,100 craft were recorded entering the river, and almost the same number left.[46] Faced with the obvious implications of this data for future growth and development, the Commissioners prepared recommendations that were sweeping and bold. If implemented, the recommendations would have radically changed the role of the river in relation to the port, as well as the face of the town. Central to improving navigation and clearing of pollution would be the widening, improved embanking and regular dredging of the river, the raising of all bridges, and the building of a boat harbour either in the river or the sea near the river mouth. The commission also examined the question of constructing a canal linking the river with Keppel Harbour and, while this was not included in their final recommendations for reasons of cost, it was seriously investigated and debated.

The River Commission proposals were followed by a number of other schemes in the following decades to improve the river, both aesthetically and as an integral part of the port. In 1905 a government appointed committee suggested ways to reduce congestion and improve navigation, and again in 1919, the question of the river and how to deal with its ecological-economic problems was raised in the Legislative Council and investigated.[47] Essentially, all the deliberations and plans from 1898 onwards reached similar conclusions. They found that the river needed to be widened and rebanked and all the bridges raised to allow greater access by lighter vessels. All attempts to implement these proposals ran into financial opposition and faced the same fate; none were adopted. While some of the suggestions in the various reports were acted upon over the ensuing decades, the main recommendations were without exception never implemented. Everyone agreed on the vital economic importance of the river and the need to tackle the persistent twin problems of congestion and pollution, but no consensus could be reached on the issue of how the various works would be funded. The colonial government and other interested private parties always backed away when it seemed they might be asked to bear the brunt of the cost.

In 1954 a further attempt was made by the authorities to tackle these important issues with the setting up of the Singapore River Working Party, which submitted its final report in September 1955.[48] The Working Party found that imports and exports conveyed along the river were in excess of 5 million tonnes annually with a staggering commercial value of 1.2 billion dollars.[49] The report highlighted the importance of the river to

Singapore's commercial and social life, stressing the need for funds to deepen the river, rebuild its walls, raise bridges and generally improve cargo-handling facilities. It also emphasised the need to reduce pollution in the river. For a time there seemed to be some possibility that the river would get much needed attention, but in the end the Working Party's recommendations were pushed aside partly as a result of financial restrictions as well as the realities emerging with respect to the long-term feasibility of maintaining the river as a major trading artery. The plan was finally laid to rest following a 1963 survey of the Port by a United Nations' authority, Dr Karl Franz, who found it to be impractical.

The century following the opening of the Suez Canal was a period of extraordinary growth and consolidation for Singapore, both as a regional entrepôt port and city. It was a century in which seaborne cargo passing through the port increased significantly. The river, although no longer the port centre, still continued to play an important role in the economic activity and life of the island and port. The river's vital role in international trade would change over time because of further technological developments and innovations in shipping and cargo handling and as a result of new local and regional political and economic realities. In the space of a hundred years Singapore had been radically transformed from a colonial city under European tutelage into an independent cosmopolitan city state. Steamships and the opening of the Suez Canal marked the beginning of a century which witnessed a universal revolution in technology and ended with major political and social change for Singapore. By the early 1970s, with almost a decade of independence from colonial rule behind it, Singapore was becoming part of an international interdependent economic system linked globally, not only by sea, but also by air and telecommunications.

New Realities: 1972–90s

Postcolonial Singapore, having unsuccessfully tried a period of union with Malaysia, was now forging a distinctive identity as an independent nation. Under this new direction, the island's dependence on the entrepôt trade or any other single economic sector was reassessed. The new Singapore was to be a manufacturer and seller of services, a regional centre for transnational trade and banking, rather than merely a sorting house for other nations' wares. This policy strategy and goal would have major implications for the future role of the river which was increasingly perceived as something of a national disgrace. Its dirty, smelly, overcrowded waters, and squatter-lined banks did not fit with the government's ideal conception of the new modern Singapore (see Map 6). All the unresolved issues of the proceeding century — congestion, pollution and how to improve its potential — were set to be resolved, conclusively.

This final phase in the river's history as a port is marked by the significant development of yet another major change in sea transportation, namely containerisation.[50] Singapore was at the forefront of this new cargo revolution, being the first Southeast Asian nation to utilise the new technology for loading and unloading containers. The port, already experiencing a boom as a result of its modern facilities,[51] was set for a further period of expansion and growth as new container facilities were brought on line. With shipping companies planning the construction of hundreds of container ships, Singapore was determined not to lose its trading edge to neighbouring countries. What appeared as a gamble in 1969, when the first piles were sunk at East Lagoon, was heralded as an indication of the foresight of the planners when the first container ship arrived in 1972.[52] Just as a century earlier, the new steamships had been praised for the speed at which they could make the round trip between Asia and Europe, so too the new container vessels were welcomed with similar comment on their speed, and more importantly, rapid turnaround time at the docks.[53] By the end of the 1970s the annual growth in container traffic was around 25 per cent.[54]

Containerisation alone, however, did not bring about the demise of the river as a commercial artery and port. While the river was now the poor cousin of the Port of Singapore, it still played the same role it always had in local-regional trade. A significant proportion of natural produce from the region, especially from Indonesia, continued to be transhipped through the river. In fact, for a brief period during the 1970s, the river was given a new lease of life via the arrival of 'China ships'. The cost of shipping goods around and from Asia was largely controlled by the powerful Far Eastern Freight Conference, a group of primarily European shipping lines dominated by the British, who held a powerful monopoly over sea transport between Europe and Asia from 1897. Faced with inflationary price hikes on European ships, under the contract system imposed by the Far Eastern Freight Conference, elements of the Singapore business community and government encouraged Chinese vessels to carry local goods for them.[55] While the aim was to break the European shipping monopoly, this stratagem also facilitated a significant increase in river trade. China ships were serviced in the Outer Roads by river lighters, only making use of Port Authority wharves when carrying particularly heavy and/or bulky cargoes.[56] By 1973 China was pledging to send as many ships as were needed to deal with Singapore's export demands.[57] This sudden influx of Chinese shipping provided a huge boost to the trading activities of the river[58] but it was a relatively short-lived boom.

By the middle of the decade the Port Authority of Singapore had secured an agreement with China to have all their ships serviced by the Authority at their wharves. With global sea trade being containerised worldwide, this new development regarding the China ships brought to an end the last great era of river trade. Ostensibly, the use of the wharves was a choice made by the Chinese on the basis of convenience and safety because there was less chance of damage to cargo handled alongside quays.[59] Other factors no doubt played a part. China ships were offered very good terms to make use of the Port Authority's facilities, while, at the same time, the new gateway of the port, Pasir Panjang, had just begun operation with the lighter industry earmarked to be resited there. Pasir Panjang's wharves were in fact designed, in part, to cater for a declining lighter trade.

From the early 1970s it was the intent of the government authorities to have the lighter industry removed from the Singapore River. In 1968, the Landing Goods Act had been passed to reduce traffic on the river.[60] Under this legislation much of the cargo which had previously been moved along the river was diverted to port facilities at Teluk Ayer Basin. Flowing as it does through the very heart of the business district, the river with its cluttered run-down appearance, noisy activities and obvious pollution was not the ideal centrepiece for a modern city. As the government's clean up campaign and urban development programme moved ever closer to the river, the official mood was that the unsightly lighterage industry should be dealt with through resiting. Pasir Panjang was the clear choice of location. The head of the Housing Board's urban renewal department, Alan Choe, in October 1970, outlined the official view, stating that as the rebuilding programme reached the river, all godowns and warehouses would have to be relocated at Pasir Panjang.[61] His comments aroused strong protest from lighter companies operating along the river with a petition being presented to the government calling on it to preserve the 'beneficial usage of [the] Singapore River when implementing the various schemes of urban renewal'.[62] The lighter industry's concerns were that the proposed Pasir Panjang berths were exposed to the prevailing monsoon, and that this would create a hazard for both craft and men working there. There was also the issue of the distance between the anchorages (Inner and Eastern Roads) worked by the lighters and Pasir Panjang (see Map 4). The added operating time caused by having to move between the Pasir Panjang moorings and ships in the harbour would, according to the Lighter Owner's Association, add both to the cost and decrease the efficiency of daily operations — costs that would necessarily be passed on to those who used the services of the lighters. While the government quickly assured the owners that there was no immediate plan to move them from the river the implication was that this was a long-term goal of the authorities.[63] But the lighter industry, mainly through petitions and protests of the owner's association and the Transport Vessel Workers Union, continued to urge the government to keep the river open to lighters.

Resistance by the lighter industry to the moving of their activities was recognised as being largely futile from 1977 when the Prime Minister, Lee Kuan Yew, 'hinted', when opening a new reservoir, that Singapore's rivers should be cleaned up within ten years.[64] In an address aimed at drawing attention to the extent of river pollution and Singapore's dependence on outside sources of potable water, the Prime Minister ordered the Ministry of the Environment to set a target to have clean water and fishing in the Singapore River and Kallang Basin within a decade. The Ministry immediately set about the task of drawing up a plan of action to deal with the various sources of pollution. The ensuing years witnessed a mammoth effort at environmental conservation and renewal, an effort which affected profoundly the lives of people who made their living on the congested, filthy waterways. Officially some 26,000 families were moved from along the rivers and resettled in public housing, a further 5,000 street hawkers were relocated to specially built food centres and some 2,800 businesses and industries were rehoused on estates built for this purpose.[65]

The lightermen of the Singapore River like the hawkers, charcoal burners, boat builders, keepers of ducks and pigs and numerous other tradesmen and industries were now caught up in this large-scale programme of urban, environmental renewal. Appeals to remain along the river were of no avail. The government had a clear plan to remove from the river and its environs any activity which detracted from the urban vision they were creating, irrespective of whether it was a real or imagined threat to the campaign for clean rivers. In rejecting a petition from the lighterage industry in 1980, the Ministry of the Environment made it clear that the Singapore and Kallang rivers were part of the face of a new beautified Singapore and as such it was important that the waterways be 'kept clean'.[66] The same communication also labelled the lighter industry as one of the main sources of river pollution. The river's role was about to change in the most dramatic way since the arrival of Raffles, as more than a century and a half of riverine trading activity was poised to end.

Faced with a down turn in business as a result of the Port Authority's handling of 'China ships', and the advent of containerisation and other more efficient methods of cargo handling, the decision by the Prime Minister to clean up the rivers delivered the fatal blow to the lighter industry. It was not just the clean up and transfer to Pasir Panjang which was to force a major down turn in the already precarious economic position of the lighterage business. One of the few cargoes still carried in large quantities by lighters was feed for livestock and the drive to clean up the rivers resulted in the complete phasing out of such local industries. Pig feed alone made up 30 per cent of the business of lighters prior to the demise of this type of farming in Singapore. In the 1970s around 500,000 tonnes of this one item were carried annually by lighters.[67] Hence, the move from the river caused severe problems of dislocation for the lighter industry while the entire renewal scheme added significantly to its woes because of the closure or removal of businesses that it depended on for its livelihood.

On the last day of August 1983 the lighters on the River began their final journey to the new mooring site at Pasir Panjang. The river was zoned off limits to all craft without a special permit on the first day of September by the Port of Singapore Authority.[68] By day's end only a handful of the 300 lighters that called the river home remained. These, much to the chagrin of officials, were in the process of discharging cargo. Some delays had occurred in the afternoon as a familiar natural obstacle had for one last time impeded the lighters' route — a high tide made passage under Cavenagh Bridge impossible.[69] But this proved only a temporary set back in what was otherwise an uneventful if not sad day for the lightermen.

Within a few days the remaining vessels had made their way out of the Singapore River for the last time and all that remained were the still waters and memories of the past.

While lighters continued to operate out of Pasir Panjang into the 1990s the total number was only a fraction of what it was in the river's hey day. The number of craft actually working was less than 100 in 1993/94.[70] While there were many more lighters still registered as in service many of these craft were in fact sitting idle never to work again. The cargoes of the past had, like the men, all but disappeared from the holds of the few remaining lighters. Of the vast array of merchandise which once made up the consignments of the lighters, only rice remained along with a small amount of ship's stores which were conveyed to vessels passing through the port but not berthing. The lightermen's despondency of the mid-1980s had given way to a reluctant acceptance of the inevitable demise of the industry. The talk was no longer of strategies for survival but rather how long the present businesses would last.

That the Singapore River played a notable role in the historical development of the island state is beyond question. One of the more enduring images of Singapore is the cluttered banks of the river and lighters laden with goods making their way along its oily surface. What remains is to demonstrate the relationship between the river and city across time and to locate in this historical drama the lightermen, who have all but been forgotten, along with their vitally important industry.

2
The River: Development of an Economic Landscape

THIS chapter examines the evolution of commercial activity along the Singapore River during the establishment years of the river as Singapore's port and town centre (1819–69). It begins by describing the transformation of the river from a muddy tidal creek into a vital economic artery — a transformation that would radically alter, by the end of this period, the ecology, character and landscape of the river. This is followed by a discussion of how the river port functioned, in which the importance of the lighterage industry is highlighted and placed in its historical context. The way in which the river evolved as the commercial centre and port of Singapore meant that the lighterage industry was crucial to all aspects of trade and commerce conducted there between 1819 and 1869. With no docking facilities for shipping, lighters provided the only means of transporting goods from vessels in the harbour to mercantile establishments along the river. As the volume of trade passing through the harbour burgeoned, and commercial activity along the banks of the river increased, the importance of the lighterage industry grew proportionately. Finally, the chapter also examines the nature and type of trade and industry that developed along the banks of the river during those formative years. These enterprises provided a variety of goods carried by lighters on the river and an examination of their operations highlights the extent of commercial activity along its banks.

Singapore River: Creation of an Ecological Landscape

The location chosen by Raffles to establish a new East India Company factory did not appear at first glance to be an ideal site to establish a trading emporium. Though Singapore island was favourably situated adjacent to the main sailing routes east of the Malay Peninsula, with a sheltered harbour for vessels,[1] the dense jungle that covered the land mass made it appear a less than desirable place to build a new port settlement. From the decks of the ships in Raffles' small fleet, it seemed there was nothing but 'impenetrable forest' to the water's edge in all directions (see Map 1).[2] Descriptions of the scene that confronted Raffles' party vary, but according to Colonel Farquhar's account, his small company, left to begin the task of building settlement facilities, were forced to pitch their tents on the only 'plot' of clear ground just above the beach near the north bank of the river.[3] Along the river itself the scene was similarly daunting with dense bush growing right up to its banks on one side and muddy low-lying swamps and mangrove wherever one looked on the other (see Map 1).[4] The only open space close to the river was on its north bank, and that was occupied by the local Malay ruler, or Temenggong. The opposite bank was extremely low and, in comparison with the Temenggong's compound, the least likely site for a future town. Farquhar described as 'formidable' both the work and expense necessary to develop this site.[5] What little bank existed was barely distinguishable from the morass behind it and at high tides vanished completely. At all times the greater part of the south bank was a marshy bog dissected by a labyrinth of turbid creeks.[6] Four months after Raffles landed at Singapore, Munshi Abdullah described the 'far' side of the river as unoccupied and 'covered with jungle, mangrove trees and mud'.[7]

The practical difficulties that might be encountered in setting up a port town were of secondary importance for Raffles as his principal aim was to thwart Dutch supremacy in the Malay world and further the interests of British trade. Raffles' studies of the Malay world had also made him aware of the strategic importance of Singapore at an earlier time and there is no doubt that the island held a romantic appeal for him. In correspondence with a friend he wrote:

> I shall say nothing of the importance which I attach to the permanence of the position I have taken up at Singapore; it is a child of my own. But for my Malay studies I should hardly have know that such a place existed; not only the European, but Indian world was also ignorant of it.[8]

Around the same time writing to the Duchess of Somerset, Raffles could barely contain his joy at the choice of location and what it represented.

> This is the spot, the site of the ancient maritime capital of the Malays, and within the walls of these ancient fortifications, raised not less than six centuries ago, on which I have planted the British flag....[9]

Notwithstanding the immediate difficulties of establishing port facilities along the Singapore River, and nostalgia aside, Raffles' judgement proved sound as the island was strategically located to protect British shipping and attract regional commerce.[10]

The Singapore River was not Raffles' first choice as a location for establishing the commercial centre of the settlement. He initially envisaged the port town further east at Campong Glam (see Map 2).[11] When this site proved untenable, any apprehension about transforming the riverine environment for commercial activity was quickly pushed aside.[12] While Singapore Bay was ideal for mooring vessels, the beach was dangerous even for small craft such as lighters. As one approached the foreshore the water became extremely shallow causing boats to strand in the surf, risking the cargoes they carried.[13] The situation was especially precarious during the northeast monsoon when huge ocean swells caused heavy surf along the shoreline.[14] With Singapore beginning to attract shipping from all quarters of Asia, there was considerable pressure exerted for an alternative haven to be found quickly. Among pioneering European merchants there was consensus that money spent on facilities along the beach would be wasted. One of the settlement's leading merchants, Alexander Guthrie, even went so far as to say he would leave Singapore if not given a safe secure site.[15]

The Singapore River, an enclosed body of water connected to the bay, proved the only alternative site along which to develop godown and wharf facilities. The suitability of the river, as a natural harbour sheltered from the vagaries of the monsoon, was readily grasped by Farquhar and the merchants on the spot.[16] It was the one site that met all the requirements of the first traders to arrive in Singapore.[17] In the words of one merchant, it was the only location near the anchorage providing 'every convenience ... for trading to any extent', and, of critical importance, the facility for boats to 'approach your godown to enable you to ship your goods'.[18] The orientation toward the river in the first years of the new settlement's life for trade and other commercial activities was a matter of necessity for individuals who arrived to set up businesses in Singapore.[19] From its banks not only could trade be conducted effectively, but also ancillary support activities for shipping, such as repairs and replenishing of vital stores and equipment, could be provided. As the settlement developed, the river also nurtured a number of key industries not directly related to its entrepôt role, such as tanneries, charcoal manufacturing, rice mills, sago production and fresh produce markets. It was also, unfortunately, a convenient place into which town and industrial waste could be dumped.

The obvious importance of the river to trade prospects and the future prosperity of the settlement resulted, during Raffles' last visit to Singapore in 1822, in a programme of reclamation and building along its banks. With his initial blueprint for the beachfront town largely discarded, Raffles was forced to accept the proliferating development as he found it three years later. The population had already grown to more than 10,000 people[20] and in spite of initial settlement difficulties there was a vibrant commerce established along the river. Reporting to his superiors Raffles stated that in the first two years after its founding the port was visited by 2,889 vessels carrying 200,000 tons of cargo. And in 1822 'no less than 130,629 tons' of goods passed through the port.[21] However, the trading community was still huddled together along only those small stretches of river which were deemed suitable for cheap development.[22] This meant building principally along the north bank and a small section of the south bank, near the river mouth, where the ground was high and not subject to flooding. Much of the available high ground on the south bank near the river entrance had already been claimed by Raffles' brother-in-law, Captain Flint, who was acting as harbour master.[23] Raffles had envisaged the south bank of the river in his first town plan (1819) as the preserve of Chinese and other 'native' groups.[24] While a Chinese quarter had developed on the high ground in 1822, with the exception of a few small 'rickety'[25] premises belonging to Chinese traders, no one had undertaken the extensive and costly work necessary to build on the swamp bordering the river along its south side. Farquhar, while recognising the importance of the river, did not develop this area because of Raffles' order to keep the settlement's running costs to a bare minimum.[26] But with the river having fast become the centre of commercial life it became necessary for Raffles to develop a plan for future growth which adequately dealt with the south bank and the entire river-scape. Through a process of consultations and committees, most notably the Land Allotment Committee (1822)[27] and Town Committee (1822),[28] the original committee consisting of CE Davies, George Bonham and AL Johnston, was established on 4 November 1822 and set the task of examining Raffles' plan for the town and then of making further inquiries and suggestions. A new committee was formed in early 1823 and given explicit instructions to carry out the plans already decided on. The findings of these committees led Raffles to revise his original town plan. The final plan which was adopted, formalised the position of the river as the settlement's port and commercial centre (see Map 3). It also placed enormous importance on how Singapore's potential could be best realised.

Recognition of the river's vital economic role led logically to the next step, a detailed strategy for granting access to it according to occupation and ethnicity. Raffles took particular care to deal with the 'power factor' of the river's 'morphology'.[29] He ensured strict control of access by fixing precise boundaries for riverside tenancy, placing government, ethnic and occupational groups in demarcated allotments according to their perceived financial worth and function. The principal objective in the spatial segregation and organisation of the river and sites along its banks was to 'secure to the mercantile community all the facilities which the natural advantages of the port afford'.[30] Raffles had been disturbed by the fact that much valuable land along the river and sea face, urgently required by the 'commercial community', was rapidly occupied by 'lower classes of Chinese'.[31] The new planning scheme, as it related to the commercial and functional layout of the river/port town interface, divided the river into four interconnected zones (see Map 3).

The first zone was reserved for the government (see Map 3).[32] On what was clearly the best land near the river, the north bank, Raffles decided the government should build its administrative centre.[33] He also instructed that all the ground along the north bank, from the foreshore to the back of the hill be set aside for future use by the government. The pre-emptive claim the government made on this tract of land was justifiable, if not contentious. It was centrally located within the settlement and immediately suitable for development. The main purpose of the settlement was to act as a trading station and this site placed the operations of government close to the commercial centre of activity. For this ground to be vacated for government it was necessary that merchants who had already established themselves on it and the Temenggong's village be relocated. The Temenggong and his followers shifted to a site between Tanjong Pagar and Teluk Blangah[34] away from the immediate vicinity of the river while the merchants moved to the second river zone.

The significance of this site for future administrative and development purposes was highlighted in 1841 when the East India Company's lease expired and it was advertised for sale. In writing to the Governor of the Straits Settlements to impress upon him the importance of retaining this land for government, Singapore's Resident Councillor, Mr Church, stressed the benefits it had secured to the administration.[35] He noted that should the government not purchase the site it would inevitably be taken up by merchants wanting access to the river for godowns and in no time be 'covered' with such premises. The response of the governing authorities in India was to buy the land and issue new instructions to reserve 'an ample portion of river frontage for all prospective government purposes'.[36] In ensuing years, all manner of government offices were to be established on this reserved land, including the chambers of government, the Law Courts, Master Attendant's Office and Police.

Zone two (see Map 3)[37] was reserved for the use of European and other merchants, most of whom had been removed from the north bank of the river. This area encompassed the sea face from Teluk Ayer around Tanjong Singapura and extended along the south bank of the river as far as the proposed bridge site. According to the Land Allotment Committee, this location was the most appropriate along which to construct godowns and other port facilities. It was, in spite of negative first impressions, 'better adapted for mercantile purposes than even the northern bank' of the river.[38] The report concluded stating it was 'impossible to select any other site combining all the advantages' of this one for carrying out commercial activities.[39] As it was developing, a further demarcation occurred within this zone between European and, in the main, Chinese merchants. Unquestionably, the best section along the river near its mouth and sea front, around Tanjong Singapura, came to be the preserve of European merchants,[40] with the Chinese establishing themselves between what is today Raffles' Place and Elgin Bridge. The better off merchants, principally European, built themselves godowns which faced into Commercial Square and backed onto the ocean where they had small jetties built. This gave them several points of access to their premises either from the sea or from the river and through the square.[41] Access to the river was especially critical, and this was frequently stressed in early correspondence between the merchants and Resident Crawfurd. The merchants claimed that for a 'great part of the year owing to a surf and a given portion of every day at certain stages of the tide' no landing or shipping of goods could be carried out along the 'sea face'. It was therefore imperative they had access to the river.[42]

Backing the mercantile area and meeting up with the river, above what is today New Bridge Road, was zone three, the 'Chinese Campong' (see Map 3).[43] Raffles' allotment for the Chinese quarter extended back from the river encompassing all the land along the beach at Teluk Ayer. His generous allocation of land to the Chinese was based on the assumption that this 'industrious race ... will always form by far the largest portion of the community'.[44] In order to encourage law and order within the boundaries of this zone, he further directed that the Chinese be allocated space along speech-dialect lines, according to their 'provincial and other distinctions'.[45] As with the mercantile zone, he emphasised the government's aim was to provide appropriate access to the river for those involved in 'every description' of trade,[46] stressing that special consideration be given to the respectable classes. There is no doubt that Raffles was here referring to those involved in commerce when allocating land along the river. He specifically ruled out other occupational groups amongst the Chinese obtaining such sites by stating:

> There does not appear any reason why the latter (craftsmen and labourers) should in any instance be allowed to occupy those situations (land near the river and seafront) which are likely at any time to be required by the commercial community.[47]

In all instances the 'commercial interests of the settlement' came first when deciding who would be granted access to the river and choice locations were reserved for the establishment of commercial premises.[48]

Finally, in zone four, space was set aside for another group critical to opening the river, the '*Chuliahs* [individuals from the Coromandel Coast, India] and others employed in boats, cooly work, etc'.[49] This ward, referred to in Raffles' plan as the 'Chuliah Campong', was located above the Chinese section of the river. The main occupation of this group was boatmen employed in transporting trade goods to and from ships in the harbour.[50] It too was a generous allocation of river front, over a quarter of a mile,[51] and proof of the importance Raffles now placed on the river as the commercial lifeline of the settlement, and the key role played by this immigrant occupational group. The Chuliah boatmen were deliberately housed in close proximity to the heart of the commercial area where the services of lighters were indispensable. Due consideration was also given to the anticipated number migrating to the settlement 'and the necessity of their residence being in the vicinity of the place where their services are most likely to be called for'.[52]

Raffles' vision of the way in which the river and town would develop was unique and it allowed, under certain conditions, individuals to readily move between the demarcated zones. Certainly amongst colonial ports of the time, with respect to ethnic groups and boundaries, this was a novel idea.[53] The smooth promotion of trade and commercial life did not, therefore, exclude any individual or groups from participating in the settlement activities of a particular zone.[54] A notable example of how this liberal attitude toward settlement patterns and town planning moved the boundaries between zones to further trading interests, was the gradual shift of Indian merchants towards the mercantile centre of town, principally congregating around Chulia Street.[55] It was a tacit policy forged out of necessity by European merchants dependent on other migrant ethnic groups to help their business transactions and trade. Chinese merchants, for example, acted regularly as middlemen for Europeans in dealing with local traders. They had a far better understanding of local institutions and social forces with respect to regional markets as well as better opportunities for access in most cases.[56] This meant their services and local knowledge were absolutely indispensable to the development and future success of the port. Thus any overt territorial disputes, regarding access to the river and trade would have been counterproductive.

In order for Raffles' plan of occupational and ethnic settlement to be accomplished it was essential that major reclamation work be carried out on the south bank of the river. Initially, the main task was the construction of a crescent shaped embankment from the road opposite Ferry Point (Fullerton Hotel) to the proposed bridge (Elgin Bridge).[57] The hitherto flood prone south side was built up and reinforced to provide a permanent embankment between the river and the land behind. With the river thus contained, the hinterland was able to be drained providing, 'extensive grounds ... rendered permanently dry and salubrious'.[58] The huge amount of land fill required for this public works programme came from a small hill which stood where Raffles Place is today. According to the only eye witness account by Munshi Abdullah, it was levelled by pick and shovel, an arduous job undertaken by Chinese, Indian and Malay labourers who were paid one rupee a day to carry soil and stone to the reclamation site.[59] The riverside land reclaimed in this manner was set aside for the business sector to conduct commerce and build godowns. The reconstruction of the bank was done in such a fashion as to create a natural wharf where lighters could load and discharge cargo.[60] It was originally estimated that between 20 to 30 spacious godowns would be created along this line.[61] In time this would prove to be a very conservative approximation of warehouse space and needs.

By the time of Raffles' departure from Singapore in June 1823, much of the ground work for the New Town[62] had been completed and the river was taking on the distinct appearance of an economic landscape. With the river being contained and transformed, extensive building work got under way as each communal group settled their allotment. Of the feverish work in progress one contemporary observer wrote, 'we may soon look for a well-built town, with numerous and convenient wharfs along the banks of the river, or rather an inlet of the sea, contiguous to which the principal mercantile part of it is marked out, and already partly occupied with ... warehouses'.[63] The river was now recognised as the centre of commercial activity, neatly partitioned into economic and ethnic zones, designed to ensure its role as the economic lifeline of the port colony. Not long after arriving to take up the post of Resident in Singapore, John Crawfurd wrote to the colonial authorities in India, highlighting the new found importance of the river: 'The existence of the river or rather creek of Singapore as the government is already aware forms one of the most valuable and striking features of the place, as a commercial port.'[64] Crawfurd, though under explicit instructions from India to bring down the factory's expenses by halting public works, authorised the completion of reclamation work along the south bank of the river and the levelling of the hill in what became Commercial Square (Raffles Place). Crawfurd was under considerable pressure from the merchant community of Singapore who petitioned him to ensure the work being carried out along the river proceeded. Their lengthy appeal provides further proof of just how important the river was to the port.[65] In correspondence with his superiors he described as 'impractical' attempts to reduce expenditure in this way as it would impede trade and the future growth of the settlement, which was not in the 'best interests of the government'.[66]

By March 1824 there were 793 substantial buildings in the settlement. The number of brick and tile warehouses and shops erected for conducting business along the south side of the river had already reached 26.[67] Many other plank and tile, and thatch buildings, also dotted the reclaimed land bordering the river. In the space of just several months the population living on the south side of the river, had swelled to several thousand.[68] The population increase and near instant success of the port pushed land prices in the best quarters of the town, including the river zones, to 3,000 and 4,000 Spanish dollars per lot.[69] Where several years earlier there had only been jungle, swamp and mud, there now stood the completed buildings of government and the more prosperous merchants. Ecologically and socially the first major transformation of the river's environment had begun. A new distinctive landscape was taking shape. Its key identifying features were no longer those associated with a near pristine environment only marginally altered by human encroachment, but rather the machines and edifices of Empire and a prosperous colonial port, namely, trading companies, shophouses, godowns and lighters. The river community was also spatially delineated according to economic, occupational and ethnic groupings, around the river centre.

While the occupational and ethnic boundaries set out by Raffles changed somewhat over time, as Singapore's population grew and its demographic composition altered,[70] they still provided the baseline for future riverine development and life. The town plan and economic landscape Raffles' inaugurated were designed to ensure control of river space by those communal groups who would further the interests of British commerce in the region. Later development along the river was also carried out with the same basic intent in mind. As pressure for expansion of the port increased, the river was further contained and land around it reclaimed and utilised for trading and other commercial activities. Later development of the port away from the river in the latter part of the nineteenth century never completely displaced the template of the early ethnic and ecological boundaries and the underlying assumption that the river and surrounding area be reserved for commerce. The river's importance in commerce and as the centre of the settlement, reflecting the basic layout of the town as prescribed by Raffles, did not alter significantly until major urban renewal schemes got under way in the 1970s. Even today aspects of the original plan are still evident with the banking sector located in Raffles Place (formerly Commercial Square) and Parliament on the ground originally reserved for such official purposes.

Functional Aspects of the River Port

Depending on the tide it was possible for large vessels to enter the Singapore River. The brig *Ganges* was taken into the river to act as a store for Farquhar and his original party[71] and other craft up to 'at least two hundred and fifty tons'[72] also entered the river during the establishment years. The river's dimensions and relatively small volume of water, however, prohibited its transformation into an area with docks where large vessels could berth and discharge cargo. Due to constraints imposed by the river's size, the port evolved in a two dimensional manner; an outer harbour, the bay, where large vessels anchored to discharge and receive cargo, and an inner harbour, the river, where goods were stored and moved to and fro by smaller craft. The link between the two parts of the port was provided by various lighter craft, plying between them.

The outer harbour provided estuary-like shelter for shipping during most of the year and was divided into areas where vessels of different nations and classes could anchor. The position of the anchorages meant shipping was largely protected from the worst weather. From most points of the compass the bay was shielded by land from the elements.[73] The only exposed side was to the south where a large 'mud bank', a mile and a half offshore mitigated the worst affects of weather from that direction.[74] Arriving at Singapore, shipping would wait off the river mouth in the sheltered waters of the bay and from there transport their cargoes by lighter to godowns along the river. The river itself, due to its pocket size, was a protected waterway rarely affected by even the severest storms, although tidal flooding did occur quite frequently in the years before embankment of the river was complete.

The interaction between the two sections of the port was bustling right from the beginning. The scene as it appeared in both areas in early travel accounts was one of intense activity and excitement. In the outer harbour, apart from lighter craft carrying trade goods from the holds and decks of ships, the water was bristling with 'hundreds of small boats of all descriptions constantly pulling about selling fruit, provisions, birds, monkeys, shells and coral'.[75] The inner harbour, or river, presented a similar scene with 'hundreds' of small craft entering and leaving with all manner of cargoes. And at night the waters of the river near its mouth were brilliantly illuminated by the lights of 'numerous boats' at rest there.[76] The two dimensional nature of the port guaranteed its future development, providing the key elements of any port, namely, shelter for shipping and safe handling of goods.[77]

Another important factor associated with the evolution of any port is its links with the surrounding countryside or 'hinterland'.[78] Singapore offered little in the way of exportable goods. Instead its role was that of a global trading 'mart'.[79] There were few major industries to speak of beyond those enterprises supporting local commercial ventures and shipping. For a time the lushness of Singapore's forests had many believing that it would, in addition to being a commercial centre, become a 'vast ...

agricultural establishment' inferior only to Calcutta,[80] but with few exceptions attempts to establish a plantation sector failed.[81] Pepper and gambier were for a time significant in the commercial success of Singapore, but proved to be unsustainable in the long term. Even the supply of fresh produce for ships' stores could not be met locally resulting in higher costs as stocks had to be brought in from surrounding islands.[82] Soil quality proved a major obstacle, as did the techniques of cultivation employed.[83] Swidden agriculture used with the cultivation of gambier and pepper, the most promising commercial crops planted, caused such land degradation that by the 1850s vast stretches of Singapore's interior had been stripped bare and abandoned.[84] With few primary industries and no agricultural sector to speak of, virtually all exports from Singapore were the imported produce of other nations: Asian, European and American.

Singapore port did not have a vast 'hinterland' unless we use the term in a more unconventional manner to include those places linked to it via sea routes.[85] Singapore's success as a commercial centre was a result of its ability to attract from surrounding areas a vast array of commodities to be traded on the world market and also to redistribute to those same locations the produce of other areas. Thus its 'hinterland' was the Southeast Asian region and beyond, linked to it by maritime transport. Unlike other major ports developing around the world, Singapore was not a location 'where ocean and inland transport lines meet and intertwine'[86] but rather a bottleneck where different maritime global-regional routes converged in the Straits of Malacca.

The port's near total dependence on a vast maritime hinterland, and, its two-dimensional nature, highlights the importance of the lighterage industry in its successful evolution and development. With no facilities for ships to dock alongside wharves, the role of lighters was absolutely crucial in the operation of the port of Singapore. The lighterage industry was the key to the port's future prosperity during the establishment years, providing the vital link and access between a vast maritime hinterland and essential facilities along the river.

The Trade of the River Port

An entrepôt is the best way to describe Singapore's role in regional and global trading. The island is situated historically in an ideal location, making it a perfect place as a redistribution centre and market. It was surrounded by numerous states and islands all within reasonable sailing distance of the port. In this establishment period, when sailing craft literally ruled the waves, Singapore's key location placed it astride the main sea routes between east and west. Vessels wanting to journey to countries east of the Malay Peninsula, such as Indo-China, the Philippines and China, had three main routes open to them during the southwest monsoon all of which brought them within easy reach of Singapore.[87] Thus, the trade passing through the port and its godowns reflected the diversity of goods and produce emanating from virtually all points of the globe as

Northeast and Southeast Asia were integrated into the world capitalist system.

It is difficult to determine the overall volume of goods that were handled along the river in the establishment period as no specific record of river trade separate from the rest of the port was ever kept. Based on the fact that the river was the principal area offering facilities for handling goods prior to the 1860s, we can assume that the rising trade figures for this period also largely reflect possible trade figures for the river.[88] (For tables showing the value and volume of trade handled at Singapore during these years see Appendix 2, Tables 2–3.) As late as 1864, there were only a 'few godowns on the western side of the town' with their own wharves, taking some business away from the river and Boat Quay.[89] While some commercial services opened in New Harbour during the 1860s, more than three-quarters of all shipping business continued to be conducted along Boat Quay.[90] The trade of the river was as varied as it was vast. It is not intended here to detail the commercial intercourse carried on between Singapore and the rest of the world, or to trace the flow of goods from one source to another, but rather to indicate the variety and volume of goods carried by lighters in the harbour and river.[91]

The assortment of merchandise that passed through Singapore was absolutely staggering. In the establishment years it was largely of a rather exotic nature — marine and jungle produce[92] while towards the end of the nineteenth-century primary commodities such as rubber, tin, copra and sugar became the main staples transhipped through the port. In the early years the trade very much reflected the Chinese and Western demand for the natural produce of the region and beyond (see Appendix 2, Table 4).[93] Any examination of the commerce of Singapore for this period reveals the port's dependence on such items as spices, ivory, dragon's blood (resin of certain trees and palms), tortoise shell, sticlac, seaweed, sea cucumber and a multitude of other items, including opium.[94] The godowns and shops that sprung up along the riverbanks were filled with such trade goods and produce from neighbouring countries and regions. The streets and alleys in the commercial part of the town were filled with the sounds of barter in a variety of languages and dialects and enlivened by numerous wares to be found on offer outside the merchant shops. According to one observer, 'here you stumble at every step over the produce of China, and the Straits'.[95] There was a carnival like atmosphere which pervaded that part of town, a permanent 'bazaar' as it was called by one observer, 'crammed', with the 'productions of almost every nation in the world'.[96]

Trading activity in Singapore revolved around two main seasons, 'the junk season and the Bugis season'.[97] Junks from South China arrived in Singapore between January and March each year. Their arrival was one of the most anticipated events on the Singapore calendar during the establishment years. They came from all points along the mainland coast, from as far north as Shanghai, carried to Singapore on the northeast monsoon.[98] The arrival of the junks each year marked the beginning of a notable increase in commercial activity, especially in the Chinese community.[99] Upon the first junk being sighted a swarm of small craft would race out to escort it to the anchorage and runners would spread the news through the town.[100] The excitement that surrounded the arrival of these junks was not without good reason as the value of cargo that could be carried on a single junk was phenomenal. One 600 ton junk from Canton in 1824 had a cargo valued at between 70 and 80 thousand dollars.[101] Another from Fukien Province, 250 tons burthen, had a cargo worth 70,000 dollars.[102] These vessels primarily carried goods to meet the needs of the growing Chinese population in Singapore and surrounding islands and countries.[103] The *Singapore Chronicle* reported on the volume and value of this trade in 1829:

> The whole of the Chinese Junks for the season have arrived and the principal part, if not the whole of their cargoes are already disposed of... The number which have arrived this year, is eight, three from Amoy, and five from Canton; and they are of the burthen of from 250 to 400 tons. The import cargoes, of both the Amoy and Canton junks are very similar, and they bring the same articles, year after year, with little or no variation. The cargoes from Amoy are chiefly composed of – earthenware – tiles – granite slabs – paper umbrellas – vermicelli – dried fruits – joss sticks – joss paper – and a few nankeens, raw silk etc., and are said to be of the value of from $30,000 to $60,000 Dollars [sic]. The cargoes from Canton, consist of the same articles, with the addition of – silk camlets – satins – camphor – sugar candy, and tea; and a much greater number of nankeens (in blue, green and yellow), and raw silk.[104]

The inventory of cargoes often included other more mundane items. To the above list one might add such commodities and products as tea, medicines, twine, flour, crackers, paint and combs.[105] A survey of merchandise carried to Singapore by junks over the years shows little variation in the type of goods shipped. Another important cargo brought from China was people or 'flesh'. The legal and forced trade in human beings was profitable and played a major role in Singapore's commercial intercourse with China as millions fled their homeland seeking better lives abroad. Singapore became a clearing house for traffic in human beings on their way to all parts of Southeast Asia.

An important source of merchandise found in warehouses and on the wharves of the river was from the archipelago itself. Collectively known as 'Straits produce' the marine, agricultural, jungle and mineral products of the archipelago were a major component of Singapore's trade with China. The trade in these products was the traditional basis of China's commercial links with Southeast Asia and the monopoly of the junk traders.[106] Most of the export trade from Singapore consisted of Straits produce because there was little demand in China for the industrial products of Britain and continental Europe.[107] Among the most desired goods from the Southeast Asian region were the following articles: edible seaweed, birds' nest, tortoiseshell, gambier, gutta-percha, sea cucumber, gold dust, ebony, shark fins, rattan, beeswax, rice, all manner of spices, tin and sandalwood.[108] (See Appendix 2, Table 4, for a comprehensive list.)

Like products that originated from China, there was always a certain amount of variation in what constituted Straits produce, and, at different times, certain items took on greater importance than others in regional and global patterns of trade and exchange.

Singapore port became a central regional emporium into which this varied and valuable trade poured. From the time of its establishment the port proved a magnet to local coastal traders carrying the goods of the archipelago. Farquhar wrote to Raffles in November of 1819 conveying news of the port's importance as a collecting point for Straits produce. In spite of the port's infancy valuable cargoes were already arriving from across the archipelago on board 'native' sailing vessels. A year later the situation had further improved and Farquhar wrote enthusiastically to Raffles about this native trade:

> It affords me the greatest satisfaction to be able to state to you that althou' scarcely one and twenty months have as yet elapsed since the first formation of the port it already far exceeds what Malacca could boast of during the most flourishing years of its long continuance in our possession — upwards of a hundred sails of Bugis prows alone have already arrived here (and more are still expected) many of them being of the most valuable class. The harbour is likewise crowded with various other trading prows and junks ... in short this seems to be the favourite rendezvous for all descriptions of Eastern traders.[109]

The Bugis of south and east Sulawesi were by far the biggest carriers of Straits produce to Singapore.[110] Large numbers of their craft, between 40 and 100 tons burthen, could be found in the outer roadstead during the 'Bugis season' between June and November each year.[111] Adept mariners and traders, the Bugis had traditionally traversed the archipelago collecting the natural produce of various islands for interregional trading. With the establishment of Singapore, much of what they collected found its way into the godowns along the river. Their voyages began with the commencement of the southeast monsoon and ended weeks or months later in Singapore depending on how far they had travelled in the process of assembling their cargoes.

There were of course many other traders in the archipelago beside the Bugis. The early official records show that a regular stream of Malay traders from Sumatra also made their way to Singapore carrying spices and other goods.[112] Pepper, coffee and sago formed an important part of this trade. In 1825 a fleet of 25 craft arrived in Singapore from northern Sumatra carrying two to three thousand piculs of pepper.[113] (See Appendix 2, Table 1 for summary of weights and measures.) George Bennett witnessed a fleet of 18 Sumatran prows arriving in the Singapore River in the 1830s loaded with unprocessed sago, and he reported that 'regular fleets of ten or more' such craft were resorting there.[114] There was also a number of sailing vessels each year from Java which were called the 'Arab ships' due to their being owned by the Arabs resident there. These craft, crewed by Javanese, carried large quantities of coffee, sugar and rice to Singapore.[115]

Similarly there were many smaller craft owned by Chinese working along the coast of the Malay Peninsula and islands close to Singapore.[116] The Malay states provided tin, gold, cotton piece goods, black pepper, rattan, salt and aloes wood.[117]

Continental Asia provided further trade products for Singapore's global-regional market, in particular Siam (Thailand) and Cochin China (Vietnam). Until the 1860s there was a steady stream of junks from both these countries sailing to Singapore each year on the northeast monsoon. Between 1829 and 1866 an average of 30 Siamese and 78 Cochin Chinese junks arrived annually.[118] Their arrival and the principal goods carried by them were detailed in the *Singapore Chronicle* in 1824. From Siam 'thirteen junks' called carrying the 'usual' articles including sugar, rice, salt, coconut oil, cast iron, culinary utensils and sticlac.[119] The article also enumerated the cargoes of the Cochin Chinese junks that had arrived, 'they have brought rice, sugar, raw silk, Tonkin lead, pickled pork, hogs lard and live stock'.[120] They also carried tea and other important items from China.

Thus far I have looked only at goods from East and Southeast Asia that passed through the godowns on the Singapore River. The river was though a truly global entrepôt and not simply a regional trading centre with goods arriving from as far away as continental Europe and North America. Trade with Britain and India was a particularly important factor in Singapore's early commercial success. Between 1823 and 1869 almost 20 per cent of Singapore's total trade annually was with Britain, while commerce with India accounted for a further 17 per cent.[121] It was after all a primary objective in establishing Singapore to further the commercial interests of Britain. John Cameron notes the extent to which European goods were readily available in Singapore, describing the scene along the river front in the 1860s. While sketching the setting along Boat Quay he stated, 'from morning till night may be seen the landing of huge cases, casks and bales of British manufactures, as well as machinery and iron-work of all descriptions'.[122] Commercial tables show the following articles as principal goods imported from Britain, Europe and America: anchors and grapnels, arms, beer, canvas, copper sheathing, cordage, cotton twist, earthenware, gold and silver thread, gunpowder, iron and steel, lead, paint, provisions, cotton piece goods, spelter, spirits, sundries, glassware, wines, woollens and ironware and mongery.[123] From India under British rule and monopoly, the following marketable goods were found in Singapore: opium, piece goods, wheat, rice, gram, gunnies and saltpetre.[124] Opium and arms were particularly profitable and sold extensively to Chinese and Southeast Asians to finance the colonial enterprise. Singapore became the biggest drug[125] and guns market[126] of the archipelago.

The bewildering array of trade goods that passed through Singapore coupled with its multi-dimensional port structure meant there was a need for the development of a lighterage industry. While some smaller trading prows were able to enter the river to discharge their cargoes, in the main all trading vessels required the services of lighters. The port regulations specifically prohibited vessels of more than 40 tons entering the river unless they were at risk of sinking.[127] And in fact, due to congestion on the river, by the 1850s no craft other than cargo lighters and small craft carrying people were allowed to enter the river. From this time smaller prows were also forced to off load their cargoes in the bay using lighters, despite protests and petitions by 22 gambier and pepper *towkays* that their merchandise was regularly damaged by exposure to salt water during transfer.[128]

The scene along the river and in the outer harbour, as attested to by numerous contemporary accounts and illustrations, was one of intense activity as lighters and small craft carrying provisions and trade goods moved to and fro amongst the ships at anchor. By the end of the establishment period in 1869 there were more than 500 small craft moored in the first reach of the river devoted solely to transporting the trade of Singapore.[129]

Other Riverine Activities

During the establishment years the river also supported activities for the port and town beyond simply by providing wharves and warehouses. Of critical importance were services for shipping such as the supply of potable water, shipwrights and chandlers. Other industries developed along the river too, taking advantage of the convenience it afforded. Many of these activities did not stand the test of time and were either forced to relocate elsewhere or they disappeared completely. Nevertheless, they played a part in shaping the early character of the river and provided further impetus to the growth of the lighterage industry. The river in spite of its small size provided a key artery for transporting materials inland. Even occasional flooding which caused problems in the town was, in the upper reaches of the river, sometimes a bonus. As the river flooded the mangrove swamps around the settlement, houses beyond its banks had ready access to the town and ocean. This allowed all manner of building materials to be conveyed by water to where they were required.[130] For sago manufacturers, the one successful processing industry that developed during these years, the river made access to factories easy (see Map 5). The raw sago could be brought up to the doors of the plant and the processed product moved with ease either for sale in town or to shipping in the outer harbour. For industries such as shipwrights and chandlers the river had obvious advantages being centrally located in relation to all maritime activity.

Amongst Raffles' earliest instructions to Farquhar were specific orders regarding works to be undertaken to improve 'the conveniences of the port for shipping'.[131] He particularly referred to facilities for 'watering, ballasting, as well as loading' ships.[132] In order for Singapore to fulfil its principal purpose as an entrepôt for British shipping in Asian waters, it was essential that these basic needs be catered for. The river played a significant role in furnishing these requirements. While some provisions had to be brought in from surrounding islands,[133] supplies of potable water were found near the river. A source near the river facilitated the water's transport to ships in the harbour. This water supply was located in a series of wells dug between the foot of Government Hill and the river.[134] A reservoir was built and an aqueduct constructed to carry water from the wells around the hill to a tank. The tank was located near the river and a spout allowed small craft to pull in beneath it and take on water.[135] Vessels in the harbour employed lighters to carry water from the river to shipside. They were also free to use their own smaller boats to collect water if they wished.[136] There were serious problems in doing this though. Until the 1840s the outlet pipe was situated above the only bridge on the river and, as it was a wooden structure, there was always a danger that a crew unfamiliar with the river's currents would ram its pilings and do serious damage.[137]

Supplies of potable water collected from the river's edge was the main source for shipping until the latter part of the nineteenth century. However, while the water was plentiful it took hours to replenish the storage tanks of a single ship as the pressure of the water flowing through the pipes was around four gallons per minute.[138] While facilities along the river continued to expand and upgrade to meet the needs of shipping, the conveyance of water was always found wanting. As early as 1823 Crawfurd wrote to the government of India complaining about problems associated with the water supply and the threat posed to shipping.[139] Although considerable monies had been spent on improving the service, Crawfurd claimed it was not adequate to handle the volume of shipping that passed through the harbour. Singapore's position as a principal port was under threat if it could not maintain a sufficient supply of potable water.[140] In the years that followed, numerous complaints were made regarding the difficulties experienced by shipping due to problems obtaining water.[141] Vessels were detained far longer than was necessary as they waited for water, and some resorted to procuring it from the Kallang River where the supply was known to be contaminated.[142] Problems with an adequate water supply for shipping continued, as they did for the town, until the building of better facilities in the final decades of the nineteenth century.

Other key industries in the busy port, were also found along the river. There were shipwrights and ship's chandlers amongst the godowns and shops along South Boat Quay and in Commercial Square.[143] These sites provided the industries with direct access to the lighters which were constantly moving between the wharves and ships in the harbour. Removed from the bustle of South Boat Quay were the shipwrights' yards. From the late 1820s until 1862 there was always at least one yard open along the north bank of the river, just behind the court buildings. For a time it was anticipated that large vessels, up to 500 tons burthen, would be built in yards along the river.[144] The 194-ton brig, *Elizabeth*, the first ocean going vessel to be built in Singapore, was launched from Hallpike Street Boat Yard in 1829.[145] This shipyard was later taken over by the company of Wilkinson and Tivendale and became one of the most important in Singapore.[146] At various times other yards were opened on land adjacent to Tivendales, but the owners eventually shifted their operations to the beach at Teluk Ayer.[147] In 1848 Tivendale's launched from their yard a small steamer, the *Ranee*, measuring 60 feet, also the first of its kind to be built in Singapore.[148] Tivendale's built several other craft in the river over the years, including a number of gunboats, and regularly serviced ships in the harbour.[149] This yard often had large vessels in the river for repairs, such as the 400-ton barque, *Lylph*, in 1836. At times the noise from Tivendale's made proceedings in the court building behind them difficult to follow.[150] While all European shipyards, such as Tivendale's, eventually relocated away from the river, there were always shipwrights found along it. As the demand for cargo lighters grew, numerous Asian (principally Chinese) artisans built and repaired them at the upper reaches of the river.

Prior to the 1860s the area below Elgin Bridge had been the focus of all commercial activity in the town and port. Cameron in his account of Singapore says that traffic and activity along the river above the Bridge was insignificant.[151] The town's growth along the river had reached only as far as Coleman Bridge. Higher up the river there were a number of properties belonging to wealthy merchants and the government's powder magazine and coal stores.[152] It was in these further reaches of the river, too, that Singapore's 'only industry of any note'[153] developed. Sago processing was the earliest and most successful of Singapore's industries and the only one to generate any real exports.[154] The production of pearl sago was introduced as early as 1819, and by 1849 there were 15 plants run by Chinese and two by Europeans.[155] The backwaters of the river were an ideal setting for sago manufacturers. The river provided easy access to their factories and a convenient dumping ground for the waste they produced. Most of the sago processing plants were located on the 'winding and branching creeks and canals of the Singapore river, a situation admirably adapted for them', because it enabled small boats to unload directly into the factory with no further transporting or handling.[156] The access to these factories provided by the river was described as one of the 'essential features of every manufactory'.[157] Sago manufacturing continued along the banks of the river long after the establishment era had drawn to a close. In the latter part of the nineteenth century, sago producers came under regular and intense scrutiny because of growing concern about the amount of waste dumped in the headwaters of the river. Municipal Reports for the 1880s and 1890s reveal regular complaints and action taken against the manufacturers of sago. Eventually, regulations were passed to try and restrict the amount of waste being dumped into the river.[158]

By the end of the establishment period in 1869 Singapore's regional role as a port and entrepôt was secure as 'the Queen of the Further East'.[159] Though vulnerable to the vagaries of global trading, by the time the Suez Canal opened in 1869, the port along Singapore River was one of the most important in the British Empire. From the deck of a ship in the harbour it would have been difficult to imagine the wilderness scene described by Farquhar only a half century earlier. The jungle covered hills and shoreline had given way to impressive merchant houses and public buildings flanking the river and the prosperous commercial centre of the town. The administrative, commercial and ethnic wards or zones created by Raffles had developed largely according to plan. From the manicured lawns surrounding government offices, on the north bank of the river, one could look across at the many fine buildings in the business centre of the settlement in Commercial Square and South Boat Quay, near the river mouth. Further along the quay, moving up the river, were many establishments belonging to Chinese merchants. And behind the commercial district, stretching inland for several kilometres, was the now extensive Chinatown.

While the upper reaches of the river, beyond Coleman Bridge, were still largely unused, their transformation into a commercial zone was already under way. With global trade about to be stimulated by the opening of the Suez Canal and widespread use of steamships, it was only a matter of time before the entire length of the river was utilised as trade burgeoned and new industries developed. The further growth of trade and commerce stimulated the already large lighterage industry. By 1869 there were hundreds of lighter craft and thousands of men employed in transporting goods between the river and outer harbour. In the post Suez Canal era, in spite of the port centre shifting to the New Harbour, the demand for more lighters, and men to work them, increased significantly. It is to these men, their origins and occupation, that I now turn.

3
Lightermen: Migration and Destiny

THE nineteenth and early twentieth centuries witnessed unprecedented migration from India and China to Southeast Asia. A combination of domestic upheaval and the promise of wealth to be made in the colonial possessions of Europe lured millions of people away from their homes and families. Faced with despair borne of poverty, war and overcrowding in their homelands, many Indians and Chinese chose to leave, attracted to Southeast Asia by colonial expansion that meant the possibility of paid work and a better life.[1] To exploit the resources and potential of the Southeast Asian region to the full, the grip of European powers on the region tightened during the nineteenth and early twentieth century, and there was a huge demand for labour. Consequently, across Southeast Asia there seemed to be limitless opportunities for unskilled labourers in mines, on plantations and in rapidly growing colonial towns and ports.

Singapore's dynamic colonial economy and growing importance as a regional and global port made it an early key destination for Indian and Chinese migrants. From a nascent population of around 1,000 in 1819[2] Singapore quickly grew to become a cosmopolitan city of considerable economic importance in the region. It acted as a conduit through which Asian migrant labour was channelled throughout the archipelago, and as a consequence of its own success absorbed large numbers of migrant workers. Those men and women who arrived and were not moved on to the tin mines or rubber plantations of the surrounding colonies, sought employment in a variety of urban occupations in Singapore. In the burgeoning settlement there were always jobs in land clearing, construction, road building and all manner of service industries, including transport, and hawking. The development and growth of the port also contributed to the overall employment situation in Singapore, providing opportunities in vital occupations like stevedoring, coal hauling and lighterage.

One of the first major service industries to develop in Singapore, the lighterage industry was critical to the port's functioning and a key source of employment. The establishment of lighterage services was an essential element in the port's initial success, and in the period 1819–1983, communal control of the industry along the river changed hands several times. Between 1819 and 1900 lighterage on the river was largely in the hands of south Indian boatmen. From the beginning of the twentieth century until lighters were removed from the river in 1983 Chinese boatmen dominated the industry. This chapter examines the origins of the men who worked the lighters of the Singapore River.

Indian Migrants and Lightermen

Contact between India and Southeast Asia had been established more than a thousand years before the first Europeans ventured into the archipelago.[3] Centuries of interaction gave rise to a succession of powerful Hindu-Buddhist city-states in the region. Though long since vanished, the early indigenous cultures and traditions of insular Southeast Asia have been indelibly marked through this extended contact with India.[4] The surge of colonialism and *laissez-faire* development in Southeast Asia at the beginning of the nineteenth century resulted in a new wave of Indian contact with the region. This new flood of south Asian migrants were desired not for their culture, religion or political skills but for their strong backs and labour potential.[5] While Indian traders and artisans continued to make their way to the archipelago, it was south Asian peasants who were in great demand as labourers to work under the growing European colonial empires of the period.[6]

Indian labour was a critical element of colonial development in Southeast Asia especially in areas under direct British influence.[7] For much of the nineteenth century impoverished Indian labourers and convicts were procured for work in the Straits Settlements.[8] With no restrictions on immigration, such as existed in China, a regular supply of Indian labour was recruited in India for Singapore and Penang under what amounted to conditions of bondage and dependency.[9] Initially, the labour-intensive spice and sugar plantations owned by Europeans in Penang and Province Wellesley, were dependent on cheap labour from India.[10] Later in the century there was a huge demand for Tamil labour on the rubber plantations that sprang up all over Malaya. Indian convicts provided a pool of cheap manual workers who could be utilised by various municipal and government authorities. And, it was to Singapore that the majority eventually found their way.

By 1845, Singapore had become the main penal centre in the Straits[11] with some 1,500 convicts serving their time there.[12] The official attitude toward convict labour in Singapore was liberal, in spite of a concern among residents over the dumping of the 'scum and refuse' of Empire on their doorstep.[13] Indian convicts were given considerable freedom in Singapore, virtually becoming their own warders.[14] Convicts were trained in useful trades and employed in all manner of activities and schemes, including agriculture, snake and tiger killing, fire control, bridge and road construction, nursing and building construction. Indian convict labour was used in almost all public works construction between the late 1820s and 1873 when the last convicts were withdrawn.[15] Economic expediency was always the primary consideration when the issue of convict labour was raised.[16] While their presence was always contentious, their removal raised the spectre of higher labour costs, particularly on major government projects. Consequently, the influential grand jury, made up of the town's leading merchants, called for a phased withdrawal of convicts.[17] This was a calculated, pragmatic approach for all concerned because of the possible increased government charges, including port fees and duties, that would arise from the absence of convict labour.

Convict labour was directly involved with and had a direct impact on the river. With the government running a tight budget, and lacking the will to levy significant taxes, the cost of land reclamation along the river was reduced by the use of convict labour. The morass to the north and west of the town was reclaimed largely by the effort of convicts. Between 1840 and 1856 up to 170 convicts were employed annually as street cleaners, scavengers and road builders in the town. These workers dumped all sweepings in the swamps bordering the river.[18] As the town refuse built up, it was covered by brushwood and dirt. Long lines of convicts engaged in reclamation work along the river could be heard singing as they daily made their way through town with bundles of brushwood and baskets of dirt balanced on their heads.[19] This method of reclamation was used until 1858 when public concern was raised as to whether it was hygienic to use town refuse in this manner.[20] Fears were raised in the press about noxious gases rising from reclaimed land and the possible health hazard posed to the town.[21] Large numbers of convicts were also employed in the construction of river walls and in cleaning the river bed.[22] At low tide these labourers would wade in the river bucketing out mud that built up near the quay walls. Not surprisingly, the first dredge boat to be used on the river was crewed by Indian convicts supervised by an overseer.[23] Indian convicts and labourers continued to be employed on many of the subsequent dredges to be used in the river.

The involvement of South Asians from the Coromandel Coast of India (see Map 7), with the lighterage industry, also dates from the earliest days of settlement. In 1819 Raffles' small fleet carried to Singapore a military force of at least 120 Indian troops, or *sepoys*, as well as Indian sailors, *lascars*, and a number of civilian natives of India.[24] These individuals were employed in various public duties including that of boatmen.[25] Singapore's early success as an entrepôt meant there was a ready demand for more settlers and skilled artisans. The Indians already in Singapore were urged by Raffles and Farquhar to encourage more of their compatriots to emigrate to the colony. Specifically, it was requested that 'sufficient masons, coolies, and the people for brick and lime kilns' together with merchants and others be encouraged to settle in Singapore.[26] It was during this initial period that Indians established themselves as the principal conveyers of cargo in the port. The extent to which they had become the primary protagonists in this industry is born out in a letter sent to Raffles' secretary in 1822 by the Town Committee, stating there were around 1,000 Chuliahs in Singapore and that it would be 'very desirable' to locate them in a situation (along the river) where they could 'have their boats at hand and ready at all times' (see Map 3).[27] Significantly, the letter does not mention any other trades with which south Indians were involved at the time; a strong indication of their prevailing strength in the lighterage industry which would last until the turn of the century.

The exact origins of the Indian boatmen are difficult to ascertain, although it is clear that they came from southern India. The boatmen were referred to variously as 'Chuliah' and/or 'Kling'. Both terms were used either together or at different times to describe Indian Muslims, primarily from the Coromandel Coast.[28] They came from the Kalinga Kingdom on the Coromandel Coast, hence 'Kling'. Until the 1880s, when large numbers of Hindus started arriving in the Straits Settlements under the indentured labour system, the largest percentage of Indians in the region were Muslims from southern India.[29] The term 'Chuliah' was used in Singapore to refer specifically to Muslim Indians from the Coromandel Coast. Later the term 'Kling' was adopted to describe individuals who were also Muslims from a broader region of southern India, including the central and west coast areas.[30]

Evidence suggests that many of the Indian lightermen who worked the Singapore River traced their roots to a group of Indian Muslims from the east coast of India, the Marakayar.[31] These people, whose name comes from the Arabic word for boat, have a long history of involvement with the sea and maritime activities.[32] Not surprisingly, then, south Indian migrants to Singapore and Malaya during the establishment era came largely from this group.[33] With their cultural-historical connections to the sea, when the opportunity presented itself, the Marakayar were naturally attracted to the occupation of boatmen in Singapore and other colonial ports. The links between immigrants' occupation in India and that pursued abroad were still strong as late as 1958 when almost 80 per cent of Indian lightermen in Singapore were born in India, and of these 76 per cent claimed to have been boatmen at home.[34] Many of the early lightermen were recruited directly from the East India Company's ports at Madras and Penang.[35] Certainly company officials such as Flint,[36] Farquhar and Raffles were familiar with Indian boatmen from their own experiences in India and Penang, and sought such capable individuals for the task in Singapore. The handling of cargo boats required a considerable degree of skill and could not be left in the hands of novices, because valuable merchandise could easily be lost or damaged through mishandling or misadventure. Finding suitably qualified boatmen was an important consideration before the advent of motorised craft, when nautical skill and strength with oar and sail were paramount to manoeuvring these unwieldy boats against tide and wind. The Singapore River was no place for an unskilled boatman, particularly in the era before motorised lighters and towing launches as the tidal movement through its narrow mouth was treacherously fast, and to avoid the rocky shoal to its seaward side, great skill in navigation was required.[37]

The earliest statistics compiled in Singapore refer specifically to the Coromandel Coast as the main source of migrants and lists among the principal occupations for this group, 'boatmen'. While Chinese and Malays were mainly employed as day labourers, porters and fishermen, 'natives' of the 'Coromandel Coast' controlled the lighterage industry.[38] A government report in 1827 stated that the number of residents from the Coromandel region was 1,121 of whom 330 were boatmen.[39]

A decade later, with the port growing and the volume of trade increasing, around 1,750 Indian lightermen were working along the river and three-quarters of the settlement's Indian population were employed as lightermen.[40] They were the most skilled in handling cargo boats and also the sole group prepared to carry out other laborious tasks associated with this trade, especially maintaining the boats and handling bulky cargoes.[41] In the 1840s Davidson wrote that 'the boats employed to carry cargoes to and from shipping in the harbour, are almost all manned by these Klings; and excellent boatmen they are'.[42] Twenty years later John Cameron described the scene along the river, providing further evidence of the extent to which Indian lightermen controlled transport of cargo in the river. According to Cameron's account the curve of the river along South Boat Quay from the mouth to Elgin Bridge was jammed with Indian lighters (tongkang) lying three and four abreast.[43] He estimated the number of craft to be around 500, and with a crew of three men each the floating population alone was approximately 1,500 individuals.[44]

The decline of Indian dominance along the river began after 1867, but it is clear that until the turn of the century Indian boatmen were involved with lighterage on the river. As late as 1911, complaints were voiced about the disturbing noise made by Indian lightermen on the river,[45] suggesting that their presence was still not inconsequential. A number of factors contributed to the decline of Indian lighters and boatmen on the river after 1867. Gibson-Hill suggests that the main cause was the administrative change which saw responsibility for the Straits Settlements transferred that year to the Colonial Office in London.[46] While there is no doubt the severing of ties with India affected the position of Indian people in Singapore, and that the decline of the boatmen began around this time,[47] there was another more important local factor influencing the lighterage industry. The shift of European trading activity away from the river to New Harbour was brought about by the increasing use of steam vessels. As facilities at New Harbour improved amidst a burgeoning trade facilitated by steam and, in the case of European trade with Asia by the opening of the Suez Canal,[48] there was a shift away from the river by European merchants and trading houses. Long in control of transoceanic trade, the Europeans found the modern facilities at New Harbour more suitable for the new demands created by steam vessels and global-regional markets,[49] hence, the centre of European trading activity shifted further west along the foreshore. The impact of this site change was significant for lightermen and the lighterage industry along the river. European merchants and trading houses were the main users of Indian lighters and as more of their custom passed over the wharves at New Harbour, the business of the lighters in the river declined. In 1884, Indian lightermen and owners first voiced their concerns in a petition to the Chamber of Commerce about how their livelihood was being affected adversely as a result of monopoly developments at Tanjong Pagar.[50] Their primary concern related to the way control of the lighterage industry along the river was gradually passing into the hands of Chinese boatmen.[51]

Witnesses during the hearings of the River Commission in 1898–99 provide a picture of the communal transition and tension happening along the river. One of the reasons why European trading houses preferred to use Indian lightermen was because of the particular type of craft they employed. (See Appendix 1 for a description of lighter craft.) Indian lighters were large, ranging in size from 20 to 120 tonnes, and while this meant they were not the easiest craft to manoeuvre in the river, in the outer harbour they offered considerably more protection to the goods they carried.[52] Consequently, up until the turn of the century it was only possible to insure goods in transit with local offices if they were transported on the larger Indian lighters.[53] Evidence was given before the Commission that 'no European firms employ twakow', the Chinese lighter craft, except on occasions when the quantity of goods was small and no Indian tongkang were available.[54] Further documentation was presented which supported this claim, and the consensus among Europeans testifying to the Commission was that Indian lighters were more suitable for the goods they transported.[55] Nevertheless, with the growing use of wharves at New Harbour there was a marked decline in demand for larger lighters by European merchants, and the fate of Indian boatmen along the river was sealed. Alexander Gentle, President of the Municipal Commissioners in 1899, in his evidence to the River Commission, specifically linked the demise of Indian boatmen to the changing circumstance of European trading houses. He said that as European godowns closed along the river they were taken over by Chinese towkay who employed Chinese lightermen and craft, replacing 'Klings' on the river.[56] This economic transformation was corroborated by other witnesses and the Chief Police Officer in his testimony candidly stated, 'Chinese merchants always use Chinese boats'.[57]

Thus, at the turn of the century a new era in the lighterage industry was beginning. While many Indian lighters were still found in the river they were under increasing pressure to clear out due to a loss of traditional business and open competition and intimidation from the Chinese — Teochew and Hokkien — the new masters of the waterway. A careful reading of the River Commission report provides evidence that Indian boatmen were still part of the river scene, but it leaves little doubt they were in steady retreat. In 1898 there were only 300 Indian tongkang, including some crewed by Chinese, compared with 700 Chinese twakow in the river.[58] The total number of twakow operating around Singapore, in the next three years, increased by more than a thousand, and many of these moved into the river forcing most Indian lighters to move out.[59] The Europeans who gave evidence spoke well of the Indian lighters but they also agreed that the communal tide had turned and the new 'masters' of the river were the Chinese.[60] By 1902 Chinese lightermen were in the river in sufficient numbers to apply enough pressure to force the Indians off the waterway. In this turbulent period there were numerous complaints from Indian boatmen about being stopped from using the river's quays to unload, and being denied places to moor their craft in the river. During the proceedings of the River Commission witnesses were repeatedly asked if there was any evidence to support the 'Kling' boatmen's claim that they were being pushed out of the river by the Chinese.[61] While most witnesses denied this was the case, over the next several years Chinese twakow did displace the remaining tongkang in the river and the years of Indian dominance on the waterway came to an end.

Chinese Immigrants and Lightermen

Chinese ties with Singapore date back well before the arrival of Raffles. By some accounts, there were 20 to 30 Chinese already living in Singapore, engaged in the cultivation of gambier, when Raffles arrived.[62] Following the establishment of the British trading post their numbers grew rapidly. Both Farquhar and Raffles encouraged Chinese to settle in Singapore and their population quickly increased to the point where they comprised the largest ethnic group in the new settlement.[63] Among the earliest arrivals were merchants from Malacca and Riau, attracted to Singapore by cross-cultural trade opportunities created by its establishment.[64] These *Nanyang*[65] Chinese with their knowledge of local conditions and languages realised the potential of the new settlement to become an important trading entrepôt. From their point of view, not only was it more favourably located than any other port in the region but it also offered the opportunity to trade without restriction. As alien traders they were often forced to deal with restrictive trading laws, heavy taxes and extortion in other settlements throughout the region.[66] Singapore offered the prospect of being able to trade across the region without undue government interference or regulation. Many of these early arrivals became important middlemen in the establishment trade of Singapore and for a time dominated the local business scene.

The number of Chinese who settled in Singapore was only a small percentage of the overall migrant total who made their way to the port town. The Malaccan and Riau Chinese, influential in the early days of settlement, were soon outnumbered by a flood of new migrants, *singkeh*, who swept in from China.[67] Throughout the nineteenth and early twentieth century several million migrants, mainly peasants, small businessmen and craftsmen arrived in Singapore from China,[68] having left rural areas of Kwangtung and Fukien (see Map 8).[69] In the streets of Singapore one could readily encounter Chinese representing all the main dialect groups of China.[70] Cantonese, Hokkiens, Teochews and Hainanese were all found in the settlement and all with one common goal, to improve their lives and acquire wealth.

The impetus to migrate was generated by the political and social turmoil experienced by China, during the nineteenth and early twentieth centuries. The chaotic state of China's domestic economy, ravaged by food shortages, war and natural disasters was a major factor in the decision to migrate.[71] For many it was a difficult choice as they came from a Confucian-centred culture that emphasised strong attachment to the ancestral home.[72] But other forces, besides the difficult domestic situation, were also at work to lure them abroad as sojourners. There was the attraction of wealth to be made in Nanyang. Not all singkeh were compelled to leave China. For some it was a calculated choice because of work opportunities they knew existed in the colonial cities and states in the South Seas.[73] From the 1870s onward there was an enormous increase in the number of Chinese embarking for Singapore, attracted by the promise of employment as a result of colonial investment and enterprise in Nanyang. This migration was also actively encouraged by colonial authorities, as Chinese labourers were felt to be the right kind of 'raw material' to foster the development of colonial capitalism in the region.[74] Escaping grinding poverty at home, Chinese bachelor migrants were an ideal source of cheap labour for colonial enterprises as they often worked under the worst possible conditions for a pittance.

It was fortunate too that the surge in demand for labour occurred at a time when technological advances meant that it could be met. The widespread use of merchant steam vessels in the latter part of the nineteenth century allowed the coolie traffic — the 'pig trade' — to be conducted year round. It was no longer a seasonal undertaking dependent on sailing craft and the prevailing monsoon.[75] This new extended system of transport and communication with vessels running on regular schedules between China and Southeast Asia also led to increased numbers of migrants making the journey to Nanyang.[76]

Most Chinese left their villages expecting to work hard, save some capital and eventually return to their families and ancestral lands. Having left their hearth and home they headed for the nearest port where they might find passage to the south. Some were fortunate, being sponsored by family or wealthy individuals from their village, but most were unable to pay their own fares and were forced to seek passage assistance.[77] Usually this contract was provided by agents of secret societies in Singapore or from a labour broker who was recruiting in the coastal ports of southern China. There were considerable profits to be made from transporting peasant labourers. Hence, not surprisingly, secret societies dominated the control and regulation of this traffic. Commonly referred to as the 'pig business', sums of money usually in the range of $33–$38 were advanced to potential singkeh.[78] Upon arrival in Singapore the contracted debt for their 'credit ticket' was transferred to an employer and they had to work it off. In most cases this took at least three years.[79]

Prior to the establishment of the Chinese Protectorate in 1877 there was no official supervision or record kept of Chinese migration to Singapore.[80] The initial influx of migrants to the British settlement was clearly dominated by Chinese, although they were not the largest population group until the 1830s.[81] When the settlement was only months old Farquhar reported to Raffles about the rapid growth of the Chinese town with new streets being added to accommodate the steady stream of arrivals.[82] Raffles claimed, in private correspondence, that the population of his settlement had grown to around 5,000 by mid-1819 and that Chinese made up the bulk of the newcomers.[83] While this figure is by some accounts exaggerated[84] it nevertheless indicates the trend that was occurring with respect to Chinese arrivals. Certainly by the time Raffles returned to Singapore in 1822 and undertook the work of town planning, there were already a large number of Chinese residing there. Chinese labourers were residing in the settlement in sufficient numbers to be used to level the hill that stood on the site of Commercial Square and to reclaim land along the river to form South Boat Quay.[85]

Within a decade of the port's founding there were nearly 10,000 Chinese living in Singapore. By the 1830s, the extent of Chinese migration raised concerns about the 'evil' influx of poor Chinese.[86] However, the growing demand for cheap labour meant no curbs were placed on this southward flow of humanity. It was only when the economy of the island slumped in the 1840s, when the price of gambier dropped resulting in large numbers of unemployed coolies on the streets of Singapore, that serious consideration was given to restricting migration from China.[87] But by 1900 the number of Chinese in Singapore had burgeoned to more than 70 per cent of the total population. Migration continued to dramatically boost the Chinese population of the island well into the 1930s with more women than men arriving for the first time during that decade. (See Appendix 2, Table 5.)

By the turn of the century Singapore had become a major Chinese enclave in Nanyang. It was a port city composed largely of transient able-bodied men, either single or separated from spouses and family. Until the 1930s there was a disproportionate ratio of males to females.[88] Few Chinese women, other than those destined for prostitution, left China until the 1920s. Women remained at home and attempted to hold together family and village life, while their husbands, sons and fathers ventured into Nanyang, hoping to return wealthy. Another notable element of this overseas Chinese community was its abnormal age structure. Until the Second World War it was a population with most of the men aged between 15 and 59.[89] From the first official census in 1871 until the 1940s more than 78 per cent of the population were bracketed in this age range with few children or elderly people.[90] The disproportionately low number of women contributed to the transitory nature of the Chinese population in Singapore. Until the 1920s, when conditions in Singapore were notably better than China the average length of stay for a migrant was seven years. Until this time most singkeh planned on a short stay and, whatever their achievements, cherished the dream of returning home.[91] From the mid-1920s, however, the nature of Chinese society in Singapore began to change as more women arrived, and the prospect of settling permanently offered more advantages than returning home.[92]

Given the enormous influx of Chinese migrants at the end of the nineteenth century it is not surprising that Chinese lighters and lightermen were replacing Indians and their craft on the river by 1900. From the earliest days of settlement Chinese boatmen had played a part in the life of the port. While Indian tongkang and lightermen were entrusted with valuable cargoes that were part of the life blood of the port, Chinese 'shoe-boats' were found in great numbers along the river and on the waters of the outer harbour carrying an assortment of people and goods.[93] These small boats regularly plied the waters of the harbour carrying various foodstuffs required by shipping such as fresh fruit and vegetables as well as livestock. They were also in demand as 'taxis' transporting passengers and their luggage to and from ships in the outer harbour. Some ships' commanders would specially hire one or two of these small craft to serve their vessel for the duration of their visit to the port.[94] This saved their crewmen from having to row daily in the debilitating heat of the Singapore roadstead.[95] It was only in cargo transportation that Chinese boatmen and craft were not heavily involved until the latter part of the nineteenth century.

As Chinese twakow displaced Indian tongkang, cargo transportation on the river entered a new phase. The Chinese takeover of the lighterage industry involved two main dialect groups, Hokkien speakers from Fukien Province and Teochew speakers from the Kwangtung region.[96] In the years prior to the Second World War it was Teochews who dominated the lighterage industry along the river. Around 70 per cent of twakow working the river at this time were operated and crewed by Teochews. Hokkiens owned and managed approximately 30 per cent of the twakow on the river during the initial phase of Chinese domination.[97] More Hokkien craft were found transporting cargo from along the waterfront (Teluk Ayer Basin) than in the river itself.[98] This situation changed after 1945 with Hokkiens becoming the principal conveyors of trade in the river. Many Teochew businesses struggled to re-establish themselves in the immediate post war era, especially during the turmoil surrounding the Emergency period. In this period it was Hokkiens who managed to secure many of the best 'jetties' along the river for themselves, jetties being sections of the river quays claimed by a particular owner where goods could be loaded and unloaded. With the exception of a small section of North Boat Quay below Elgin Bridge, the lower reaches of the river (between Cavenagh Bridge and Elgin Bridge), including the full length of South Boat Quay, were now dominated by Hokkiens (see Map 9).[99]

Like fellow sojourners from China who became rickshaw pullers, coal coolies and manual labourers, the lightermen were induced to enter the industry by the economic opportunity it offered them. They were seeking a better livelihood than was found in their homeland, as the Indian boatmen had done before them. Sweating, hauling the great trade of Singapore through the river, they only had to reflect on the situation they had left behind in China to once again turn their perspiring faces to the task at hand. Destiny had brought them to this 'better' place and home was something to reflect on and dream about during those spells when the twakow lay idle at its berth along the river.

4
The River and the Government

Regulations

THE importance of the river to the commercial well being of Singapore invariably led to some government regulation of trading activities and involvement in the development of the river as a port. Early attempts to control and manage the port from 1819 were rather ad hoc with a significant degree of authority being in the hands of the port's Master Attendant. Various regulatory measures were instituted in the intervening years before the Straits Settlement Port Ordinance of 1912 constituted the Singapore Harbour Board. The Board was succeeded by the Port of Singapore Authority, established in 1964. However, official concern and involvement with the waterway until the 1970s might best be described as minimalist.

In line with Singapore's status as a 'free' port regulation of trading activities was kept to a minimum and focused for the most part on protecting property and trade goods. Primarily this was achieved through regulation of the lighterage industry with measures and rules being put in place relating to sea worthiness of vessels, cargo capacity and storage and protection of goods while in transit. There were also regulations to keep some sections of the river clear of moored lighters and stipulations on how lighters were to be secured in the river when not in use. Similarly, with funds for improvements to the waterway always short, regulators and planners confined themselves for the most part to ensuring that the river was kept navigable through dredging. These two issues, protection of trade goods and river maintenance, above all else are constant themes in the regulatory history of the Singapore River.

A plethora of regulations was promulgated over the years to control the lighter industry and protect the property they transported. Regulatory control of the industry was initially handled by the Master Attendant and later, as the port grew, the Singapore Harbour Board and more recently the Port Authority of Singapore. The port authorities, however, in no way owned the river and worked with other agencies to ensure regulations introduced were upheld. For example, the Master Attendant's Office was responsible for registering lighters, but it was the Police who ensured that unregistered craft were not used in the port. Similarly, river maintenance was shared with other agencies such as the Public Works Department. The extent of actual involvement in regulating river trading operations by the port authority was also always limited. The trade of the river was completely 'laissez faire'.[1] The regulations affecting the lighter industry in the main fell into two categories, those related to fees for services and those that sought to protect property transported in lighters.

While the port was still in its infancy the matter of regulating activities of cargo vessels fell to the Master Attendant. Before Raffles left Singapore in February 1819 he placed Francis Bernard in charge of the port as Acting Master Attendant.[2] Bernard filled the position until the arrival of Raffles' brother-in-law, Captain Flint, in April 1820. Raffles' instructions regarding how the port would be regulated were vague at this early stage. Beyond the need to establish watering facilities for ships and for Singapore to have the status of a free port, little direction was given to those whose job was to get the port running.[3] This initial lack of a clear direction and guide lines placed considerable regulatory power in the hands of the Master Attendant giving him near complete control over lighterage activities in the port.

Bernard, as acting Master Attendant between February 1819 and April 1920, introduced a number of controversial charges to be paid by vessels using the port.[4] These fees were used to defray the cost of stationery and consumables in his office and constituted the first regulatory measures adopted by the port.[5] When Raffles' brother-in-law Captain Flint took over the position from Bernard, the ambiguity that surrounded the regulation of the river and port gave him ample opportunity to exploit the situation for personal gain. While Bernard's introduction of port fees caused some consternation in the Governor General's office in India, they were considered of minor consequence compared with his successor's activities. Flint ran the port as if it was his own commercial fiefdom, introducing ever more fees while at the same time exercising complete control over the lighterage industry.[6] In writing to Flint to express his concerns, newly-appointed Resident Crawfurd described his control of the port and lighterage as 'complete'. The imprecise regulations on administering the port and rapid growth of the settlement during the first three years of Flint's administration as Master Attendant, 1820–23, allowed this situation to develop.[7] Flint had arrived in Singapore before its future was fully determined at the international conference table in 1824. Given the political uncertainty that surrounded the settlement prior to 1824, there was considerable opportunity for the Master Attendant to frame and reinterpret port regulations to great personal advantage. He built and crewed with 'Chuliah' lightermen a fleet of cargo boats which he then hired out to government and private individuals. He also managed through his office to undertake, without perceived conflict of interest, many of the repairs that needed to be done on visiting ships.[8]

The *laissez-faire* interpretation of Raffles' instructions by his brother-in-law meant in the early years of the port's life that regulatory measures and transport of cargo and servicing of ships was totally monopolised by him.[9] Vessels frequenting the port were left with no option but to pay fees set by him for everything from anchorage and port clearance to hire of lighters for transporting cargo and supplies. Private individuals attempting to establish a cargo fleet or operate on a smaller scale, with perhaps one harbour boat, were faced with the awkward dilemma of having to compete against the authority that was responsible for their development and regulation.[10] It seems from the correspondence between Crawfurd and Flint that others may well have been operating cargo lighters, but they were always at a disadvantage because of Flint's position as Master Attendant and Magistrate. Thus, both control and profits from the lighterage industry, were for a time monopolised by the Master Attendant while the work was done by Indian boatmen.[11] Understandably, during the initial months of the port's operation, it was considered both desirable and necessary to have a super-ordinate authority to ensure that cargo carrying and servicing the demands of shipping were adequately met. It is unlikely that Raffles intended for this operation to remain in the hands of a single official beyond the time necessary to get a proper port service established. Clearly, there were benefits for the port in allowing independent cargo lighters to operate without restriction.[12]

There is no doubt that Flint exploited his family relationship with Raffles to the fullest extent. Lieutenant Farquhar found it arduous to deal with Flint who always seemed to have the ear of his brother-in-law, a situation made all the more difficult because he had to answer directly to Raffles. When Flint and Crawfurd fell out, Raffles' correspondence with his sister clearly indicates that he took his brother-in-law's side.[13] The influence of the Flints is evident in Raffles' port regulations of 1823 which legitimised the Master Attendant's monopoly of lighterage services and control of port facilities. The ordinances, in fact, further extended the Master Attendant's powers by conferring on him the position of magistrate and bear the hallmark of Flint's influence.[14] While never officially adopted, and quickly overturned by Crawfurd in 1823, the regulations provide insight into how the Master Attendant controlled the lighterage industry and port. They stipulated that 'all applications for cargo boats and water' were to be made at his office. Crawfurd pointed out these regulations would have legitimised the existing unfair monopoly.[15] While some provision was made for vessels, on payment of a small fee, to use their own boats for stocking firewood, water and ballast sand, the general practice was to arrange such services through the Master Attendant. On the other hand no concession was given for carriage of cargo which had to be handled by special craft arranged by the port's central authority, the Master Attendant.[16] Paragraph 11 of the regulations also explicitly stated that all cargo boats and crews in the port came under the 'control' or jurisdiction of his office.[17]

The Master Attendant's initial monopoly of the lighterage industry and port was constrained to some extent in August of 1823 when Crawfurd, as the new Resident, redrafted the regulations. His Provisional Regulations for the port opened the lighter industry to fairer competition for individual operators:

> The business of supplying wood, water and ballast for ships and the employment of cargo boats shall not be considered subject to any official restriction ... and the mediation and assistance of officers of the Government with regard to them is deemed in the present advanced state of trade of the port no longer necessary.[18]

There was more at stake than simply the monopoly of the lighterage industry. The Master Attendant's monopolistic control of the port had opened up opportunities for fraudulent activity. Crawfurd stripped Flint of his excessive powers. He then launched an inquiry into the 'imperfect manner' by which tonnage of cargo was measured in lighters belonging to the port, suggesting Flint had been lining his pockets by unfair means.[19] In response to Flint's protests Crawfurd replied: 'It will not escape you, that the exercise of the power of fining and inflicting corporal punishment upon your competitors in the business of wooding, watering and ballasting ships and furnishing cargo boats ... could not be continued with justice.'[20] Flint was left with no choice but to sell his fleet of cargo boats. Angry with the situation he now found himself in he suggested the government should purchase his lighter fleet.[21] From this time onward the lighterage industry was opened to competition, and regulation of the port was placed on a more formally recognised footing.

Beginning with Crawfurd's 1823 Regulations all cargo-carrying boats in the port were to be 'regularly measured, numbered, and registered in the Master Attendant's Office'.[22] It also stipulated that each boat would have its registration and tonnage marked on the bow. A regular problem for merchants and shippers using the port was water damage to cargo as it was transported from ships in the bay to wharves along the river. Crawfurd placed responsibility for such conveyance and damage squarely on the shoulders of boat operators, requiring them to provide 'coverings adequate to protect ... goods from damage'.[23] He also placed controls on fees that could be charged for various transport services, ensuring the newly-privatised lighterage industry did not overcharge. These basic measures to control and regulate the lighterage industry were to form the basis of all future port rules affecting small cargo carrying vessels.

Modification of port regulations in later years gradually extended the jurisdiction of the Master Attendant, the port's principal authority, further upriver. In 1856, the official port extended as far as Coleman Bridge.[24] This expanded in later years to include Kim Seng Bridge area,[25] which was the navigable limit of the river. From around 1850 the first serious complaints of overcrowding in the river started to appear in the local press. In the main they refer to the area below Elgin Bridge which was at the time still the main trading area of the port. By 1856 regulations were introduced for the first time to deal with the problem of overcrowding in the river.[26] The relatively small area available to load and discharge cargo along the waterway was the usual cause of delays and bottlenecks as craft were forced to queue for berthing space. To alleviate the congested situation lighters not loading or discharging goods were forced to move out of the river or moor upstream away from the commercial centre around South Boat Quay.[27] As the port continued to grow there were fewer and fewer locations where lighters could moor out of the way of working craft. Later efforts to reduce congestion on the river entailed limiting the amount of time lighters could berth and marking a clearway through the river in which no craft were allowed to moor.[28] Larger lighters, particularly tongkang, were required to berth parallel to the shore to create more room for navigation while no more than three craft of any description were allowed to lie beside each other.[29] The problem of river traffic and congestion continued to be vexatious, and no amount of regulation in the end could ultimately resolve this problem.

As twakow replaced tongkang as the dominant lighter craft in the port, attempts were made to introduce new measures to regulate their construction. Evidence presented to the Singapore River Commission in 1899 first raised the issue as to whether Chinese twakow were suitable for use in the port.[30] It was conceded by larger mercantile firms that they preferred Indian tongkang for transporting goods as they were more seaworthy in the waters of the outer harbour. There were tongkang losses but these seem to have always been attributed to overloading and not any design fault.[31] The question of twakow suitability remained an issue as more and more of them took over the river trade. In 1907, the government proposed legislation that would have required a particular construction design to be adhered to, but at the time the matter went no further.[32] The concerns expressed by merchants proved to be well founded, as demonstrated by a single incident in October 1917 when 50 twakow were sunk during an early morning squall, many of which were loaded with valuable cargoes of rice, sugar and dried fish.[33] By 1923, cargo losses and complaints were of such a magnitude that a special committee was appointed to investigate ways of ensuring that twakow were seaworthy given the loads they normally carried.[34] It was reported in the *Singapore Free Press* three years later 'that for a great number of years past there has been a serious overloading of these twakow with the result that they have very often foundered, cargo has been lost and the lives of the men endangered'.[35] Insurance companies were the main advocates of reform and an array of recommendations was put forward concerning future construction of twakow.[36] However, pressure from the Singapore Chamber of Commerce, fearing the strong measures proposed would push up the cost of transporting goods, resulted in most of the recommendations being dropped.[37] Even the introduction of a load line to be painted on the sides of lighters in order to easily ascertain whether or not they were being overloaded was rejected. Instead, the Chamber of Commerce counter-proposed that current rules and regulations be more strictly adhered to and that twakow be built and maintained according to existing codes.[38] Concessions occurred though, enabling closer supervision of twakow construction and more exacting inspection.[39] Modifications to regulations and rules affecting lighter craft in the river continued to be implemented and enforced by Marine Police up to the time of the river's closure to trade in 1983.

By the mid-1860s the regulation of charges for lighter hireage had been taken out of the hands of government and passed to the Singapore Chamber of Commerce. This arrangement was advantageous to individual owners and operators of lighters as it meant that they were not subject to arbitrary governmental interference and decisions. Prices and fees were fixed only after consultation with various interested parties, namely, the Chinese Chamber of Commerce and lighter owners. While the fee system worked quite well, there were times when the interests of merchants and shippers, the dominant force within the Chamber of Commerce, did not coincide with those of the lighter operators, and transport costs were deliberately kept low. This was the general situation at the turn of the century when boatmen and owners complained bitterly that they were unable to make a decent living as the prices were artificially set by the Chamber of Commerce.[40] In a 1901 petition to the Chamber of Commerce the river men pointed out the important role they played in the running of the port and asked that this fact be taken into account in considering their appeal to raise fees.[41] The behind the scenes power of the merchant houses was evident in the Chamber of Commerce's refusal to increase hireage fees.[42] It was not until 1903 that a revision of rates resulted in a tariff increase for lighter operators,[43] but only after the leading merchant houses urged new rates be approved so that 'this important work' could be 'carried out efficiently'.[44] This Chamber of Commerce system of the negotiated setting of lighterage rates continued with some modification into the 1990s.[45]

Keeping the River Open

Ensuring that the river was an effective artery of trade was the most important area of government involvement with the waterway. For the lightermen, the state of the Singapore River as a navigable channel was of critical importance to their day to day existence, but they had little control over how it was managed. The question of responsibility for river development and maintenance was from the very beginning a contentious issue of debate between commercial operators and the government. Invariably, the government took responsibility for ensuring that the river remained open for trade. Since the river was critical to conducting business in the port, especially in the establishment years of the port, merchants and other private citizens were able to pressure the government to take charge of its maintenance. Nevertheless, until the 1980s the government's involvement with the river would be marked by the lack of affirmative action. Perplexing to both officials and citizens was how to keep the river from progressively silting up and becoming unnavigable. While other areas of river management, such as construction of safe bridges, would involve lengthy debate and procrastination, it was the problem of silting that took up the most time and attention of those concerned with the regulation of the waterway. Throughout the years that the river acted as the principal trading area of the port, there was always more talk than action when it came to solving the problems of river maintenance created by silting, pollution and overcrowding.

When Crawfurd took over the reins from Farquhar in 1823 he was confronted by extensive unfinished river works around South Boat Quay. The initial reclamation work started by Raffles had stopped after his departure.[46] These half-finished public works caused real problems for the mercantile community as they struggled against the tide and mud to establish themselves on the river's south bank.[47] Crawfurd, under instructions to cut expenditure, was forced to explain to the government in India why he permitted the work to be resumed.[48] Having failed to persuade the merchants of their responsibility to carry out the work, Crawfurd, recognising the vital importance of the river to the island's future prosperity and trade, committed government to the task.[49] This was the beginning of ongoing government involvement in maintaining the river, a role that over a century-and-a-half saw various government authorities take some responsibility for development along its banks and for keeping it clear and open for trade.

The natural ecology of the waterway deteriorated as commercial activity extended along the river. During Crawfurd's Residency, only four years after the port's founding, the general problem of silting and degradation of the river was first encountered. In late 1822, a committee set up by Raffles inquired into the state of the river and found in the short space of time that the port had been operating a considerable amount of sand had built up around the river mouth.[50] This was due in part to the construction of jetties on the North Boat Quay side of the river. These structures were interfering with the natural course of the river causing a build up of silt near its mouth. The Committee urged removal of the sand bar at the entrance as well as work on clearing a 'rock bar' just outside the river to further alleviate the situation.[51] It was not uncommon during the first years of settlement, as land clearing occurred along the river, for individuals to dump trees and other refuse in the water, further exacerbating the problem of silting.[52] Within months of Crawfurd's arrival, he urged the government to provide the necessary funds to clean up the river mouth as silt had just about blocked the entrance.[53] He impressed upon his superiors in India the commercial importance of the river and called for a dredge to be built and operated by Indian convicts to clear the waterway before it became unnavigable.[54]

Ironically, dredging machinery was sent to Singapore but it was never put to use in the river. The engineer who was to assemble the dredge died several months after arriving in the settlement.[55] As a consequence, it would be years before the government was prepared to spend money again on a large, expensive proper dredge for the river. The problems of inadequate funding and expertise meant major initiatives to clean up the river were often placed on hold during the nineteenth century. In the absence of a concerted strategy, ad hoc measures were usually adopted to deal with the problems that plagued the waterway. For example, there were occasions when entire sections of the river wall collapsed and no measures were taken immediately to repair the damage.[56] Even the commercially important South Boat Quay was not free of such mishaps as parts of it washed away in 1850, placing godowns and shophouses situated along it in jeopardy.[57]

As already discussed Indian convicts were used as a cheap source of residual labour along the river during Crawfurd's term in Singapore.[58]

They undertook much of the reclamation work done along the river's banks and also worked at low tide clearing mud from the riverbed with their bare hands. Attempts to remove the troublesome 'rock bar' beyond the entrance illustrate how inept the early authorities were when it came to dealing with the river. Though a genuine hazard to navigation, it was nearly 20 years after Crawfurd first recommended its destruction that blasting of the bar was carried out. An unsuccessful operation as the press noted the blasting merely removed the crown of the reef visible above water.[59] Ironically, danger to craft entering and leaving the river had increased significantly as mariners could no longer see the rocks as they negotiated the hazardous entrance to the river.[60] It would take more than 60 years before this irksome problem was finally dealt with in a conclusive way, and then only after several further inquiries into the state of the river were held.

In the 1850s numerous petitions[61] to government finally resulted in a dredge being built for use in the river. Governor Butterworth, because of continuing problems to navigation, moved to clean up the river and urged that a dredge be constructed.[62] Again, this progressive step was to prove largely in vain. In the first place the dredge, contracted to be built locally by Tivendales,[63] took more than two and a half years to complete due to difficulty in obtaining the teak required for its construction. It was further delayed when machinery sent from England proved faulty. All the while the silt build up in the river continued unabated.[64] When the dredge actually began operation in 1856 it became apparent that it was not up to the task of clearing the river mouth. The *Singapore Free Press* reported that it seemed to sit in one place stirring up mud while, 'cargo boats taking goods to ... shipping are as exposed to as much inconvenience as ever in crossing the bar of the river'.[65] The damming report called for an 'honest confession' as to what went wrong with the dredge and whether it was a total failure.

The dredge continued to be used for some time but was never able to effectively deal with the constant silting of the river. To make matters worse the dredge was also unable to clear the river channel at its upper reaches as it was too wide to pass under Coleman Bridge.[66] In light of this manufacturing blunder, the Chamber of Commerce was duly informed that it was not the responsibility of the government to ensure the river was dredged but rather the Municipal Commission.[67] A request that convicts be employed once again in cleaning the river was denied on the grounds that they were fully employed on major public works projects being undertaken in the town.[68] Eventually the faulty machinery was removed from the dredge and sent to Malacca. In 1857, the ill-fated boat was turned over to the police to be used as a 'Marine Police Station'[69] and in 1861, after a request from the Reverend Nicolson, it became a 'floating chapel' for sailors.[70]

By the last quarter of nineteenth century the rapid growth of the town and port was placing a huge strain on the river and its resources. To many residents the river appeared to be little more than an open sewer exuding an 'extremely disagreeable' smell.[71] It was clear to all concerned that it was no longer possible to ignore the plight of the river without putting at risk the burgeoning trade of the port. In May 1875 the government provided funds for the Municipality to clear the build up of mud and debris in front of South Boat Quay which was threatening to close it off from cargo boats.[72] An expedient, albeit temporary measure, it involved manually bucketing the mud and sludge away to achieve the minimum depth required for small craft to approach the quay. Two years later, in 1877, with the situation again reaching crisis point, a government committee including the Master Attendant and Colonial Engineer, was set up to further investigate ways of clearing and deepening the river.[73] Several schemes were proposed as a result of this committee's deliberations. For a time it seemed that South Boat Quay might be further extended into the river, creating a narrower channel to increase the flow of the current on the ebb tide and improve the natural scouring.[74] Ultimately though, it was felt this solution would solve one problem but only exacerbate another, that of overcrowding in the river. In the end it was decided once again to look at purchasing a dredge to scour the river bed.[75] Not surprisingly, the administrative wheels moved slowly when it came to actually purchasing a suitable machine for clearing the river. So slow in fact was the process for building the dredge that, in November 1881, one member of the Legislative Council told fellow members in despair, 'there is something grotesque in our helplessness. Rather than go on in this way we had better do as the ancient Egyptians did with their canals — turn ten thousand men into the river to clean it with their hands.'[76] The urgency to act was also stressed by the Colonial Engineer who pointed out that over the past decade more than 40 acres had been reclaimed at the upper reaches of the river, drastically reducing the amount of back water available to flush out the lower end of the waterway.[77] This reclamation development, coupled with an estimated 3,000–4,000 people living on boats in the river basin, were the main causes of continued silting which could only be alleviated by regular dredging.[78] A steam dredge was purchased and put into operation on the river in 1884. Many of the basic environmental problems plaguing the waterway remained and would become the focus of later investigations.

Dredging operations in the river became a regular feature of life from the mid-1880s. Despite the dredging, it was agreed among engineers there would be considerable gain in narrowing the river to increase the outward flow of water, but this scheme was never undertaken because of the property concerns of merchants and owners along South Boat Quay.[79] As mud and sludge, to a depth of more than seven feet above the river bed, continued to build up,[80] dredging was considered the only viable alternative to keep the river open.[81] In 1884, extensive clearing operations finally got under way with the arrival of a new bucket dredge. It was put to work immediately, clearing the entrance of the river and in front of South Boat Quay.[82]

In 1898/99, following a further commission of inquiry, into the congested and polluted state of the river, another dredge was purchased at a cost of 100,000 Straits dollars to further lower the level of the river bed.[83] By this belated measure the Commission drew to the public's attention just how important the river was to the future welfare and prosperity of the port and how its wellbeing had been neglected over the previous half century.

The river, besides being a trading artery, had become the town's primary sewer. As a consequence, the years following the turn of the century witnessed unprecedented efforts to improve the life of the river. The situation was summed up in 1912 by the Colonial Engineer when he stated: 'The river must be dredged and so long as the town drainage is discharged into it, and so long as a large population lives on it this annual dredging will be necessary.'[84] It was estimated that the new dredge, *Mudlark*, would require up to 80 twakow attending it to keep pace with the volume of material to be removed.[85] This calculation was not exaggerated, as by 1903 more than 2,000 tons of silt had been removed from the river, as well as 600 tons of rock from the bar at its mouth, long the bane of craft using the waterway.[86] When the dredge was working at full capacity it could clear 700 tons of mud from the river bed per day and, by 1912, over 482,000 tons of silt and waste material had been cleared from the river by the *Mudlark*.[87]

A further benefit from these scouring operations was the reclamation of land with soil dredged from the river. In fact, the amount of material taken from the river proved so great that the question of what to do with the refuse became a waste removal problem. The cost of dumping the dredgings at sea was lower than utilising them as landfill, but it was recognised that, with so much silt being extracted from the river bed, the opportunity existed to undertake reclamation work,[88] public projects that would enable rapid extension of commercial activity along the river and improve the character of the town. By 1912, soil from dredging had been used to reclaim 10 acres of swamp at the upper reaches of the river, and this reclaimed land was planted with coconuts, while the esplanade was extended into the ocean by more than 200 feet.[89] The land reclamation in the upper reaches of the river proved to be of dubious value beyond the immediate extension of commercial premises which it permitted. Every report on the river noted insufficient backwater for flushing as a major cause of the river's silting and the continued reclamation work in the catchment only further exacerbated the situation.

Dredging proved to be only a partial solution to the problems the river faced. Constant dredging could only maintain the status quo. The effectiveness of dredging operations was always hampered by the earlier poor construction of quays along the banks, and the ever-present possibility of the collapse of the embankments, hampered efforts to clear the full width of the river.[90] In 1905, the local press blamed dredging for the collapse of a large section of river wall, jeopardising godowns and other buildings.[91] Dredging had been one of a number of key recommendations in the River Commission's Report of 1899. Other shelved proposals for long-term improvement of the river included the construction of a new boat harbour above Pulau Saigon where craft would moor when not working.[92] The report argued that if a large inland basin was constructed it could shelter lighter craft and open up more ground for godowns, and it also would increase the volume of water in the river, thus further alleviating the age-old menace of silting. The removal of two 'projecting points' along the river was also recommended, one where Ord Bridge stands and the other near the river mouth just above Cavenagh Bridge.[93] Straightening the river in these areas would have increased the outward flow of water, also contributing to a reduction in silt accumulation. These turn of the century recommendations highlighted a basic dilemma faced by government and municipal authorities. Containment of the waterway had been carried on for almost a century without any systematic forethought as to how it would affect the river's natural existence and functioning. The original meandering course reshaped with trade demands in mind no longer had sufficient backwater to flush the river out. Any further significant alterations to correct previous blunders would be achieved only by a complete realigning of the river. Such an undertaking, either by government or the private sector, would have entailed huge financial costs as property would have to be purchased and all the bridges spanning the river either replaced or, raised at great expense. Under these circumstances, for the most part, only cosmetic measures were adopted for dealing with the river's future existence.

Nothing more of real benefit was accomplished in river management between the Colonial Commission's Report of 1899 and the establishment of a post-war working party to examine recurrent problems in 1953.[94] By then the river was sorely in need of extensive works and refurbishment if it was to have a long-term commercial future in the life of the port. The Second World War had created serious problems for river regulation and maintenance. In 1945 the British Military Administration found that the Singapore River had been totally neglected by the occupying Japanese. The six dredges owned by the port had either been taken away or stripped of their components.[95] Throughout the period of the Japanese occupation, from 1942–45, the river had not been used for serious trading activity. Nearly all the twakow and tongkang had been confiscated by the Japanese and either used elsewhere or fallen into a state of disrepair.[96] In fact many twakow were sunk in the harbour at the request of the colonial authorities in the last desperate hours before the onset of the Japanese occupation. Although steps were taken to re-establish trade in the river, in September 1946 this initiative continued to be hamstrung because of a lack of equipment to clear the river of wrecked lighters and silt which blocked the river to even the smallest boats.[97] Less than 50 per cent of the pre-war lighter fleet was operational two years after the re-establishment of British rule. Other areas of the port and waterways requiring clearing and dredging had to wait until the Singapore River was dealt with by the military administration. Desperate efforts were made to secure additional dredges to speed up the process of reopening the river to trade in the immediate post-war years.[98]

By the early 1950s, the river was functional again, but it had suffered considerable neglect. The Singapore River Working Committee began deliberations in 1954 to find ways of dealing with the post-war problems facing the river's recovery and future as a trading artery.[99] Two years of investigation revealed the neglected state of control and regulation of the river and the extent to which pre-war mismanagement had enabled unbridled economic activity to occur so as to severely impair future development. The Committee found more than 1,000 lighters used the river and most were operating from South Boat Quay, causing inordinate congestion.[100] The reasons for the congestion were apparent. In the first place, there was insufficient space under some bridges for lighters to pass when fully loaded. Coleman and Ord Bridges had only between 5 feet 8 inches and 4 feet 2 inches of clearance at Low Water on Spring Tides (L.W.O.S.T.)[101] making it impossible for many lighters to proceed beyond them.[102] With such low levels of clearance it was also inconceivable to dredge under the bridges. Soundings, in 1954, found that at low tide in the upper reaches of the river there was less than three feet of water while at the mouth there was barely six feet.[103] The same environmental and engineering problems that had haunted previous administrations for more than a quarter of a century were again highlighted, but by the 1950s, the ecological situation had progressively deteriorated. The precarious state of the river's nineteenth-century walls made it impossible to dredge the channel in places for fear they might collapse and carry fronting godowns with them. It was revealed, too, that the embankment problem had been exacerbated because of previous uncertainty as to whether relevant government ordinances, principally the Foreshores and Municipal Ordinances,[104] could be enacted to force river front owners to repair walls belonging to them. While the government exercised authority over construction of new quays it was by no means clear that they could force owners to maintain and repair private quays. To further complicate matters, letters issued to property owners requesting indemnity from claims against the government should old walls collapse during dredging operations, were categorically refused with the result that such operations could not be expeditiously carried out.[105]

Like the River Commission 50 years earlier, the Working Committee recommended a range of options to resolve the ecological problems associated with river use and maintenance. It was a scheme that would have cost $30 million to implement in the early 1960s.[106] Despite the huge sum involved it seemed definitive action was to be taken at last, not only to clean up the river but also to enhance its capacity to act as a trading artery. The Public Works Department was so confident the proposals would be acted upon that other key maintenance projects were postponed for several years.[107] But, as in the past, little came of the committees' bold recommendations, it was decided officially that 'the present facilities on the Singapore River should remain undisturbed' and 'development should be limited to normal maintenance dredging'.[108]

Despite the familiar conservative colonial financial refrain, real change was about to occur in the life of the river. Singapore became an independent state in 1965. By 1969, the government of the new republic was taking seriously the river's problems and carried out its own investigations as how best to resolve them. At the Prime Minister's behest the first concrete steps were taken to deal with the vexing problem of pollution in the river.[109] Over the next decade, as part of the republic's housing and development programme, squatter communities along the river totalling some 3,959 people were relocated,[110] while steps were taken to reduce the discharge of industrial pollutants and domestic effluent into the river. Laws regulating pollution control were enforced vigorously and new legislation was introduced. By the end of the decade, the diminishing importance of the river to the commercial future of the republic, coupled with the development of new technologies in cargo handling, ruled out the necessity of a large lighter fleet, providing the government with a context in which to rethink the future role of the river in the port city. In the ensuing decades, affirmative environmental and economic measures were taken with respect to the river's future. These measures had nothing to do with furthering traditional trading activities along the river as they were already becoming defunct. Rather, they were driven by a desire to develop a new ecological and economic face for an independent and affluent Singapore.

The Singapore River and City

In the first section of this study I have examined the historical development of the Singapore River as an integral part of modern Singapore's economic and physical landscape. The transformation from tidal creek to port and commercial centre was necessary to the rapid growth of the island as an entrepôt in Southeast Asia. The river provided an ideal natural artery around which the city could flourish as trade ebbed and flowed across the archipelago. Labour to work the river and government and municipal regulation to keep it open to trade were key elements of this transformative process.

The river became for generations of south Asians, and later, for Chinese boatmen whose labour helped build the trade and wealth of Singapore, the means of their own financial salvation. For the authorities, colonial and post-colonial, keeping the river open to trade was a paramount consideration because of the commercial importance it had assumed in the life of Singapore. This was achieved through a process of control and regulation, as well as practical measures, albeit inadequate, especially dredging to ensure the waterway remained navigable.

In the next part of this study I examine more closely the working conditions and lives of the men who made the river their home, the lightermen.

Part Two

Life on the River

5
Lighterage Work Conditions and Organisation

FOR thousands of Indian and Chinese who worked on lighters along the Singapore River arduous toil was a daily reality. Forced to leave their villages and homelands because of grinding poverty and political turmoil, they arrived in Singapore prepared to take any sort of job. At the very least the port city offered a chance of employment and escape from a rural life with little or no future. There was always the hope among even the poorest sojourners that, like others before them, they might return home prosperous and with some dignity. Stories told by kin and friends about the wealth that could be made in Singapore were often familiar to those who embarked on the hazardous journey in search of work and a better life. Such accounts and gifts brought home[1] by neighbours who periodically returned from Singapore sometimes fired their imagination and fuelled their dreams. Furthermore, the spectre of unemployment and starvation at home made even an uncertain future in distant Singapore appealing.

This chapter examines the nature of work done by migrant lightermen and the way they organised themselves as an occupational group. Initially there is a discussion of lighterage work, including how lightermen organised their day-to-day activities entailed by life and work on the river. This is followed by an analysis of the nature of the relationship between lightermen and lighter owners. Conditions of employment for lightermen were to a large extent determined by the nature of the relations between labour and private capital. Finally, efforts of lightermen to organise themselves to deal with the difficulties and uncertainties of their work and work place conditions are examined.

While Indian boatmen are not ignored, the primary emphasis of this chapter is on the Chinese in the lighterage industry. Indian boatmen were still a visible part of the river scene up to the turn of the century. As previously noted, one of the issues considered by the River Commission of 1899 was whether or not unfair treatment by Chinese boatmen was forcing Indian lightermen out of the river. Sayna Mahomed Mustan told the Commission there had been a substantial 20 per cent fall in the number of 'Kling tongkangs' using the river in the years immediately proceeding the inquiry.[2] The period 1869–1979 is notable for the rise of Chinese lightermen and industry on the river. Much of the detailed information in this chapter is based on interviews and time spent in the field, observing Chinese lightermen who previously worked along the river. Some aspects of the discussion relating to work done by Chinese lightermen was also pertinent to their former south Indian counterparts. The form and manner of the labour performed in transporting cargo from ship to shore via the river did not change a great deal in the last century. The strenuous and hazardous nature of the work was a shared experience for Indian and Chinese lightermen.

The Work and Social Organisation

The work of lightermen along the Singapore River was commented on from the earliest days of Singapore's incorporation into the British East India Company's trading network and empire. In the nineteenth century, few visitors writing of their stay in the port failed to mention the intense activity along the river's banks or the constant shuttling of cargo boats between godowns and ships in the bay. When George Bennett visited Singapore in the 1830s he had this to say of life along the river:

> The river at the low part of the settlement, always presents an animated scene, from the arrival and departure of native boats, with fruit, vegetables, and livestock, as well as from the number of sampans plying for hire... At night the flickering and brilliant lights of the numerous boats upon the river, make an animated appearance.[3]

In the years following Bennett's visit this singular scene was variably described. John Cameron, fully aware of the port's commercial significance, placed additional emphasis on the lighter craft in the river:

> The river is alive with boats of all sorts ... the last which [Indian tongkangs] are by far the most numerous, are employed in bringing up and down the river the cargoes of ships in the harbour ... and so numerous are they, that they generally lie three or four abreast along the entire western bank of the river, from its mouth to Elgin Bridge above.[4]

To the casual observer, even in depressed times, activity along the river seemed to continue, unabated. 'Rubber shares may be down, and business in the bazaar generally dull, but Boat Quay is always full of life.'[5] While such fragmentary accounts provide colourful descriptions of daily activity on the river they tend to gloss over the harsher aspects of the life and work of lightermen.

The principal task of lightermen was the transport of cargo between ships in the harbour and warehouses along the river. They were responsible for both the safety of their craft and the cargo it carried. Teo Ah Lea, after a lifetime on a twakow, had this to say about the work and duties of lightermen:

> The duty of twakowmen was to look after the goods once they were loaded on the twakow. We had to count the goods, stack them in proper order, and cover the goods whenever it rained. We could not relax until all goods were cleared. The responsibility was very heavy.[6]

While the transfer of goods from godowns, bullock carts, lorries and ships to lighters was traditionally carried out by stevedores, referred to as *chor coolies* (rough labourers) in Hokkien and *lau ah hia* (old brothers) in Teochew,[7] and in more recent times, cranes, boatmen were in charge of the actual loading of their craft.[8] The consignments of crates, bundles and sacks had to be carefully stowed in the vessel.[9] A badly loaded lighter could readily flounder in ocean swells once outside the river, especially if the sea was whipped up by a sudden squall. Preparing the cargo for transport was a task that required lightermen to skilfully handle all sorts of goods. Chang Ham Chwee observed:

> The work of lightermen was very heavy work. Making sure everything was stacked properly in the twakow meant hard work had to be done. Good stevedores would help by putting cargo in the correct place but mostly they just wanted to get their part of the job done. So of course our men had to help stack the cargo. It was their responsibility.[10]

The duties of lightermen often went further than stacking the cargo. Prior to the Second World War, many were required by their towkay to assist the stevedores carrying goods between the lighter and quay.[11] Kwek Ah Lam, a lighterman for 26 years, specifically mentioned this particular aspect of the gruelling work, 'we load and unload heavy bags of rice, bales of rubber, cartons of merchandise and most of them on our bare backs'.[12] Another elderly lighterman also recalled that 'sometimes we had to carry the goods up and down until our legs were cramped'.[13] Even the use along the river of mobile cranes (tiao chin) in the 1960s,[14] to lift goods from the holds of lighters did little to make the work less backbreaking. It still fell to the lightermen to ensure the proper loading of their vessels. Cranes not only replaced chor coolies but sped up the process of loading and unloading lighters.[15] Many lightermen felt their job was more demanding than that of chor coolies. While stevedores had only to convey goods to the lighter, the crew were held accountable for the cargo until it was removed,[16] sometimes days later. It was a cause of pride amongst lightermen that their work involved more responsibility and skill than other manual labouring occupations.[17]

Hence, in spite of the hard work, securing a position as a twakow man was considered a fortunate fate. Working as a lighterman was preferable to many other unskilled jobs and it paid better than most.[18] As late as 1980, the Industrial Arbitration Court found that lightermen earned 'far above' the average wage of other 'manual and non-skilled' workers.[19] Ironically, while risks to life and limb were readily acknowledged, working in the industry was considered a healthy way to earn a living.[20] Labouring outdoors, particularly on the ocean, led to the commonly held belief that this type of work was more salubrious than other occupations.[21] Historically, twakow men were amongst the fittest of 'coolies'. Giving evidence to the 1908 Opium Commission, the Coroner, Alexander Gentle, commenting on the general health of lightermen said, 'look at these twakow men. Stronger, finer men you do not see anywhere'.[22]

In order to understand how physically demanding the work was along the river it is necessary to examine the packaging and weight of frequently carried commodities. Cases of dried fish weighing more than 200 kilograms were among the heaviest goods handled. These large roughly cut crates were particularly difficult to move because of their bulkiness.[23] Before the advent of cranes it took three chor coolies to lift one of these cases onto the back of a fellow worker who would then struggle with it to a waiting lighter. Lighter owners spoke highly of the strength and stamina of these stevedores.[24] A great deal of physical strength, precision and stamina was also required to shift this cargo once it was placed in the hold of a vessel. Rubber was another exceptionally heavy and bulky freight item frequently handled by lightermen. Sheets of rubber tied in bales weighing up to 100 kilograms had to be stacked carefully in the lighter to ensure proper weight distribution and stability of the craft.[25] As with dried fish crates, it was the awkward and unwieldy nature of baled rubber that made it so hard to handle. Chuan Hian Chuan remembered how difficult it was to just secure a proper grasp on those unwieldy bundles.[26] Somewhat easier to handle were staples carried in sacks such as rice, sugar, coffee, spices, maize, beans, copra, cereals and cement.[27] Nevertheless, shifting and loading such cargoes was still gruelling work. Even the fittest lightermen felt the physical strain of several days on end spent stacking hundreds of sacks, weighing up to 100 kilograms each.[28] Manual work of this sort on the riverfront was aptly described by an insider as 'bone-breaking'.[29]

It was not simply the bulk or shape of various cargoes that made the lightermen's work physically demanding. Compounding problems of handling unwieldy cargoes were the difficulties of working in the hold of the vessel itself as goods were loaded and unloaded.[30] The deep broad bellies of particularly large lighters tended to be very hot, almost oven-like, at certain times of the year. Further adding to the discomfort caused by searing heat and humidity was dust, and depending on the cargo, a noxious smell which could be overpowering in the confined humid space of the lighter's hold. Add to this the constant rocking and jarring, caused by the ocean swell, while tied alongside a ship in the harbour, and the lighterage work became even more difficult and dangerous. It was a challenge to keep one's footing while at the same time avoid being accidentally crushed by goods as they were hoisted down over the side of a vessel. I witnessed first hand how hard this work was when I followed one of Ow Chin Seng's lighters to take on 120 tonnes of rice from a Thai freighter. For four hours without a break two lightermen worked at stacking the 100 kilogram bags of rice as they were hoisted by the ship's crane into the twakow. There seemed barely enough time to sort one sling load of bags before the next one was swinging overhead. Yet, I was assured, on better equipped ships the transfer would be even quicker and the same men had handled similar tonnages in two hours or less.[31] The work of twakow men called for not only exceptional strength but also 'skill and balance'.[32] A momentary loss of concentration could mean serious injury or even death. Though injuries occurred, lightermen accepted the risks as an occupational hazard. The more time a man spent on the job the better he became at avoiding possible danger and injury to himself although 'accidents were always likely to occur during loading and unloading of cargo'.[33] According to Chang Ham Chwee most injuries were of a minor nature although from time to time more serious accidents occurred.[34]

In the lighterage industry there have never been regular working hours or regulation on how many hours lightermen might reasonably work. When work was available 'it had to be done'.[35] Two factors influenced when lightermen would work, the diurnal rhythm of the tide and the arrival and departure of shipping, the latter being dependent to a large extent on the state of regional and global trade. Trading vessels could arrive in port at any time and if they required 'fast clearance'[36] lighters were sent to service them immediately. As Kwek Ah Lem explained, 'you never know when a cargo vessel will come in. It may come in at 1 am, 10 pm or just when you are trying to catch a quick dinner'.[37] Despite working long stretches there was no guarantee that twakow men would not be called to clear yet another cargo. To quote Kwek Ah Lam again, 'even after our regular hours, there is no such thing as total off-duty for us. We stay on stand by ... round the clock.'[38] There were many frantic occasions when lightermen worked without a break for more than 24 hours, using a brief lull in the work to snatch a bit of sleep or something to eat.[39] Indeed, even taking time off to holiday and celebrate Chinese New Year was forsaken if a vessel had to leave port, quickly.[40]

The rate charged to a ship owner for failure to load or discharge the ship within the stipulated time also affected the hours worked by lightermen. It was a common complaint of lightermen that, once their craft was loaded, they could not do anything except patiently stand watch over the cargo until it was discharged.[41] From this standpoint, it was preferable for cargo to be removed the same day it was loaded on board. When cargo could be discharged was dependent upon being able to enter or leave on the tide and other factors, such as congestion on the river, availability of transport to convey goods away from the quays and customs clearance.[42] As the trade and town of Singapore grew, only a small percentage of goods moved along the river were actually stored in godowns along its banks. Most cargo was transported away from the river to factories and wholesalers immediately after it was taken from the hold of the lighter.[43] While most lightermen lived on their craft in the days before it became more common to marry, guarding cargo against theft meant they often had to stay riverside even when not working. Hence, lightermen often worked round the clock, only being free from the relentless routine of their occupation when there was little or no activity at all on the river or waterfront.[44]

It was not uncommon for lighters to stand alongside a ship for days waiting for cargo to be off-loaded. Freighters often carried a mix of goods which had to be unloaded in turn.[45] If lighters waited in a queue at their berths until called, and then found the tide would not permit them to exit the river, discharging cargo would be unduly delayed. Consequently, when a ship was ready to unload freight, all necessary lighters had to be alongside.[46] In most cases lighters from several companies would be standing by at the ship's side to take various consignments of goods. If a contracted company did not have lighters waiting when they were required, the boats of another company could be called into service. Under such circumstances, the company who provided the emergency lighters invariably charged more for their service, inflating the cost to shippers.[47] The owner of the consignment ultimately bore the increased cost which could be three times as much as the usual fee.[48] If the lighterage company originally contracted to do the job did not repay the difference to the charterer it risked losing his service.[49] The risk of having to pay an indemnity and lose business in the process was a compelling reason for lighter owners to make sure their craft were at the ready. Hence, this sometimes meant waiting days at sea beside vessels. Lighterage companies from the 1850s received a demurrage fee for the time their craft had to stand by.[50] Mr Ow recalled how sometimes his lighters waited up to a week for cargo to be unloaded, and all the while the crews stayed on board.[51] For lightermen the time spent tied to a freighter in the harbour was often trying. They experienced boredom and little or no privacy as eating, sleeping, bathing and even going to the toilet were done on, or over the side of, the lighter.[52] Until the 1960s, there was no extra pay for lighter crews as they waited on vessels in the harbour. Most owners would send out meals at regular intervals, but that was the limit of their liability to the boatmen standing by.[53]

The number of men working on a lighter varied over the years, while the structure and organisation of the work force remained relatively static. Before the advent of motorised vessels and the use of tugboats, lighters were generally small. Indian tongkang at the turn of the century ranged in size from 30 to 100 tons fully loaded while Chinese twakow tended to be smaller.[54] (See Appendix 1, 'Lighter Craft of the Singapore River' for a discussion of the various craft.) In fact, until the 1960s, the average size of lighters operating in the river was just 38 tons.[55] The number of crewmen on either tongkang or twakow would vary from two to four individuals. Larger craft, propelled by sails and 'punt-poles',[56] required more crew to navigate the crowded river. Manoeuvring fully laden lighters of up to 100 tons in the narrow confines of the river using only two long punt poles, one on either side of the craft, was difficult work that required great skill. The craft was moved slowly by two men, one on each side of the vessel, pushing the punt-pole into the river bottom, a method of propulsion that required great shoulder strength on the part of crew members. Tan Ah Poh recounted his early experiences using such a pole:

> It was rough. When I came as a singkeh, I was not used to it. My shoulder was painful and swollen. In normal conditions, it took more than an hour from the river mouth to *Cha Chun Tau* [Read Bridge].[57]

Serious injuries could occur when the pole snapped under the strain, including men being impaled.[58] Once they had passed under the last bridge a collapsible sail was raised for the rest of the trip. On occasions, if the freighter was not far from the mouth of the river, the lighter would be poled some distance in the harbour. In the post Second World War era mechanisation of the industry led to the building of larger lighters. In the decade following 1945, the average size of lighters increased to between 100 and 200 tons fully loaded, as the volume of global and regional trade grew.[59] There were also some bigger, special purpose, motorised vessels built, some weighing over 300 tons fully loaded. But even on the largest cargo lighters it was still standard practice for there to be only two or, at most, three crewmen.[60] Motorised craft were easier to manoeuvre in the river with its narrow channel and low bridges and consequently, fewer men were needed to safely operate the big lighters.

While changes occurred in lighter size, the social organisation of the labour force remained constant. On each lighter there were always two types of crew members, the *taikong* also referred to as *twaylo*, helmsmen, and one or more *swaylo*, ordinary crewmen. Taikong were always men of considerable experience, initially having worked for years as swaylo.[61] The taikong took responsibility for the lighter and its cargo. It was his job to ensure safe passage of the craft in and out of the river and to check cargo weights and tallies. Chan Hian Chuan recalled how this division of labour and responsibility had deterred him from becoming a taikong:

> I am a swaylo. This is the job I have done since I became a lighterman. I could have been a taikong by now. But this means much more responsibility. You need to be able to count and calculate the amount of your cargo and I was never able to do these things well. Also as a taikong you are considered responsible for the lighter and this is a big responsibility ... Moving around in the river was always very difficult. You had to watch out for other boats and also the bridges. For these reasons I never wanted to be a taikong.[62]

The taikong on each lighter needed to be aware of all possible hazards to navigation in the river. He had to be particularly familiar with tidal variation, bridge clearance and water depth in different sections of the river. If a lighter was not properly loaded, or if the tide was higher than anticipated, passage under any one of the low bridges was impossible, even dangerous.[63] A twakow could just as easily be damaged hitting submerged rocks in the river or stranded on its muddy bottom if not loaded correctly. Parts of the river were always badly silted, and knowing how a loaded lighter would pass over such hazards was indispensable knowledge that a taikong had to possess.[64] Just as important to a taikong, was a working understanding of port regulations affecting the movement of lighters in the harbour. There were rules relating to speed, obstruction, mooring and how long lighters were permitted to stand alongside certain sections of river quays. To become a taikong, it was not only necessary to have the constitution and personality to take charge of a lighter, but one also needed to be literate in order to tally cargo and keep track of port rules and regulations.[65]

Prior to the advent of motorised lighters in the 1940s there were no formal qualifications necessary to be a taikong,[66] however, this changed as lighters were fitted with motors, *tian chun* (motorised twakow).[67] (For a detail discussion of various lighter craft, see Appendix 1, 'Lighter Craft of the Singapore River'.) Post-war mechanisation brought more direct government involvement and more explicit recognition of the skills necessary to be a taikong. The principal concern of authorities was the safety of shipping in the harbour, as the increasing number of motorised lighters posed a far greater threat to other craft than poled and sailing lighters. So motor lighters had to be under the command of a Class II Helmsman who was the only person permitted to train another operator.[68] Taikong on non-motorised lighters also now had to be licensed as Class III Steersmen.[69] This meant that no lighter could operate in either the river or harbour without a licensed taikong on board.

A further responsibility of taikong was the recruiting of swaylo. While the employment of taikong was in the hands of lighter owners, swaylo were often engaged by the helmsman of each lighter.[70] While river boat experience was a principal criteria for the job, being recommended by a reputable taikong was also required to secure a position.[71] Typically, taikong recruited men based on kinship and communal ties.[72] It was a recruitment system based on dialect and clan links which worked well. While owners wanted to be involved in hiring the person in charge of their lighter, crew selection was better left to the taikong. Obviously, it was in the taikong's interest to take only people who would work hard and cooperate in the smooth running of the craft. It also fell to the taikong to pay other members of the crew. There seem to have been few industrial problems caused by this system, and it was possible for owners to dispense with a taikong's services if they were dissatisfied.[73]

Apart from the additional responsibilities of the taikong, there was little to distinguish them from swaylo. When it came to the heavy work of cargo handling both shared the burden equally. However, swaylo were often expected to take care of more menial tasks. For example, swaylo were required to clean the lighter while it was idle and to cook the meals.[74] Even with respect to these chores though there were no hard and fast rules. Ow Chin Seng noted, half jokingly, that based on his experience the person who did the cooking was 'the best cook'.[75]

A Patron-Client Relationship

The patron-client relationship between lightermen and lighter owners played a critical part in shaping the work environment of Singapore boatmen. The reciprocal ties between a 'good towkay' and his lightermen went beyond that standard for an employer and employee under capital. It was a relationship based on mutual trust and reciprocity.[76] A trusted towkay was looked up to for more than just employment. He played the role of benevolent patriarch. Yap Aik Kun compared the role of the lighter owner to that of the village headmen in rural China.[77] In times of financial need or personal difficulty the towkay would be the individual to whom the lightermen turned for help.[78] When a crisis arose the towkay would often advance pay or lend money to their lightermen without interest. If disputes between lightermen occurred it would likely be the towkay who stepped in to resolve the conflict.[79] Chang Ham Chwee described how lightermen came to him with all manner of problems and, depending on how long they had been in his employ, he would attempt to assist them.

> I think I have been involved in some personal matter for all the lightermen that have ever worked for me. Sometimes they [lightermen] might come to me for a loan if I knew the person well enough then I would help him out. Except with gambling debts, although I have even lent money to pay these at different times. Usually my lightermen would only borrow money though if it was for an urgent family matter, such as paying a medical bill. I have also, in the past, helped men who found themselves in trouble with the law. Providing it was only a small matter, I would try to help.[80]

For lightermen who spent a lifetime in the industry, the extent of social welfare offered by a good towkay extended beyond their working life. It was accepted that, after years of arduous service, if a lighterman was unable to do hard physical work then the towkay would provide support.[81] Usually this meant providing some less laborious work, perhaps around the office or in a godown. Another common practice was to pay their passage costs to China if they had family there and wished to return.[82] Such social welfare measures were particularly important to lightermen who neither married nor had kindred in Singapore.

The socially responsible nature of this relationship was tied to patterns of recruitment and the fact that most owners had also worked as lightermen in the past.[83] For owners, employing boatmen with a common dialect and surname background meant fostering an extended family and they knew this was beneficial for the industry.[84] From the towkay's point of view, it was recognised that a work force would be more cohesive, loyal and productive coming from the same dialect group.[85] People recruited from the same province and village shared more than language as they had a common heritage and ethos which enhanced the social bond between them.[86] Wang Aik Mong grew up along the Singapore River in a world of lighters and river boatmen. His father was a large operator of cargo boats before 1940, and he recalled that all the men employed on the lighters were Teochew and referred to as 'family'.[87] While many lightermen were not actually related, he explained the meaning of family.

> That is how we described them. At that time it was considered proper to employ people who came from the same area and spoke the same dialect, sometimes even from the same village. This was natural. We felt some kind of affinity with these people that we didn't have with the others. This is no longer the case, in the lighterage industry at least.[88]

The President of the Lighter Owners Association expressed a similar opinion about the basic link between kinship and recruitment in the industry. Following his father's death in 1949, Chang Ham Chwee found himself, at the age of 14, in charge of the family business. Recalling that time he stated,

> I was able to manage the task at such a young age because most of the lightermen were 'family'. They at least came from the same village or

> province of China as my family. Most were not really related to us, but we spoke of them in this way. The majority of lighter companies in the past were staffed like this.[89]

This positive social and cultural attitude toward recruitment along dialect lines was shared by lightermen as it gave them job security and a sense of belonging. Considerable merit was placed on maintaining good relations with their towkay and fellow workers. They rarely changed jobs unless there was a falling out with the towkay or other crew member on their lighter.[90] Lightermen occasionally moved employers if the company changed hands or went out of business.[91] Changing jobs too often was frowned upon by both owners and boatmen. Men who did this were viewed as untrustworthy and unreliable. The work of lightermen entailed a high degree of cooperation, and the men on each lighter had to see themselves as part of a team.[92] Unnecessary disruption of this pattern and the resultant organisation of work was recognised as counter productive to the interests of owners and the safety of the boatmen.

The recruitment of lightermen along kinship lines by family and friends strengthened the close knit nature of the river boat community. Even in the post Second World War era lightermen still entered the profession this way.[93] Vacancies within the industry were commonly filled by a nephew, cousin or friend of someone already employed. Teo Ah Lea recalled how friends working on lighters helped him to get a job as a twakow man. Out of work and with little formal education he seized the opportunity to work on lighters when it was offered.[94] The experience of Chan Hian Chuan was similar.[95] As a child growing up, the area around the river was his home and playground. His father was employed in a godown nearby and had friends in the lighter industry. For Chan there was not much choice when it came to employment, especially without formal education:

> In this case you had to take what you could find. For me it was easy. I grew up along the river and knew much about the work of lightermen. So when it was time for me to find a job my father arranged for me to get work on a twakow. This was not bad as the money I made was better than I could earn anywhere else.[96]

Despite the hard work, the fellowship of family, friends, and countrymen from the same province or village in China gave the lighterage industry a strong basis for solidarity and socio-cultural organisation.[97]

A notable aspect of recruitment in the post-war era amongst family members was the reticence to bring next of kin, especially sons, into the industry. As more lightermen married in the post-1945 period it was rare for them to encourage their children to follow in their footsteps.[98] Though proud of their occupation, most opted to educate their children for careers that did not entail such strenuous work and, in more recent times, possible unemployment.[99] Without exception the lightermen interviewed for this study who had families said they had worked hard to ensure their children received a good education so they did not have to work as lightermen or labourers. None wanted their children to have to work as they had. Even owners of lighters rarely encouraged their children to become involved in the business believing that there were better opportunities for them in other careers. Consequently, a lighterman might find a job for a nephew or more distant relative in the industry, but he would not readily recommend his own child.

Fee Sharing

The way lightermen were paid reflects the patron–client bond that existed between themselves and lighter owners. With the exception of lightermen who worked on company-owned twakow, such as those owned by the Shell Oil Company, they were all paid on a piecemeal basis. Tan Chee Soon was paid a flat rate of 2 Straits dollars per week by Shell to work on one of their twakow.[100] There were no fixed wages paid in the industry to these men,[101] nor for years were there any written agreements between lightermen and owners about a wage index. The contract was verbal, based on trust and reciprocal obligations.[102] Traditionally, lightermen received a share of the fee charged to transport cargo.[103] This system of payment was discussed by all the people interviewed for this study. The figures quoted throughout this section are based on information provided in the various interviews quoted. Ow Chin Seng described the rational for this wage arrangement.

> The people who own lighters see themselves as providing the materials and, most importantly, the contacts ... Lightermen provided the manpower or muscle. It is a sharing arrangement where both parties need each other to survive ... The lightermen understood this well.[104]

Fee sharing was practised in all areas of water transport. It was common for tongkangs in Singapore that freighted goods, such as foodstuffs, timber and rubber from neighbouring islands, to also operate on a fee-sharing basis.[105] It was an arrangement that satisfied most lightermen. They earned relatively good wages compared to other labouring occupations. This, at least, was the impression that most lightermen and owners had of the system as ascertained from various interviews. Labour Department Annual Reports in the 1940s and 1950s appear to support the fact that lightermen were quite well paid, especially in comparison with labourers and semi-skilled workers in the employ of the government. Chang Ham Chwee suggested also that these reports were not necessarily an accurate reflection of the actual income that lightermen received. Labour Department reports reflect official rates and many lightermen were on higher rates. Also, they do not take into account other benefits such as being able to live on the lighter (see Appendix 2, Table 6).[106]

The profit-sharing system meant there was no guarantee as to how much income would be earned in any given period. Stories circulated amongst lightermen highlighting the financial insecurity associated with fee sharing. These adages point to the economic uncertainty of day-to-day work in the lighterage industry, for example, 'twakow one day earn three dollars, no earn must run away'.[107] Chan Hian Chuan recalled the boom days but also the financial insecurity of an industry dependent on the fluctuating fortunes of regional-global trade.

> Working as a lighterman you could make good money. If there were many ships then you could work hard and make more money. But it will never last. If it is good today you know that tomorrow or the next day it will not be the same. There are always changes happening.[108]

Their income was calculated as a share of the transport fee. The amount a lightermen earned was contingent on a number of factors, including the size of the lighter, type of cargo and frequency of trips, as well as changing tides and weather.

Over the years there have been small variations in the way that profits have been divided between the parties. Since the 1950s, the usual has been fifty-fifty.[109] That is half the profit from each consignment went to the lighter owner and the remainder was divided amongst the lightermen. Prior to the 1950s, on twakow over sixty tons, owners would take a larger share of the profit. This arrangement developed because bigger twakow carried more cargo on a single trip, earning their crews more money for fewer journeys, than smaller lighters. Conversely, on smaller lighters the share of the fee that went to lightermen was larger. In craft under 60 tons the fee paid was as high as 60 per cent. The logic behind the fee disparity on different sized lighters ensured that crew working on smaller craft were not disadvantaged at the expense of their counterparts on larger vessels.[110] Whether it had the desired affect across the board is debateable, but, what is clear, is that owners of bigger lighters were financially better off.[111]

The shared income was calculated on the net value of the transport fee. The running expenses of the lighter and maintenance costs were subtracted from the gross fee before any profit was divided between owner and crew.[112] For lightermen, any additional costs incurred, such as expenses for food, had to be deducted from their share.[113] It was common for taikong to receive a slightly larger percentage of the split than swaylo, usually between 5 and 10 per cent.[114] Understandably, the incomes of lightermen fluctuated considerably over time. Tan Chee Soon noted that in the early part of this century it was possible to earn as much as S$32 one month and as little as S$8 the next.[115] In 1946, government statistics reveal that lightermen's wages varied from S$70–S$120 per month.[116] This pattern of fluctuating income continued into the post-war era. In a 1960 government report, monthly average income for lightermen varied from just over S$200 to almost S$400 depending on boat size and position.[117] In the 1970s, during a boom period monthly earnings reached as much as S$1500. It was pointed out by Ong Ah Cheng that while the 1970s were years in which lightermen made better wages than in any other period, they were also years in which lightermen worked many long hard hours.[118] They were heady days for the industry and the few remaining lightermen who remember that time reflected upon it wistfully. By the 1980s their average monthly earnings had been slashed to between S$400 and S$650.[119]

The patron-client or towkay-coolie relationship was the primary form of protection boatmen had against hard times when the industry slumped because of global recession or a downturn in trade. During idle periods boatmen received a living allowance of S$7 per week from the owner of the twakow.[120] In most cases this subsidy was barely enough to pay for the cigarettes and coffee consumed in a week.[121] Furthermore, they had to be unemployed for at least a week to claim the gratuity. This small advance was fixed across the industry.[122] Some owners preferred to provide provisions for their lightermen when they were out of work. They then could be certain that the men were eating properly, since cash could be squandered on some whim of the boatmen, such as gambling.[123] As a result the wage structure of lightermen was a further reflection of the traditional socio-cultural organisation of the Chinese river boat community with the economic and social welfare of boatmen largely dependent on the good will of lighter owners.

Industrial Organisation

It is a measure of the cultural strength of the bond between lighter owners and lightermen that the political organisation of boatmen as a union did not occur until 1937.[124] Historically, labour disputes in the industry and on the waterfront were rare and usually not related to work conditions. The earliest record of lightermen striking is 1842. It was a strike linked to a large-scale protest by the Indian community against the government's refusal to allow a religious procession through the streets of the settlement. The *Singapore Free Press* commented on the 'temporary inconvenience' especially for merchants who were 'deprived of the services of their boatmen and boats'.[125] A similar strike occurred in 1857 with the passing of the Municipal and Police Acts. This time it was the Chinese community that protested, resulting in all shops shutting and coolies and boatmen refusing to work.[126] In both these early cases the choice to strike by boatmen was a consequence of broader community concerns, rather than matters relating directly to the lighterage industry.

The Lightermen's Union was born during the latter part of the Depression, in the late 1930s, when boatmen and other labourers wanted to rectify long-standing grievances over working conditions in the port city.[127] In spite of the seeming harmony and communal loyalty lightermen felt for their employers, by the 1930s there was real tension over wages and conditions in the work place. In the volatile pre-war social and political environment of Singapore, the nature of the traditional patron-client bond was strained to the limit. This was a period marked by considerable union activity and social unrest in Singapore. Amongst the labouring masses there was a growing sense of political awareness as strident demands were made for better work and wage conditions. Labourers in a range of occupations, from boatmen to warehouse workers, were forming unions. Lightermen, too, became increasingly aware of their political strength when united.[128] A measure of the degree of solidarity and cooperation that existed between workers at the time was seen in the assistance rendered by the pineapple workers to the lightermen's union.[129] Already unionised, the pineapple workers provided invaluable advice to boatmen trying to unionise themselves and their support even went so far as to help organise the first union strike by lightermen.[130]

In forming a union it was not the lightermen's intention to radically transform the industrial system under which they lived and worked. They accepted the fact that working on a profit-sharing basis meant there was always a degree of economic uncertainty in earning a livelihood. Their principal concern was to ensure that they were treated fairly under the existing profit-sharing arrangement.[131] Boatmen understood that to a great extent they were dependent on the benevolence and honesty of their towkay. Oral evidence suggests not all owners acted honestly toward their staff. They were 'businessmen trying to make as much profit as they could', and, in some cases, they used 'unfair means' to evade the terms of the contract they established with their workers.[132] A major complaint of boatmen was that owners did not calculate the profit split properly.[133] Some owners cheated lightermen by not stipulating the correct amount paid to carry a cargo.[134] By under valuing the transport of merchandise they reduced the boatmen's share. It was also a simple matter for owners to claim the cargo weighed less than it actually did. This fraud was apt to occur when dealing with 'general goods' such as produce or rattans.[135] The other major complaint of lightermen pertained to the hours worked. They resented not receiving a larger share of the profit when working long and irregular hours.[136] Lightermen felt, that when they worked through the night or had to stand alongside a ship for days on end waiting for cargo, they were entitled to receive a subsidy. Another equally important concern to boatmen was lack of proper compensation and rehabilitation when injured on the job. Some unscrupulous owners did what they could to avoid helping injured workers.[137]

Established on the eve of the Second World War, the Lightermen's Union did not really come to fruition until the post-war period. It was reorganised along different communal and administrative lines after the war and registered as the Transport Vessel Workers Association (TVWA).[138] Originally set up as a union for all lightermen, it had, by 1947, come to represent almost exclusively Chinese boatmen on the river. Because of the 'communalistic' attitude and rivalry pervading the Chinese section of the industry,[139] Indian lightermen employed in the Teluk Ayer Basin resigned en masse in that year to form the Singapore Lighter Workers' Union.[140] As a union, however, it failed to satisfy the demands of its Indian members and was racked by scandal and controversy. It seems that many of the people involved with organising this union proved to be less interested in their members' interests than their own. There was talk of union funds spent on luxuries for officials and a general air of distrust seems to have hung over these men. The Singapore Lighter Workers Union eventually collapsed.[141] Although several other attempts were made to organise Indian lightermen, these too proved unsuccessful. This left only the TVWA as the principal organiser of lightermen. Though always dominated by its Chinese majority many Indian lightermen opted to rejoin following the failure of their own union.[142]

The efforts of the TVWA to ensure their members received proper wages and improved working conditions were generally successful. It achieved its aims in the ensuing decades primarily through arbitration and negotiation. The TVWA united lightermen and gave them a powerful public persona and voice. Lightermen who previously felt intimidated and unable to voice their complaints now spoke out.[143] The union fostered a sense of class solidarity amongst lightermen that cut across clan and dialect boundaries and reduced the number of territorial clashes between rival dialect groups.[144] The age-old rivalry between Hokkien and Teochew boatmen was contained after the union was established. For many swaylo, joining the union was now preferable to affiliation with a clan association, as union membership was important in keeping a job.[145] Many petty monopoly issues traditionally fought over by dialect groups, such as accidents and conflicts over which boat bumped another, or who claimed the territorial right to use a particular jetty, no longer mattered.[146] Lightermen now began to think of themselves as an occupational group with common goals and interests, irrespective of earlier traditional communal affiliations. Ong Ah Cheng noted that it made no difference any longer whether you belonged to the 'Kim Mui clan' or the 'Hui Wan clan' as the work you did was basically the same and the sorts of 'difficulties you faced were the same'.[147] Lightermen realised the constant rivalry was not conducive 'to do business, to make money, to make ends meet'.[148] The early success of the union enabled the boatmen to realise that united, the TVWA could ensure fair and proper treatment for all concerned.[149] Ong Ah Cheng felt the key to the union's success was the sense of unity it fostered amongst lightermen.

> By bringing together all lightermen the union achieved its success. This was the most important accomplishment of the union. Everyone, the owners and the shippers, realised that now the men had real protection and could no longer be treated as if they did not count.[150]

The majority of lightermen supported the union and the majority of owners came to grudgingly accept and respect the union as a necessary industrial body in the political economy of post-war Singapore. They, too, stood to gain from the marked reduction of communal rivalry amongst lightermen.[151] Greater solidarity and cooperation between lightermen also meant operations along the river generally ran more smoothly.

Cooperation and Decline

In spite of the benefits of a unionised workforce, work place difficulties remained and the relationship between unionised lightermen and owners was not trouble free. In 1961 the most serious falling out occurred when lightermen went on strike over issues of pay and conditions. The aim of the union was to secure extra money for working on Sunday.[152] The strike lasted two tense weeks during which time a number of waterfront fights broke out and several minor incidents occurred. Violent confrontation was sparked by some shipping companies using non-union labour to break the strike.[153] Lightermen successfully stopped the strike-breakers from working and many of their demands were subsequently met by owners. This strike was heralded as an important success by the lightermen. In the aftermath of the strike, they were confident enough of their newfound strength to insist that all lighters had to fly the union flag to get work.[154] It was an unparalleled act of militant unity, hitherto unseen in the industry.

Chang Ham Chwee believes the matter could have been resolved peacefully if the political climate had been different.[155] The strike occurred right at the time when left wing members of the People's Action Party (PAP) broke away to form the Barisan Sosialis (Socialist Front) opposition. According to Chang, most owners were prepared to meet the demands of their workers but everyone got emotionally caught up in the milieu of unfolding political events. As he explained:

> We found ourselves on opposite sides of the political fence. The union [lightermen] supported the Barisan Sosialis while the owners' association [lighter owners] supported the PAP. I think the differences we had and the fighting had nothing to do with working conditions. Everyone was very hot about their own side in the political debate of the time. Because of this things that would otherwise have been settled without incident became troublesome.[156]

Tension between the lightermen and owners continued to fester for a number of years and the consultative process fell apart.[157] The situation was not helped by the war of counter-insurgency being waged in Malaya. The so-called 'emergency' resulted in the Lightermen's union being accused of harbouring communists. While it was true that some members were affiliated with or sympathetic to the communist movement, the accusations made against the union that it was a front were false according to Ong Ah Cheng. 'Its principal aim at all times was to look out for the interests of its members.'[158] The TVWA, along with other labour organisations, was considered by the Internal Security Department to be a front for the Malayan Communist Party in Singapore.[159] Its leaders were harassed and imprisoned at various times, even though the number of lightermen 'infused with political thought were in the minority'.[160] As a consequence of these turbulent years the union began to chart an independent course, avoiding affiliation with any political party.[161] The union realised the need, albeit painfully, to put the immediate occupational interests of its members before any broader political concerns.

The majority of lighter owners realised, too, that by cooperation with the union the industry could improve its business performance. As early as 1949, the owners had encouraged the establishment and registering of a committee to coordinate various interests in the industry, including the TVWA. Known as the 'Joint Committee',[162] it comprised the following unions and associations: The Singapore Lighter Owners Association, The National Lighterage Company, The Singapore Transport Vessel Workers Association, The Singapore Lighter Workers' Association and the United Motor Sampan Association.[163] The reframed 1955 Memorandum of Agreement summed up the aims of this body.

> To secure the largest possible measure of joint action between the employers and the workers for the development of the industry as a part of the economic life of Singapore and for the improvement of the conditions of all engaged in the industry ... Regular consideration of wages, hours and conditions of employment generally in the industry ... Representation of the needs and opinions of the industry as a whole to the Government, and/or other appropriate authority.[164]

The Joint Consultative Committee struggled through the 1950s and 1960s to achieve these aims and virtual became defunct. However, in the 1970s it became a formally united body, as new technologies and changed attitudes toward working conditions foreshadowed the demise of the industry.[165] The Committee secured consensus between its members to pay standard rates and pay extra wages for certain services such as demurrage time.[166] Most importantly for owners there was no explicit demand to change the traditional task system of wages based on profit sharing. While some in the union wanted to push for set wages, the majority of lightermen never supported the idea.[167]

Owners and lightermen agreed that liaison and negotiation between the TVWA and the owners' association, facilitated by the Committee, helped create a better working environment on the river and waterfront. Both parties gained by ensuring that all lightermen received the same share of profits. It meant that no company could undercut the prices of a competitor simply by reducing the percentage paid to their boatmen.[168] Occasionally, there were instances when a company did cut prices or lightermen agreed to work for less, but these were dealt with quickly by both the union and owners. These sorts of disputes arose when a new company was trying to establish a customer base in what was a highly-competitive industry.[169] The usual method of dealing with such cases was to boycott the company concerned if negotiations did not resolve the problem. If all other measures failed lightermen physically blocked the offending companies' lighters so that they could not leave the river.[170] Sometimes a lighter was loaded with up to two dozen men who would proceed to verbally harass anyone working on the 'black' craft.[171] Though rare, there were instances when force was used to 'persuade' lightermen against working for companies not abiding by industry standards.[172] For example, poaching customers was considered bad for all concerned as it was often accompanied by lower wages.[173]

As the spirit of solidarity and cooperation developed, the union pursued the 'relatively small number of owners' who continued to deal unfairly with workers.[174] In the 1970s, some owners still did not take out adequate insurance on behalf of their lightermen, despite the fact that each year there were a sizeable number of accidents in the industry. There were on average one or two serious accidents a year, resulting in death or permanent injury and many minor injuries. Most injuries were the result of crushing, resulting in broken bones, and in more severe cases, severed limbs. Explosions and fires also occurred from time to time causing injury, and it was not uncommon for lightermen to drown.[175] These owners clung to the mistaken notion that, because lightermen were paid on a piecemeal basis, this aspect of rehabilitation and welfare was not their responsibility.[176] By winning a number of important court cases the union was able to convince all owners to accept their responsibility for compensation. The sobering thought of losing their own property and wealth in a compensation claim was sufficient incentive for even the most intransigent owners to cover themselves.[177]

Cooperation between the lightermen and owners under the auspices of the Joint Consultative Committee also meant they had a more united voice when it came to dealing with the government, and in particular, the port authority. Throughout the 1970s a string of joint appeals was made to the government as the lighterage industry struggled in the face of technological and political change. In 1971, petitions were lodged concerning the economic necessity to keep the river open to trade in face of urban renewal.[178] Similarly, when the Port Authority restricted access to Keppel Harbour for lighters over 100 feet in length, it met a storm of protest from both lightermen and owners. Jointly they took up their concerns with the Port Master and the Minister for State and Communications, as well as making sure their concerns reached the press.[179] Another issue taken up jointly was the impact of Lash (lighters aboard ship) ships on the lighterage industry. In 1975, the Joint Committee called on the government to investigate the impact on the local industry of vessels bringing their own lighters into port.[180] By far the longest most difficult battle fought together by lightermen and owners was to prevent the government moving them out of the river. Even when the battle was lost they continued to use their united strength to secure the best possible deal for the future.[181]

The late 1970s were the years in which traditional ties between owners and lightermen were strengthened in the face of adversity, as both parties faced the prospect of extinction. During these years the Joint Committee worked frantically to increase the overall level of efficiency and the profits of all concerned through negotiation with interested parties, namely the various chambers of commerce, business and industry.

Hard work and economic uncertainty were hallmarks of a lighterman's life along the Singapore River. The demanding work called for not only sheer physical strength but also a measure of manual skill and dexterity not required in other labouring occupations. The safe handling of the enormous wealth that passed through the port was entrusted to these men. Their occupation required that they were part skilled labourer and seafarer. To be a boatman required strength and agility to handle bulky cargo and also the skill to manage the craft as it threaded its way through the harbour. Lightermen earned better wages than other non-skilled persons but never shared the luxury of regular working hours. Their work routine was inextricably tied to fluctuations of trade activity and tidal variation. They might work for days on end and then remain idle for just as long a period waiting for the next ship.

Organisationally, the labour system of the lightermen reflected particular Chinese socio-cultural traditions. It mirrored the ties that bound clan and kin associations with sojourning networks and home. The quasi-kin based patron-client relationship between owners and lightermen determined the conditions under which boatmen worked. The cultural sense of reciprocity and exchange with respect to labour and security that pervaded the industry restricted the types of industrial claims made by either party. Even during the 1960s when the union was at its zenith the cultural basis of the lighterage industry was never seriously challenged by the TVWA. The profit-sharing system favouring owners was never rescinded. Throughout the period under consideration, lightermen wanted equitable treatment but they were not prepared to sever the bonds of the traditional patron-client relationship between lighter owners and boatmen. This traditional arrangement provided lightermen with the only security they had against fluctuations in the fortunes of their trade. The industry continued to operate in this manner into the 1990s.

6
Life Along the River: Domesticity, Rest and Recreation

THE lives of lightermen were inextricably bound up with the river and the craft they worked aboard. The river became the lighterman's neighbourhood haunt and the vessel his home. It was a way of life tied to the rhythms of trans-oceanic trade, tide and weather. The amount of work they did and when they did it was not simply a matter of choice. A rickshaw puller could choose to work longer hours or to work at night instead of during the day, there was no limit to the time he could put in running along dusty dangerous streets beyond the constraints of his own fitness.[1] For lightermen this kind of workplace choice did not exist. Usually, the hours a lighterman worked were dependent on factors beyond his control. Even when the trade of the port was thriving there was always the tide and general congestion to contend with on the river, determining the number of trips made to vessels anchored in the roadstead. Consequently, there was often time for other activities beyond the immediate work as lighters lay idle waiting for the next consignment, tidal change or break in the weather.

Nevertheless, the river tended to be the focal point of social activities outside of work for lightermen who often sought pleasures and distractions away from work, yet close to their place of employment — the river. They never knew when their lighter might be called into service, so the river quays were crowded not only with lightermen at work but also with those temporarily idle, waiting for their next trip. 'Good lightermen' never strayed far from the ambit of the river and their twakow. This characteristic was the mark of a reliable man.[2] As late as 1983, on the eve of the removal of the industry from the river, lightermen continued to congregate along its banks on a daily basis, while waiting for work. This practice still occurred despite the fact that, by this time, most men were married and lived on a housing estate where they could be reached by telephone when their services were required.[3] The attraction of being on the twakow and on the river, though, was not just economic, as both were places to socialise, and, for many men, they provided the sole place where they actually felt at 'home'.[4]

This chapter examines the social and recreational world of lightermen along the river, analysing their lives beyond the routine of work. It begins with a discussion of the way in which their social world was shaped by the transitory nature of labour migration and urban life in colonial Singapore. The social life of lightermen, the entertainment and distractions they sought, were created by their bachelor status and limited opportunities to put down roots. The discussion then focuses on the types of leisure activities in which lightermen engaged during their free time.

Bachelors, Marriage and Home

Like many of their compatriots in Singapore, lightermen found themselves living a life devoid of most things associated with personal contentment. They had left their kin in China with little hope of establishing a family in the difficult environment of colonial Singapore. Most lightermen lived a solitary life prior to the Second World War as they contemplated on how best to work toward their eventual return home. The majority clung to the dream of returning with savings to their ancestral homes and loved ones in China. Most maintained contact with their family and village, in spite of the great distance and difficulties of maintaining regular communication. Ow Hin Kok recalled that even after the Second World War many lightermen still talked of returning 'home to China as if nothing had changed'.[5] For many, this distant contact was the strongest consolation as they worked through the monotonous grind of their daily lives on the Singapore River. There was always talk of China on the lighter and wherever lightermen congregated of distant family and friends, remittances of money and of the day when one would journey home.[6] It was customary for groups of twakow men to sit huddled around cups of strong tea or a bottle of rice wine talking of such things.[7] The haunts of lightermen buzzed with concerned conversation about what was happening in China during the 1930s, and most men were kept up to date with the latest news from home during those fateful years. When contact with family was either intermittent or nonexistent there were still always new arrivals to question about what was happening in the village and neighbouring areas. The river quays were an ideal spot to seek out personal information and news because craft in the harbour carried not only cargo but news of home from ships' crews and passengers. Invariably, men who had only recently arrived, with memories of family still fresh in their minds, were eager to relate accounts from home and tell their own story.[8]

For some of these sojourners the dream of modest wealth became a reality. They returned home after several decades or more in the lighterage industry, content to see out their days with the hard-earned money they had managed to save. Others, however, were repeatedly drawn back to work along the Singapore River. Some had worked hard, saved enough and married in China, but eventually the lure of money, combined with difficult political conditions, persuaded them to return to their twakow on the Singapore River.[9] The more successful lightermen, those able to save and manage their incomes, made regular trips to China. Ow Hin Kok recalls that some men who worked for him before the war made the journey to China at least once every five years, often staying for a year or more. These were the men who did not spend their income on 'gambling, opium or women (prostitutes)'.[10] Less frugal individuals made fewer trips and tended not to stay away as long.[11]

There were other reasons besides the transient nature of life as to why lightermen chose bachelorhood over marriage in Singapore. In the main, these other considerations were financial and work related. Lighterman earned better money (see Appendix 2, Table 6 and note 107, Chapter 5) than most labouring groups in Singapore. However, they generally believed that they did not earn a sufficient wage to maintain a family and thus opted for bachelorhood.[12] For many the choice of a solitary life also concerned filial commitment to family in China. A wife in Singapore meant there would be less or, perhaps, even no money for remittance to loved ones and kin, and in most cases, little or no chance of returning to see family unless the work and years were kind.[13] Life was hard enough for a single person before the war, so to have a wife and children was not something to be undertaken lightly.[14] Chan Hian Chuan recalled, that when he started work as a lighterman immediately after the War, few boatmen were yet married. As he explained:

> Most were single at that time. People (lightermen) did not think marriage was a good idea in this industry ... because the wages you earned were not enough for the responsibilities that came with marriage. And even if you met a woman who was working what would happen after you married and children came along, life would be very difficult.[15]

The elusive goal was to get rich in Singapore and return home to settle permanently. Marriage was considered a dangerous step. It could lead to impoverishment and a life in Singapore cut off from home and family in China.[16] For most pre-war lightermen, it meant the end of the sojourning dream of returning home wealthy.

When a lighterman decided to marry locally there was always the problem of where he and his wife would live. Lightermen often paid for lodging in a *coolie keng* run by individuals of the same surname or clan association, but they rarely ever stayed in these cramped accommodations, choosing instead to live on board the lighters.[17] The rental cost of these tenement quarters was reduced by large numbers of men living together, paying around S$1 per month plus miscellaneous expenses for food and other necessities.[18] The standard of living conditions prevalent in these older two and three storey houses was shocking in the extreme.[19] Cubicles measuring only a few feet across were shared by several men, and sometimes even families, taking it in turn to rest and work. With little light or ventilation and even less provision for sanitary requirements, morbidity and mortality from communicable diseases such as dysentery and tuberculosis were common place. The Commission of 1918 found the population density of some areas, such as Chinatown, to be between 796 and 1,304 persons per acre — even higher than the average for Bombay, India. Not surprisingly, the infant mortality rate in such densely populated housing near the river was high. More typically though, lightermen lived on their craft or in one of the many godowns that dotted the river bank, rather than in the coolie keng, thus avoiding some of the more dangerous aspects of life in the tenements.[20] The coolie keng was considered a place of last resort — a haven for unemployed men or those too sick to work.

Living on the lighter was a practical, healthier arrangement for single men, as it meant rent was less and boatmen were always on hand for work.[21] Wang Aik Mong who managed a fleet of lighters along the river in the immediate post-war years, remembered that 'most' of his twakowmen 'cooked, bathed and slept' on their lighters.[22] For many of them the lighter represented a clean and healthy place to stay. The alternative was a crowded cubicle, or duckling bed, in a coolie lodging house.[23] As late as 1982, Mr Tan was still sleeping on his lighter, preferring to spend his nights on the river where a cool ocean breeze made sleeping more comfortable.[24] He only used his room in the coolie keng, shared with six others, to shower and change. Given a choice, lightermen would always opt for staying on board the lighter.[25] Some lightermen even preferred to live outdoors under Read Bridge, despite its traffic noise, rather than in the coolie keng.[26] The underside of the bridge's superstructure allowed planks to be erected, creating a living space. There was always a risk that the local authorities would evict lightermen from under the bridge and other such locations, treating them as vagrants.[27] In spite of the river being polluted, it seemed like a safe outdoor refuge compared with the cramped conditions prevalent in the lodging houses.

Housing problems aside, marrying and moving away from the lighter meant being away from the river and work, something most men could not afford, even if they could manage the rent. Given the periodic nature of lighterage work, there were difficulties for anyone attempting to make a home away from the vicinity of the river. Owners were not prepared to chase after their boatmen when a consignment of goods suddenly arrived or an unannounced ship reached the harbour as they expected their crews to be on stand by at all times.[28] Equally difficult for a married man were the number of days on end spent on a twakow to protect goods against theft and weather damage, waiting to get out of a congested river, or similar periods spent tied alongside vessels in the harbour waiting for consignments to be off-loaded. As far as lighter owners were concerned, lightermen were responsible for the cargo on their twakow until it was discharged.[29] Thus, shedding work commitments to tend to family responsibilities or an emergency was extremely difficult for lightermen to manage well.

Furthermore, when it came to the issue of marriage for lightermen in Singapore, the unequal ratio of females to males was as significant a factor as financial and work considerations. The small number of Chinese women living in Singapore before the 1920s meant there were few opportunities for marriage, even if a lighterman felt his income was adequate to support a wife and family. Singapore was still very much a bachelor-migrant-coolie town. In the 1880s the demands of the colonial economy for unskilled manual labour resulted in a huge influx of young males. In 1884, there were only 6,000 Chinese women living in Singapore, a sizeable proportion being prostitutes, while there were more than 60,000 Chinese men.[30]

Census data shows this discrepancy in the sex ratios and gender imbalance to have been a constant feature of Chinese immigration to Singapore for more than four decades from the 1880s onward.[31] Until the 1920s, comparatively few Chinese women, other than those procured for prostitution, immigrated to the region. Ee points to a steady increase in the number of Chinese women arriving during the 1930s, but it was not until the post-war era that the ratio of females to males began to approach acceptable levels.[32] A wealthy Chinese man might return to China, find a bride and bring her to Singapore,[33] but few such opportunities existed for lightermen and other labouring groups. Ow Hin Kok one of the oldest surviving lightermen and owners described the demographic situation prior to the Second World War this way, 'anyway there were few opportunities to marry at this time because there were many men living here but few women from China'.[34]

Quay Side Leisure and Vice

The impact of living in a predominantly male environment where an individual's personal value was measured in terms of the physical work he accomplished, shaped the kinds of social recreation lightermen sought outside of work. There was a void in the transient urban lives of lightermen which craved to be filled. They came from village homes and a rural culture that placed primary value on the extended family, often with several generations living under one roof. Whilst affiliation with a surname or occupational group provided a measure of security against the unforseen,[35] it could not fill the personal void created by the absence of kin and loved ones. The lack of genuine family ties, especially female, coupled with harsh working conditions, combined to create a sense of frustration and loneliness[36] that was often relieved in ways that were not necessarily healthy or socially acceptable in village China. Separation from family also meant there were fewer constraints on behaviour in Singapore.[37] The moral exhortations and standards of home seemed far removed from the harsh realities of life in Singapore. Foremost among the rest and recreation pursuits of lightermen were visits to brothels and opium dens that dotted the Chinatown area. Brothels in the area of Nankin Street, Hokkien Street and Teochew Street were popular with lightermen.[38] Those who did not succumb to either of these temptations could either gamble or drink as a pastime to part with their hard-earned wages. Ong Ah Cheng, describing the lives of lightermen in the past, stated that, 'these were people with no family living lonely and often harsh lives. They turned to whatever forms of relaxation and entertainment they could find and afford.'[39]

Prostitution and opium played an important role in the political economy of Singapore.[40] The unfettered immigration of male coolies was critical to the colonial economy and growth of the city. Whilst the extent of traffic in women and children and brothel prostitution in the port city proved an embarrassment to its colonial overlords, they were dependent on vice as a means of social control. The disproportionately small number of Chinese women meant there was a need for sexual services to cater to the enormous number of bachelor migrant-labourers in the city, including the lightermen. The colonial government was acutely aware of this social fact and acted accordingly to control and regulate prostitution rather than prohibit it. Official voices in the colony would repeatedly point to the particular social conditions that existed in Singapore as reason enough to sanction brothel prostitution and its regulation for the safety and benefit of all.[41] Such efforts were aimed at eliminating the worst aspects of the vice trade, namely, forcing women and girls against their will to work as prostitutes, and the control of venereal disease.[42] The Contagious Diseases Ordinance of 1870 gave the colonial authorities wide-ranging powers to ensure that both brothels and women working in them were registered. It authorised the Registrar General's office and later the Chinese Protectorate to investigate premises under suspicion of operating as 'sly' brothels — establishments that were not legally registered.[43] More importantly, the Contagious Diseases Ordinance helped contain the spread of venereal disease through compulsory medical examination of women of all nationalities working in the brothels of Singapore. While voices of protest and pressure from England by the late 1880s saw a relaxation of government control of brothel prostitution, there was little attempt to abolish the industry due to the singular economic and demographic dynamics of Singapore. The campaign against the Contagious Diseases Ordinance was led in England by the charismatic and persistent Josephine Butler. While the campaign was successful, it had disastrous consequences in Singapore, unleashing a venereal disease epidemic.[44]

Visits to brothels by lightermen satisfied not only their sexual urge, but the desire for female companionship and intimacy, however fleeting.[45] Accepted social norms of morality and orientation towards one's family and kin were of little consequence when there was long separation and isolation in a city like colonial Singapore.[46] Honourable intentions were often not enough to withstand temptation.

> Many men deny they ever visited with prostitutes but most did when they were young and before there were many wives here. Some men made promises to their families before leaving China, saying they would work hard and not get involved in anything bad, and tried to keep them, but for most these promises were forgotten after some time had passed.[47]

For these hardworking young men, whose days were either occupied by the grinding toil of lighterage work or monotonous waits for the next job, the lure of the nearby brothel quarters in Kreta Ayer was irresistible. Especially at night, these red light districts were flooded with labourers and artisans from all over the city.[48] They came for the food, gambling, opium and prostitution, which occupied entire streets in that area and other quarters of the city. The officially recognised brothels of Chinatown were located in the following areas: at the western edge of the town on Sago Street, Smith Street, Temple Street and Trengganu Street; the central part of the town on Upper Nankin Street and Upper Hokkien Street; and behind Ellenborough Market on Chin Hin Street. An elderly resident of Chinatown recalled how in the Kreta Ayer area especially, the brothel district was lit up as 'bright as day every night'.[49] During quiet nights along the river lightermen resting on their craft or cramped in their 'duckling beds' would hear the sounds emanating from the bustling heart of Chinatown and think of their next excursion on pay day.[50]

The repeal of the Contagious Diseases Ordinance in 1887, followed by the increasingly hostile view that the authorities exhibited towards prostitution by the late 1920s, did not change the reality of social life for lightermen. The closure of the brothels in 1927 and new regulations against traffic in women were belated remedial measures of a government under siege from the British public, with little regard for the continuing social isolation of these labourers and tens of thousands of others. The lightermen were still, until the 1970s, bachelors who felt they had little chance of marrying, and found themselves driven by force of circumstance to seek the services of prostitutes.[51] Sanctioned brothels had disappeared but there were establishments in Desker Road as well as the 'bumboat girls' at the steps behind the Fullerton Building or Collyer Quay whose services could be readily obtained.[52] In the style of Jack Flowers,[53] some lightermen earned the sexual favours of these women by transporting them to ships in the harbour where the real money could be made on foreign vessels. Twakow men were also accused of stealing from vessels in the harbour and of being peddlers of pornographic magazines and postcards.[54]

In much the same way as 'womanising' relieved the stress of daily life, opium smoking was also an escape for lightermen from the harsh reality of their situation. These two vices, sex and drugs, were linked together. Evidence provided during the 1908 Opium Commission suggested many opium smokers first acquired the habit while visiting brothels.[55] Further, opium was often used to relieve pain caused by the ravages of venereal disease, contracted, more likely as not, while visiting one of the town's many Chinese brothels. Not surprisingly, just as brothel prostitution can be explained by severance from home comforts, so too can the widespread use of opium amongst the Chinese labouring classes in Singapore.[56] Opium was often referred to as the 'pill to peace and happiness' by those who used it.[57] In the short term at least, it provided relief from the physical pain of strenuous work and the mental anguish of loneliness and isolation. Deprived of ordinary comforts, opium acted as a powerful sedative creating a sense of 'indifference to all external discomforts and wretchedness of any kind'.[58]

The extent of opium addiction amongst lightermen was high. Heavy opium use was particularly evident with men working in physically demanding occupations such as lightermen, coal coolies and rickshaw pullers.[59] As early as 1848 Singapore had 15,000 opium users, equivalent to one-third of the male Chinese population and most of them came from the coolie ranks. Of course opium use cut across all class and occupational boundaries. The evidence suggests, however, that amongst the labouring and artisan classes the level of use was inordinately high.[60] According to Dr Robert Little's 1848 survey of opium use in Singapore, up to 85 per cent of boatmen were addicted to opium.[61] The use of opium by lightermen did not decline over the ensuing decades, leading up to the Opium Commission of 1908. Giving evidence to the Commission, Alexander Gentle, Singapore's Coroner and a resident of Singapore for 43 years, stated about the boatmen and their drug habit, that 'the very large class of twakow and sampan men, I should say almost to a man indulge in opium'.[62] He went on to discuss the nature of lightermen's work, their exposure to the elements and the strenuous physical demands placed on them, as major factors in their use of opium.

Lightermen often began using opium medicinally as a way to relieve the aches and pains they felt after days of hard manual labour. There were times when its sedative and pain relieving qualities were absolutely necessary. Accidents resulting in broken bones and crushed limbs were common on lighters as they jolted against the side of ships rolling on ocean swells, and crane cables snapped, spilling heavy crates, sacks and bundles of goods onto the men working below.[63] The use of opium after such accidents meant somewhat less suffering than otherwise would have been the case. Many men also used the habit-forming drug because, in the short-term, it made them feel refreshed and able to face yet another day or night of gruelling labour.[64] It was a widely held belief amongst boatmen that opium use in moderation made them stronger and better able to cope with the strenuous work. Lim Buck Chua's father owned seven lighters and employed over 30 lightermen, half of whom took opium daily to 'renew [their] vitality'.[65] The addictive trap for many began because the drug seemed to have therapeutic qualities. In 1908 regular opium users appeared to be in excellent health and were described by one knowledgeable observer as generally fitter than men found almost anywhere else.[66] One lighterman described the beneficial effect opium had on them this way, 'there were some men who could only work well after they had taken some of the drug. It made them strong like tigers and you could really see the difference'.[67]

The initial experience of drug taking usually resulted from the recommendation of a friend or a prescription from one of the many medicine shops which dotted the streets of Kreta Ayer area.[68] Opportunity and temptation to take the drug abounded. The initial prompting of peers was just one aspect of a cycle which often ended in addiction. The colonial government depended on revenues raised through the manufacture and sale of opium and there was always an abundance of outlets. Between 1848 and 1900 the number of licensed opium shops in Singapore increased from 45 to 550 with many illegal dens operating as well.[69] The government became heavily dependent on the revenue raised from opium, initially through a system of farming out the rights to sell opium to Chinese capitalists and later through direct monopoly, manufacture and sale of the drug.[70] For decades, more than half the capital raised by the colonial government was acquired at the expense of opium users.[71] For lightermen, access to the drug was literally on their doorstep, or perhaps one should say, quay. Licensed opium shops were found all along Boat Quay and in nearby streets. The opium dens of Boat Quay, Pagoda Street and Duxton Road filled the air with pungent 'whiffs of the drug'.[72] The wealthy Opium Farmers of Boat Quay also created a carnival atmosphere in the area during certain Chinese festivals. For example, during the Hungry Ghost festivities they provided a large-scale banquet as an offering to the dead and afterwards distributed the food to those living in the area, including addicts. One such occasion, sponsored by Seng Poh and Wat Seng, the leading opium revenue farmers on the quay, was described in the *Singapore Daily Times*:

> Opposite the offices of the Opium Farmers in Boat Quay, were ranged a series of tables giving an entire length of over 200 feet, and the whole was laden with a feast such as folks at home would go many miles to see ... some of the pyramids of food stood at least 10 feet high ... the whole was brilliantly lit by fantastic designs in gas laid on for the occasion.[73]

There were of course lightermen and owners who did not use opium or sanction its use. For a long time, however, they were the minority. Chang Ham Chwee's father was not keen on employing lightermen who were habitual users of opium, but since so many lightermen smoked the narcotic, it was impossible to not have employed some addicts. He accepted, too, that the conditions under which the men lived were such that the use of opium was inevitable.[74] Those who did not take the drug had little choice but to work alongside users, despite the fact that this could prove dangerous. Some men who used the drug habitually 'acted as if drunk when working' and were not in full control of either their mental or physical faculties.[75] There is little doubt that serious accidents occurred as a result of lightermen being under the influence of opium, and older, long-term users of the drug, were more likely to be injured on the job than lightermen who did not smoke.[76] A momentary lapse of concentration or the slightest error of judgement was all it took for either a horrific injury to occur or for a man to be killed while loading or unloading a lighter. Addicts were also more prone to minor injuries which resulted in lost work time and wages and, in some cases, ultimately leading to permanent disability.[77] The inattention of just one addicted individual could also lead to the death or injury of his co-workers. Improperly secured cargo accidentally falling into the hold of the lighter did not select victims. How many lightermen drowned simply falling from their craft into the harbour while in a drug induced stupor will never be known. Such incidents occurred and were invariably reported as accidents or suicides.[78]

The effects of long-term opium use and addiction on lightermen were devastating economically, socially and physically. Most lightermen found the feeling of well being brought on by opium use quickly gave way to a craving that could not be readily satisfied. The wages of the addict were frittered away as they became ever more dependent on the narcotic. Such users lost sight of the original purpose which first brought them to Singapore, namely remitting money to support family in China and, ultimately, to return to their ancestral home with some wealth. Various surveys and reports conducted throughout the nineteenth and early twentieth centuries found all classes of hard labourers spent up to three-quarters of their income satisfying their craving for the pipe.[79] In 1906, twakow men were earning 75 cents a day and those addicted spent between 30 to 40 cents on prepared opium or chandu.[80] Lim Buck Chua recalls that opium users who worked on his father's lighters in the pre-war years spent half their daily wages of S$3–S$8 on opium.[81] Some twakow men, as they sunk deeper into addiction and ever more of their income literally went up in smoke, became increasingly unreliable or simply unable to work.[82]

Debilitating illness and unemployment combined with opium addiction were a fatal combination. Robbed of the ability to earn money, the addict was forced onto the charity of friends or was left destitute to fend for himself. Either way he was unable to finance his habit. Driven to despair, many men chose the only path open to them and took their lives. While the Opium Commission found that chandu was rarely swallowed in order to commit suicide,[83] there was no doubt that opium addiction was a major contributing factor in cases of suicide. Ho Cheok Goo, a twakow man for 10 years, was found hanging on board his lighter in late June 1927.[84] The Coroner found he had been addicted for some time and was a habitual opium smoker. With no money to purchase the drug, Ho was driven, out of desperation, to take his life. The previous year the life of Lee Chye ended in a similarly tragic way. Not having worked for some time due to illness, he was unable to buy either food or opium and, despite receiving assistance from friends, took his own life.[85] Some elderly lightermen, who earned the respect of their peers were able to survive the worst rigours of the job and possible addiction by having younger, stronger men do the bulk of the heavy work on their behalf. The owner of a lighter, in some cases, took responsibility for the welfare of a man who had been in his service for a long time, ensuring that he received the necessities of life, including a regular ration of opium.[86] For most, though, opium addiction meant loss of well being and work and an increasingly desperate situation from which there could be no outcome, short of death.

Quay-side Entertainment

There were other less harmful ways in which lightermen could occupy their leisure time besides drug taking and the pursuit of prostitutes. A great number of social activities presented themselves in the heart of town, near their work, that provided relief from the stresses and strains of work on the river. Most often lightermen would seek out rest and recreational activities to occupy their free time in the company of their work companions. It was rare to find them with men from other occupations unless they had a connection with the river or were kin.[87] The social intercourse of lightermen was usually limited to those with whom they came in contact on a daily basis, such as crane operators, lorry drivers and coolies employed to help load and unload lighters or who worked in the godowns along the river. The river front labourers were a tight knit bunch and often suspicious of outsiders, preferring to keep to themselves.[88] Generally speaking, most other leisurely pursuits of the lightermen fell into two categories — routine and festive. Routine activities were those that filled the days or hours between jobs and were considered part of the everyday life of a lighterman. Festive activities were those cyclical events associated with cultural and religious ceremonies during the year.

Eating out together was a routine social activity. Food played an important social role in the life of coolies such as lightermen. Eating in hawker stalls, open air markets or teahouses, and drinking coffee, tea or rice wine were favourite pastimes of lightermen, sometimes combined with other recreational pursuits like gambling.[89] The low price of hawker food made it an ideal attraction for men whose pockets were rarely lined with money. At a quayside food stall it was possible to eat your fill for an entire day for only a few cents.[90] When circumstance permitted, the day would typically start with something light to eat and coffee prepared by the most junior person on the twakow. Alternatively, food would be purchased from one of the perambulating hawkers operating along the quay. A more substantial meal would be taken later, usually after midday, when the morning work was finished or time permitted.[91]

Where food was concerned clan and cultural boundaries sometimes tended to break down. Hokkien and Teochew coolies would rub shoulders in the open air stalls while partaking of Cantonese fare or other delicacies.[92] Lightermen got to know which itinerant hawkers and eating houses served the best food or drink and frequented these places between working hours.[93] They did not have to go very far to get a good meal. Perambulating hawkers serving a variety of noodle or rice dishes were found all along the river at any time of the day or night, catering for the manual workers in one of the busiest parts of the city. Alternatively, if time permitted, a short stroll to the Kreta Ayer district provided a wide range of eating choices. Obtaining prepared cooked food was never a problem as hawkers and most eating establishments operated until the early hours of the morning. It might just be a nourishing meal one sought, but the cooking aromas and lively atmosphere generated by the people around could also suddenly transport a lighterman back home to China for a brief moment.[94] Sitting around eating and drinking provided an opportunity to discuss not only local events but also news from the village and homeland.[95]

Another diversion for lightermen and the quayside community were storytellers and readers who set themselves up along the river bank. They became a regular feature of the river's landscape in the cool of evening. Reading by candlelight or kerosene lamp these literate individuals would read extracts aloud from local Chinese newspapers or tell stories from the Chinese classics about bandits and emperors to crowds that would gather round. On quiet nights, after they had eaten, lightermen would relax by sitting for an hour or so listening to the storytellers.[96] This oral form of entertainment and news service was meant for the entire community of

River Valley Road — which lay along the upper reaches of the north bank — but the closer the storyteller's site was to the river, the more lightermen there would invariably be in the crowd.[97] One of the earliest accounts of Chinese storytellers providing entertainment for the labouring masses in Singapore dates to 1849. The *Singapore Free Press* recorded that it was the custom of the 'lower classes of the Chinese' to listen to tales read aloud by an 'intelligent reader' in the evening, after work or close of business.[98] There were two locations where lightermen could always find this sort of entertainment in the evening, the first was near Read Bridge, and the other near Coleman Bridge.[99] Readers also used other quiet, spacious locations, but these two venues were well known to all around Chinatown. Where one went to listen to stories or hear the latest news was partially dependent on the dialect spoken. Readers speaking Teochew would commonly be found at Read Bridge as this was where Teochew lightermen and others regularly gathered.[100] Those who spoke Hokkien would usually congregate near Coleman Bridge or China Street.[101] Sometimes there would be more than one storyteller speaking at the same time and the throngs of listeners numbered well into the hundreds.

For men who, by and large, were illiterate these storytellers were an important source of information about the wider world beyond the river and port. 'They were like reporters', informing and entertaining.[102] They charged a small fee for their services, but this was considered nominal by those who listened to them.[103] The fee was based on the amount of time spent reading or storytelling and was measured by the burning of a joss stick. For five to ten cents a lighterman could listen for up to an hour to international news and classic stories.[104] If a twakow man chose to stand at the back he did not have to spend a cent, but the moment he sat down he was obliged to pay the fee. Lock Heng Huat recalled storytellers at Read Bridge charged between one and five cents in the immediate post-war period when he used to listen to them. Like others he went for news about his homeland and to hear traditional epic tales such as the fable of the Monkey God.[105] The skill of the storyteller depended in large measure on turning such stories into epic accounts and in holding the attention of the audience through dramatic oratory, mime and facial expressions. In order to guarantee an audience on subsequent nights it was common practice to leave the dramatic ending open until the next session.[106] Some storytellers were also more than happy to debate with the audience and give opinions on issues that were of current interest to all concerned.[107] Their seemingly learned opinions were valued by illiterate listeners as their literary skills placed them in a sage-like position to discuss a particular issue or problem. It could either be a bill introduced by the Singapore Legislative Council or the politics and social affairs of China. They might talk about such matters and offer an opinion if there was an interest professed by the audience.[108]

Chinese street opera or *wayang* provided another form of entertainment for lightermen. Street operas, like the visiting storytellers, provided an opportunity for river boatmen to collectively relax and enjoy themselves for a while.[109] While concerts took place throughout the year there were special holiday occasions such as New Year celebrations and the Festival of the Hungry Ghosts when wayang was a nightly occurrence along the river.[110] During these festivals, at various spots on the river, wooden stages were erected between the embankment and shops along the quay, for street opera performances. Sometimes the stage would be built on pilings out over the river itself, allowing for more people to observe the opera being staged.[111] No seating was provided for such performances so a lighterman had to bring his own stool or crate or sit on the ground. The extraordinary singing and brightly coloured costumes were all a part of a performative spectacle that was eagerly looked forward to by the boatmen. The area around the quays took on a carnival atmosphere during these special festival celebrations. From the river to Chinatown the roads, buildings and walkways would be brightly lit up with lanterns, candles and electric lights. Everywhere, hawkers were selling food, much of it prepared especially for the festive occasion, alongside all sorts of stands selling novelties. Joan Hon captures the mood in this passage:

> Houses were spruced up, banners of red appeared everywhere. Well-decorated shops burst with wares — pussy willows, kumquats and cakes. Lights sprung up all over and the area never seemed to go to sleep. Business thrived all through the night. Throngs of people filled the streets ... the entire quay ... exploded with noise, colour and activity.[112]

Lighter owners would also celebrate on these holidays, distributing gifts of duck and chicken to their workers and clients, as well as sponsoring some of the festivities.[113]

Lightermen were conscious of their cultural and religious heritage and these festivals and celebrations provided an opportunity to stop work for a while to participate in the collective rituals of their faith and culture, especially during the Hungry Ghosts' festival. Obviously lightermen felt a desire to propitiate the spirits of those who had died violently and ensure a safe year ahead.[114] The dangers inherent in their particular work made it absolutely necessary not to tempt fate and upset the spirits.[115] Often, men who died in unfortunate accidents or accidentally drowned were suspected of having offended the spirits.[116] In order to propitiate the spirits, many lighters carried on board a shrine to the Goddess of the Sea, Mah Chor, the protector of seamen, and at various places along the river, small shrines were erected where lightermen could pray before venturing out to sea.[117] While they enjoyed the festive aspects of these annual cultural and religious occasions, their participation had a far more profound spiritual significance than mere recreation and the enjoyment of the holiday atmosphere.

Another less well known festive occasion on the lightermen's calendar was the annual trip to Kusu Island (Pulau Tembakul) to pay homage to Datok Pek Kong.[118] This deity, the God of the Land, was, in the eyes of lightermen, responsible for protecting the waterfront and ensuring their prosperity.[119] Annually, during the ninth lunar month, lightermen would spend the day travelling to the island to make offerings of food and pray for a safe and prosperous year. Just as Mar Chor was paid homage to safeguard them while at work on the sea, so too was the favourable disposition of Datok Pek Kong sought. Teo Ah Lea recalled that this important religious and social event was considered necessary to gain the favours of Datok Pek Kong in order to ensure a 'safe and prosperous future'.[120] While lightermen from different clans worshipped various local and regional deities brought with them from China, all paid homage to Mar Chor and Datok Pek Kong.[121] Lighters would be loaded with industry people and all sorts of food for the trip to Kusu Island and the day's festivities. After paying their respects, the lightermen would spend the rest of the day celebrating and relaxing. Those with families would bring the children and relatives as well as friends and spend the day eating, swimming and beachcombing.[122]

The social aspects of life for lightermen along the Singapore River were very much influenced by their economic and ecological circumstance. They were dominated for more than a century by a political and economic milieu over which they had little control. Until very late in the history of the river, as a lifeline for the port and city, the bachelor status of lightermen, particularly the lack of opportunity to settle and put down roots, was the single most important factor in how they lived their lives and sought rest and recreation from the harsh nature of their work. Cut off frequently from family and friends in China, and with little hope of marrying, many succumbed to the lures of a social world that could forever destroy any hope of fulfilling their sojourning goals.

For all lightermen the nature of their work meant the river became the focal point in their lives — including their social lives. Their recreational activities as well as spiritual undertakings were directly connected with the river. In a real sense, for more than a century, the river and its immediate vicinity was home, playground and temple to the lightermen.

Life on the River

This section of the book has analysed the actual conditions of life for lightermen on the Singapore River. It has examined the nature of lighterage work, the terms and conditions under which boatmen laboured, and attention has also been paid to aspects of social life along the river. Whilst the work of lightermen demanded they be on stand by almost all the time, they enjoyed a range of social activities close to the river and built a community along its banks. It was a social world though distorted by issues of gender imbalance, labour and colonial policy and practice and this had significant, if not grave, implications for the way in which lightermen spent their leisure time, especially in the pre-war era.

In the following chapters the clean up and future role of the Singapore River are described and analysed. In the last decades of the twentieth century, as the economy of Singapore became less dependent on river trade, the drive to have clean waterways in the Republic of Singapore has meant the demise of the lighterage industry and the development of a new economic and social role for the river.

Part Three
Looking to the Future

7
The Clean Up

THE clean up of the Singapore River and the end of its days as a lifeline and trading artery was well under way by late 1983. In September 1983 the river was nearing the end of an incredible transformation in its role and appearance. Its stagnant and polluted waters were clearing. The last symbol of its trading history, and source of life for more than a century-and-a-half, the lighters, were also removed to new facilities at Pasir Panjang. According to a popular view, this was the culmination of seven years of work instigated in 1977 after the Prime Minister, Lee Kuan Yew, called on all arms of government to clean up the Kallang and Singapore Rivers.[1] Lee wanted fishing in both waterways within a decade. In reality, the campaign to clean up the river was the culmination of a much longer period of determined effort and official intervention. The post Second World War colonial government first initiated action to improve the river and this initiative was further intensified under an independent government. Significantly, by 1977 Lee had already been involved with the river clean up programme for almost a decade. Lee's speech was, in certain respects, a formal public announcement, warning the lighterage industry and others using the river, that there was to be a major change in its role and destiny, and in types of activities permitted on its waters and along its banks. This chapter examines the various stages and processes in the clean up, eventually resulting in the last lighters being forced from their berths along the river to a new home at Pasir Panjang.

The Post-War Colonial Years

In the years immediately following the Second World War the returning British authorities were faced with an urgent need to get the society and economy of Singapore back on its feet. They began a massive rebuilding programme to restore the war torn city and get its economy back on a pre-war footing. The river was crucial in this reclamation process. Singapore was desperate to re-establish pre-war river trading links with surrounding countries. The British Military Administration handed over lighters left after the war to individuals to promote the resumption of trade.[2] Until Singapore's regional trade balance was restored, the chronic shortage of basic commodities such as rice and fish would continue unabated.[3] Rebuilding inter-island trade links around the river was made a matter of high priority. It was never an easy undertaking, though. Throughout the Japanese Occupation the river had been largely unused and neglected.[4]

No dredging or other maintenance work had been undertaken between 1942 and 1946. Along its entire length silt had built up to levels which made it unnavigable in places.[5] Further exacerbating the situation, the returning colonial authorities found much of the dredging equipment had been either removed, partially dismantled for shipment to Japan, or simply left to rust away.[6] The Singapore Harbour Board estimated it would cost $42,000,000 to restore the port and river to pre-war conditions.[7] The hulks of abandoned lighters could be seen sunk in the mud at low tide, their rotting timbers just visible above the water. In spite of the seemingly impossible nature of the task, dredging was undertaken at a frantic pace with new equipment especially brought out from Britain.[8] A measure of both the haste and seeming success of this operation was how quick regional trade activity resumed. By May 1948, the port authorities estimated river traffic was five times that of the pre-war period.[9] The initial dredging and refurbishment, started in the first years after the war, became part of an ongoing process which, after independence, focused more on the clean up than the port role of the river.

By the early 1950s, the river was once again at the heart of Singapore's trading activities, but still suffering the same problems it had faced in earlier years as part of the port. As a major modern trading artery it was in desperate need of improvements and expenditure to facilitate the growing amount of regional trade it attracted. However, the river's quays were in a terrible state. It was also polluted and foul smelling, and for much of its length, still too narrow and shallow for safe, unhindered navigation.[10] Lighters were routinely forced to wait in queues to pass along certain hazardous sections of the river.[11] Added to this, was the problem of navigating under the half dozen bridges spanning its width. Without exception, the bridges along the river did not provide sufficient clearance to allow larger lighters to pass under at all stages of the tide. The situation became more desperate as larger and larger lighters continued to be built. Depending on the season and tides some of the largest lighters might take several days to pass from the upper reaches of the river to the roads, waiting for the tide to rise along a particular stretch of the river and, then, waiting for it to fall so they could pass beneath one of the bridges. Every report on the river and its trade highlighted the problem for lighters of not having adequate clearance under the bridges.[12]

In light of these serious navigational and trade problems, a committee was set up in 1953 to attempt to find lasting solutions.[13] The Singapore River Working Committee, which began its deliberations in February 1954, marked the end of an era. It was the last in a long line of such committees commissioned by colonial authorities to try and map out an improved future for the river. Like so many of the final reports before it, this one also had the stated aim of improving the river as an artery of trade. Its members considered the river's 'primary' role to be 'the means for the efficient and economic loading or unloading of the goods of trade'.[14] The Committee's report, which took more than a year and a half to complete, suggested action on two fronts. These were wide ranging improvements to the river and surrounding areas for trade, and a concerted effort to remedy the chronic pollution problem. They estimated the cost of implementing the recommendations would be around S$15 million, and in 1960, revised this figure to more than S$23 million.[15] Typically, the report was hailed as providing the answers needed to both clean up the river and improve its trading capabilities. Finance Minister Goh Keng Swee talked at length to the Legislative Assembly about the importance and extent of river trade and the need to make improvements to the river.[16] Just as typically the report was to languish for years in chambers as debate continued as to whether the expense was warranted.[17] It seemed at times as if the project was certain to proceed as various preparatory works and surveys were undertaken.[18] However, the project seemed always to be just one stage of decision making away from full implementation.[19] This process was far more complicated than in the past, though, as Singapore was going through the painful throes of becoming an independent nation. Ironically, it fell to the newly independent government of Singapore to finally make a decision as to whether or not the Committee's recommendations would be adopted. A decade after the foot dragging colonial Committee was first convened, the new government of Singapore decided not to implement the recommendations in the now aging report.[20] The government's decision was based, in part at least, on an independent report by Dr Carl Franz, a United Nations expert who determined the project was not feasible.[21]

The working party's report, although not formally adopted, nevertheless highlighted the run down state of the river, and resulted in tentative steps being taken to improve the overall situation. While the report was primarily concerned with the river's role as a trading artery it had also focused attention on the polluted and generally filthy state of the waterway. Between 1954 and 1964, while deliberations on its recommendations continued, the report featured prominently in numerous communications between the Public Works Department (PWD) and other government agencies, as funds were sought to carry out clean up operations and rebuilding work along the river.[22] Consequently, some funding was secured for the most urgent work to be undertaken, also prompting some action to clean the river. The PWD file on the future of the river was kept open until the 1980s even though the major recommendations of the report were not adopted. The report was to become a key reference point for all future river projects and many of its principal concerns were ultimately addressed, even though the role envisaged for the river had changed.

A New Start

Singapore as an independent nation state embarked on a massive programme of urban renewal and reform. The end of the colonial era left many basic town planning problems to be resolved by the new government. Urban overcrowding and lack of basic amenities such as piped water and sewerage were pressing issues of major public concern, especially in the city's heart near the river. The 1957 Census indicates 'gross residential densities', in the most populated parts of the city, had reached '370,000 persons per square mile'. Even this figure was down on an earlier report from 1953 that pointed to a population density in the city centre exceeding '640,000 persons per square mile'.[23] Between 1947 and 1957 the population of Singapore grew from 938,144 to 1,445,929. The population residing near the city centre increased by 63 per cent, straining the city's public utilities to the maximum.[24] Unlike its colonial predecessor, the new administration could not afford to turn its back on the public for the provision of these basic needs. Under the newly-formed Housing Development Board (HDB),[25] the 1960s ushered in a period of unprecedented urban renewal, as run down and dilapidated sections of the city began to be redeveloped and slums gave way to modern high rises. By 1963 the HDB had completed more than 31,000 low cost housing units.[26] To facilitate the modern building programme large-scale projects were undertaken to provide adequate drainage and sewerage. Reclamation work around Pasir Panjang and the southeast coast of Singapore, between the river and Changi, created vast tracts of dry land for building sites where once there had been sea. Between 1965 and 1985 almost 40 square kilometres were claimed from the sea around Singapore, adding 6.71 per cent to the island's land mass. This figure does not include reclamation that had been carried out on many of the off-shore islands.[27] This was a period when a 'demolish and rebuild'[28] attitude prevailed in government and urban planning circles. The rapid pace of urban redevelopment in this period of Singapore's post colonial evolution completely changed the face of the urban landscape. During the 1960s thousands of public housing units were constructed. It was a mammoth rehousing effort that set the pace and tone for future projects. Earlier colonial efforts to rehouse people were a dismal failure by comparison.[29] During this time, much of Singapore's population was uprooted and moved to the new towns growing up outside the central city district. Although the area around the Singapore River remained the business and administrative heart of the island, the population residing in this part of the city was rapidly reduced by resettlement to the new housing developments which were springing up.

By the 1970s, the earlier colonial Master Plan for the island's development was found to be wholly inadequate and was revised accordingly to address the emerging contemporary social situation in Singapore.[30] The new document for town planning, known as the Concept Plan, provided a more complex forward looking vision for future development. The Concept Plan took into account the way urban renewal had begun to shape the island's future growth, landscape and development, in particular the outward migration of population from the city centre. The plan called for further development of high-density residential and industrial zones in a ring formation around the central business district.[31] It also allowed for these new housing and industrial estates to be linked via a modern transport network.

With a powerful blueprint for redevelopment and modernisation of the city well in hand it was only a matter of time before the Singapore River again became the focus of attention of the urban planners. It seemed ironic to some that, in the midst of all the ongoing renewal and talk of refurbishing the city, the river continued to flow as polluted as ever with no attempt being made to improve it. To the critics, the river was a source of major embarrassment. Barely five months after the decision not to proceed with the Working Party's Report, Sim Kee Boon, a government insider,[32] described the situation as 'scandalous considering that the city is now embarking on a cleaning up campaign'.[33] He claimed, with considerable anger, that the river was, 'absolutely black', and due to rubbish perennially floating in the rancid water, navigation by boat was all but impossible in the upper reaches. His letter finished by stating this is 'another example of Singapore barking more than she bites'.[34]

Almost immediately, some action was taken to identify the worst sources of pollution and attempts made to prevent further environmental damage. The main cause of pollution was the dumping of rubbish by businesses and individuals in either the river or canals feeding into it.[35] This included hawkers and others who operated along the river and used it as a convenient sewer. Certain sites such as Ellenborough Market were identified as major sources of rubbish and effluent, with all manner of vegetable and animal matter being unceremoniously dumped into the river at the end of a day's trading.[36] PWD files covering the period in question indicate something of a paper shuffle went on for a while as various departments, the Ministry of Health, PWD and Port of Singapore Authority (PSA), accepted responsibility for only part of the works which needed doing. In spite of confusion over who was responsible for maintaining the river, various measures were taken to deal with problems identified as the main causes of pollution, including the cleaning up of floating debris and utilising more inspectors and patrols at night to curtail rubbish dumping in the feeder canals and river.[37] It appeared that the new administration, despite its hard line on urban reform and clean up, was going to act much like its colonial predecessor and put off the necessary major work to keep the river functional. It seemed pragmatic cosmetic efforts were the order of the day, dredging only when absolutely necessary and rebuilding river walls only after they had collapsed.

The situation changed dramatically in March 1969. The years of hedging were about to end as Prime Minister Lee intervened in order to do something about the poor state of Singapore's waterways. Cleaning the waterways of Singapore was about to become an official national goal and the concern of all departments of government under the scrutiny of the Prime Minister himself. In an initial memorandum to Wong Chooi Sen, head of the PWD, Lee called on the engineers and the Public Utilities Board (PUB) to develop a plan to solve the environmental problems associated with the island's rivers and canals.[38] He called for an end to pollutants being dumped in the waterways and a programme of beautification to be undertaken. His future environmental goal was clear, 'keep these rivers and canals with more or less clean, translucent water, where fish, water lilies, and other water plants can grow, and both sides of the waterway be planted with trees, like willow'.[39] Interestingly, this minute was written eight years before his much heralded 'Clean Up the Rivers' speech at the opening of the Upper Pierce Reservoir.

His urgent request received an immediate response from all concerned parties. Preliminary meetings and discussion of the Prime Minister's directive took place between the main agencies within two weeks beginning on the 7th April, with representatives from the Public Utilities Board (PUB), Ministry of Health and PWD present.[40] Early discussions covered much the same ground as had been dealt with in the past. The usual sources of pollution were identified, and typical measures that could be adopted to reduce levels of pollution in the river were presented. Lee's interest now was to ensure that more than just discussions occurred. Minutes from various meetings and interdepartmental memos regularly referred back to the Prime Minister's instructions, giving a clear indication that rapid results were expected.[41] The tone of debate and discussion took on a new urgency and manner of discourse. In line with the expectations and aims encompassed in the recently passed, strict Environmental Health Act (1968) which allowed for the prosecution of anyone found to be polluting the island's rivers and waterways, the discussion from all quarters began to highlight the 'environmental health' benefits of cleaning up the rivers and canals of Singapore.[42]

In the months following Lee's first memo on the subject, tests were done to ascertain scientifically exactly the levels and extent of pollution in the river. A committee, the Atmospheric and Effluent Pollution Study Group, carried out detailed analyses of the river bed, water and air to determine what pollutants and gases were present in and around the river.[43] The results of their testing confirmed what concerned citizens with a sense of smell and sight had long known — the river was highly contaminated with organic matter.[44] At all levels of the tide, water in the river, especially in the upper reaches, was black and had such low oxygen content no marine life could survive, nor could any natural process of breaking down organic matter occur.[45] Small scale tests were carried out near Kim Seng Bridge and Magazine Road to determine whether a chemical solution might be found to clean up the river or at least remove the foul smell that emanated from it. Several tons of sodium hypochlorite were spread in the river at these locations with some success but it was conceded that this method was not practical on a large scale to combat the serious pollution problem of the river.[46]

By October 1969, the various departments developing a strategy to achieve the Prime Minister's goal of clean rivers were obliged to submit a full report on progress to date and future actions to be taken.[47] The report identified three main sources of river pollution: firstly, 'the discharging of domestic wastes', secondly, 'the throwing of refuse into watercourses', and finally, 'the discharge of industrial wastes'.[48] The solutions offered to solve these chronic problems would change the face of the river and its surroundings as the area was redeveloped in line with the planning goals of the city. It was clear much of the domestic waste discussed in the report came from nearby tenement buildings and squatters living along the river or in its catchment area.[49] The densely populated and unsewered Chinatown, with much of its domestic and commercial waste run off finding its way into the river, was a source of considerable pollution.[50] The immediate targets, though, were the rows of squatters' huts, food stalls and small industries that lined sections of the river bank, constituting part of the river scape since the first settlement under Raffles. But now they had to be removed. Efforts were already in hand to clear the river banks of all unauthorised structures including latrines, food stalls and makeshift industrial buildings and storage premises by the time the report reached Lee's office.[51] No one, with the exception of the lighterage industry, for the time being at least, was to escape the tide of change. Hawkers and others, who made their living along the river, were to be removed or housed in controlled areas.[52] The days of squatting and preparing food wherever people congregated along the river were over. A range of other occupations associated with riverine life and culture were also earmarked for removal and relocation as early as possible. The boat builders along a short stretch of Pulau Saigon Creek, who traditionally played a vital role in the lighterage industry and river trading activities, were among the first to be given notice in August 1969.[53] These craftsmen occupied small boat yards in the upper reaches of the river and feeder creeks such as Pulau Saigon Creek, Kim Seng Road Creek and Robertson Creek. On the muddy banks of these shallow, tidal rivulets they plied their vocation constructing lighters for the trade downstream. The yards were strategically located to both construct lighters and provide ongoing maintenance and repairs for those already in service. Their sudden removal was a cause of considerable concern in the lighterage industry.[54] There were seven firewood and charcoal dealers still operating along Boat Quay[55] and they, together with boat builders, were deemed a principal source of pollution and began to be removed in numbers.

From this point onward, as the boat yards and charcoal dealers were forced away from the river, the environmental campaign gathered momentum. *The Straits Times* reported in late 1970 that the PWD was undertaking a S$200,000 clean up of the 'foul-smelling' river, and it would, they suggested optimistically, become Singapore's 'Seine'.[56] All along the river notices were served on businesses and individual premises that they had to move. Provision was made through the Housing Development Board (HDB) for affected individuals and businesses to receive priority for rehousing and new commercial sites away from the river. Censuses were taken of each stretch of the river, in most cases demarcated by bridges, for example, 'Illegal Structures and Extensions along Boat Quay Between Ord Bridge and Read Bridge', and so on to determine the number of people and businesses who needed to be relocated.[57] The upper reaches of the river quickly began to disappear. Above Kim Seng Road Bridge, the river was rapidly turned into a large concrete lined drain. All the feeder creeks, such as Pulau Saigon and Kim

Seng Road Creek, disappeared as they were filled in or converted into drains.[58] Much of the silt and mud dredged from downstream was used as fill in the creeks. The boat builders worked frantically to complete partially constructed lighters before they were evicted from their yards, in some cases seeking extensions to their clearance notices.[59] The boatmen working lighters carrying goods from godowns in the upper reaches of the river, could literally see the river 'disappearing behind them'.[60]

To say there was reluctance and resistance on the part of those affected by the resettlement and clean up is an understatement. Compensation and offers of new housing or locations to run businesses were not enough to get many of the affected population to readily move. The PWD was responsible for issuing notices to vacate sites and was forced to issue repeated orders in many cases. It was a cause of considerable concern and frustration to those given the thankless task of enforcement that after each round of removal notices little seemed to happen.[61] 'None of them is showing any readiness to leave', wrote David Chow, a senior engineer with the PWD.[62] Further complicating their efforts to remove people and businesses was the press coverage the campaign was receiving. The various departments involved were keen to carry out the operation with as minimal confrontation and bad press as possible.[63] Their frustration with how slowly the removal was proceeding and the lack of enthusiasm to comply, was evident in many interdepartmental letters and memos.

Not surprisingly, the majority of those being told to move were among the most socially and economically disadvantaged in the country and they were understandably concerned about what the future held for them. Tan Guek Eng, recently widowed with three young children, was renting living space in an illegal building along Kim Seng Road Creek when she received notice to quit.[64] Working as a domestic and a washerwoman, she could not afford other private accommodation and had little hope of receiving an HDB flat within the 14 days stipulated before she had to quit her home. In this case an extension of one month was granted on compassionate grounds.[65] Mr Lee Lian Seng was not as fortunate. He already had permission and a licence to construct a boat near Kim Seng Road Creek when, with the craft already partially built, his permit was revoked and action taken to remove him.[66] The PWD put pressure on the Fire Department to revoke the granted licence so they could proceed to issue a clearance notice.[67] Mr Lee had neither the money nor time to take the PWD to court. Both his trade and the river were vanishing before his eyes. Others simply attempted to resist by carrying on as if nothing out of the ordinary was happening. Koh Cheow Sok, after repeated notices to move his boat building operations to a site in Upper Serangoon, simply began building more boats on a site adjacent to his old yard. His conscious attempts to ignore the impending forced move were described as 'mischievous' by the PWD.[68] Similar foot dragging actions and responses were widespread all over the Singapore and Kallang catchments.

For the lighterage industry, too, early indications of its ultimate fate were already apparent. In September 1970, while announcing a soon-to-be-built warehouse complex at Pasir Panjang, Alan Choe, head of the HDB's Urban Renewal Department, in what seems to have been an ill-timed and premature statement, told the press when urban renewal reached the river all godowns there would have to be relocated.[69] He added that the Singapore River was 'no longer suitable for the handling of goods from ocean-going vessels'.[70] This statement came at a time when the river was still playing an important role in Singapore's regional trading activities.[71] Choe's comments caused considerable alarm amongst lightermen and lighter owners who immediately petitioned the government to consider 'preserving the beneficial usage of the Singapore River when implementing the various schemes of urban renewal'.[72] The industry felt its impact on pollution in the river was minimal and that it had a strong case for special consideration given its vital historical links with the river and Singapore's trading history. It seemed incredulous at a time when business was booming and the river lined with active trading houses, lighterage companies and godowns,[73] that anyone would suggest something as drastic as the removal of the industry from the river. There was in fact at the time a shortage of godown space in Singapore, partly due to redevelopment going on in the city, but largely as result of an increase in trade in the early 1970s.[74] The owners and boatmen were subsequently assured that there were no immediate plans to shift them and there would be no redevelopment of the riverbank, 'soon'.[75] Consequently, for the immediate future, this meant business as usual. But there was now an air of uncertainty about the prospects of the industry and a growing awareness that its destiny was no longer necessarily linked to the cycles of trade and market fluctuations. The growing uncertainty had a stifling effect on the industry as many owners, like Ow Hin Kok, decided, in spite of what appeared to be boom times, not to further expand or invest in more or larger lighters.[76] His decision proved to be a prudent one.

1977–83

The year 1977 marked the beginning of the final phase of the river clean up operation. Eight years had passed since Prime Minister Lee first took an active personal interest in cleaning up the island's waterways. Now he was about to go public with his vision of sparkling waters and a thriving marine life. The moment he chose was the opening ceremony for the Upper Pierce Reservoir. A more appropriate occasion for the public airing of his clean waters plan is hard to imagine, given the effort that had been put into building and cleaning up the catchment area for the Pierce Reservoir project.[77] Lee was brutally candid in his public appeal to make the rivers clean. He noted that the ongoing redevelopment of the Singapore and Kallang River catchments would see the entire area properly sewered and drained within 10 years, which meant the only sources of pollution then would be those 'stupid and ignorant enough to believe that canal, that river is his [sic] free rubbish dump'.[78] While his speech instigated a new round of inquiries into pollution sources and how they could be eradicated there was nothing new in what he said with respect to pollution control in the rivers. In fact there is a great deal of similarity between his comments in this 1977 speech and the memo of 1969. Much of the clean up and environmental work he foreshadowed in his speech was already under way or slated for future development by various authorities working on the river. There remained several serious problems across the two catchment areas targeted by Lee. Some 44,000 squatters were still living in unsanitary conditions in the vicinity of the rivers. But, even worse, from the point of view of pollution control, there were 610 pig farms and 500 duck farms draining untreated waste into the creeks and canals feeding into the main waterways.[79] The effluent dumping by markets and hawkers also continued to be a problem in spite of efforts to relocate and house them in modern facilities.[80]

Lee's speech about cleaning up the rivers was a public warning and confirmation of future direction. The years of uncertainty about Singapore River's future were over. The urban renewal envisaged by Alan Choe in 1971 had finally reached the banks of the river and now nothing was going to stop it. Redevelopment of run down inner city areas such as parts of Chinatown were overdue but now such initiatives were given additional impetus as they were linked to the clean up of the river. The clean up that had started quietly along the banks of the upper reaches of the river almost a decade earlier was now expanded into the public basin near its mouth. There were still 3,959 people identified as squatters contributing to the pollution of the river.[81] Most of these were individuals living in run down and unsewered premises in the central area of the city.[82] This figure also accounted for some 50 industries and 180 shops, many of which were involved in river trading activities. While a programme of moving hawkers off the streets and out of makeshift stalls had been initiated in the early 1970s, there were still many unlicensed individuals operating in unsupervised and insanitary conditions near the river. In 1978, there were still more than 2,500 hawkers in the Singapore River catchment area,[83] most of whom were located in Chinatown, namely, on Tew Chew Street and China Street, with the remainder scattered in various avenues and lanes near the river.[84]

Individuals and businesses affected by the government redevelopment scheme were still being offered fixed compensation and given priority for housing in the new estates, but they had to move. The amount of compensation paid varied, but was entirely at the discretion of the government. 'Residential squatter houses' were paid $110 per square metre and farmers $205 per square metre. Other payments were made for removal and individuals could obtain HDB housing with no deposit.[85] The government's hard line position was clear. On this matter there could be no compromise. By late 1983 the clean up operation was nearing completion. Close to '90% of the pollution load' identified at the start of the operation had been removed.[86] More than 80 per cent of the people initially designated for resettlement had been relocated, and throughout the central city area, redevelopment was going ahead at a frantic pace.[87]

Singapore's reputation as a modern and industrious state is understandable when one considers that throughout this transformative period the housing authority alone built 30,000 new accommodation units each year.[88] A proper sewerage and closed drain network now also snaked under most of the city.[89] Of the 2,500 hawkers still in the river catchment in 1977, more than two-thirds had either been closed down or provided with an alternative site in one of the newly-constructed hawker centres.[90] Two of the new multistorey hawker complexes were situated right on the banks of the river just above Cavenagh Bridge — Boat Quay Food Centre and Empress Place Food Centre. Hundreds of tonnes of rubbish were removed as the last hawkers abandoned their sites or were forcedly moved out. In Chinatown alone 807 street hawkers were removed and 390 tonnes of their refuse cleaned up.[91] The government publicised the post removal clean ups to partially justify the social dislocation caused by the uprooting, and to encourage a more responsible and pollution conscious citizenry.[92]

After 1977 the lighterage industry knew for certain, too, that it was destined for relocation. Much had changed in the intervening years since the suggestion was first made that Pasir Panjang should become the new home of the lighter fleet. The emergence of the modern Singapore of soaring glass and steel, symbolic of transnational capital and regional trade, was now encroaching onto the banks of the river. The imperative for drastic change was immediate and everyone working lighters on the river felt it. There had also been significant economic changes within the industry itself. While there was still sufficient work the volume was not the same as in years gone by. The number of lighter operators declined, and more lighters increasingly sat idle.[93] At the beginning of the decade, the outlook for the river had been more optimistic as it still played an important role in Singapore's regional trading activities. Industry insiders felt it was only a matter of time before major improvements would be undertaken to further enhance trading along the river. And, for a short time, in the early 1970s, there was a resurgence of activity in the industry when 'China ships' (see Chapter 1) started making Singapore a regular port of call.

Times quickly changed, and by the end of the decade the PSA was handling most of the cargo moving through Singapore. Throughout the 1970s there had been unprecedented development of the port authority's facilities. The port of Singapore was fast becoming one of the busiest and most modern harbours in the world. Technological change in cargo handling, especially container shipping, played a major role in this rapid development and transformation. From the arrival of the first container vessel in Singapore, the *Ottawasan Maru*, in 1972, the global move was toward this method of cargo transport across the industry.[94] The PSA enthusiastically embraced the new technology.[95] Consequently, by mid-1972 Singapore was already opening the first container port in the region with two more under construction and due for completion in 1978. PSA sources confidently predicted in 1979 that container traffic would increase by at least 25 per cent per annum.[96] There was little the lighterage industry could do to offset the impact of these dramatic changes in the ocean shipping industry.

The fact that the lighterage industry no longer played the key role it once had in Singapore's port commerce gave the government the whip hand in its drive to clear lighters from the river as part of the clean up operation. In the years immediately proceeding Lee's 1977 public announcement the moribund state of the lighterage industry was apparent to all. The hulls of abandoned lighters were strewn all along the river. Several newspaper articles described the river as a 'graveyard for derelict lighters' and blamed the downturn in trade for the industry's demise.[97] It was estimated that only 40 per cent of the river fleet was still utilised in 1975.[98] In some places, there were so many derelicts, that they were blocking the river for other traffic. Under such circumstances, the PSA was forced to intervene and make owners remove idle lighters, and in cases where ownership could not be established, the port authority undertook the work itself.[99] In desperation, lighter owners called on the government to intervene and take measures on behalf of the industry to save it.[100] Many other business people were also concerned about the declining economic role of the river and the impact it was having on riverine community life. The Tally Clerks and Checkers Union also called on the government to support the industry claiming that 5,000 jobs were at stake.[101] The lighterage industry was struggling and not in a position to plea bargain when the time eventually came to be moved.

Between 1977 and 1983 the industry campaigned vigorously to be allowed to continue working along the river. The Lighter Owners Association and the Transport Vessel Workers Association presented a united front in their attempts to sway the government.[102] Rivals in other areas of industrial relations, they were, where the future of the lighterage industry was concerned, united in their perception of the PSA as a 'bully'.[103] They were told in the course of difficult negotiations their 'time was up' and that they had to make a 'sacrifice for the good of the country'.[104] The lighter owners argued from the start that the facilities the government provided at Pasir Panjang were too exposed to the sea and that there was insufficient space for all the lighters that were expected to operate from there.[105] Another tack taken by the operators was to highlight the historical character of their industry, claiming it was an 'instant tourist attraction'.[106] Furthermore, they believed they could continue to operate and not pollute the river providing all lighters were fitted with proper sanitation facilities. They steadfastly refuted claims that the industry was responsible for river pollution.[107] It was even suggested out of desperation that a special toll could be levied on goods passing through the river and that the tariff collected could then be used to ensure the river was kept up to a proper environmental standard.[108] The authorities, however, were not going to budge. The lighters had to be removed. The Ministry of the Environment summed up the government's position:

> Rundown urban areas in the Singapore and Kallang river catchments will also be redeveloped. It is important that the two rivers be kept clean ... one of the main sources [of pollution] being lighterage and related activities. The only practical and economical solution is to resite the lighters.[109]

Ultimately the efforts of the industry focused on getting the best deal possible under the circumstance to resite the lighters. The authorities, too, were fully aware of the strong ties the industry had with the river and did make some concessions to ease the pain of relocation. Further work was carried out to improve the facilities at Pasir Panjang for the lighterage industry,[110] including extensions to wharves, a 100 metre breakwater to shelter lighters, 160 mooring buoys, a lighter repair site on nearby reclaimed Terumbu Retan Laut and supporting amenities such as offices, toilets, canteens and rest areas.[111] The new facilities were also generously provided at lower rents and fees than might have otherwise been the case.[112]

Barely past the half way mark of Lee's ten year environmental plan for the rivers, the waters were not yet clean, but many sources of pollution identified at the beginning of the decade had been eliminated or greatly reduced. Now all that remained were the lighters and the date of their removal was set for 1 September 1983.[113] For the industry it was a historically miserable day, in spite of the fine weather.[114] From early morning onward, there was a procession of lighters, some towed, others moving under their own power, streaming out of the river. Altogether some 270 lighters belonging to 30 companies left the river for the last time.[115] Only a handful of craft, in the process of loading or unloading riverine cargo for the last time, were given several days grace. A high tide temporarily halted the large scale removal during the day as it suddenly became impossible to pass under Cavenagh or Anderson Bridges. Those caught by the tide were forced to wait until evening before resuming their journey.[116] Even up to the very end the river remained fickle.

The Singapore River's days as a lifeline and trading artery were over. It was now on the verge of becoming the clean waterway teeming with marine life that Lee wished for future generations. Much environmental work remained to be done, but the future of the river was now clearly flowing in a different direction. The questions remained though — would clean water be enough to grasp the imagination of the public, and what would it take, after the removal of the lighters, to inject 'soul'[117] back into the river.

Beyond the River: Pasir Panjang

On the wharves at Pasir Panjang there was, in the first months at least, still an air of optimism with respect to the immediate future:

> The wharves were very busy and crowded with lightermen then. There were still goods to be carried and people (lightermen) even without a job for that day would come along to catch up with friends and just see how things were going. It was like the way things were along the river.[118]

Nevertheless, all of the activity was short-lived and any sense of similarity with the way things had been on the river quickly vanished. The lighterage industry continued to decline and appeared in 1993/94 to be near vanishing from Singapore's commercial landscape.[119] While almost everyone involved with riverine trade predicted the industry's future would be bleak after relocation, nobody foresaw just how quickly the demand for lighterage services would dry up. The worst case scenario contemplated by the lighterage industry prior to relocation predicted that in the decade following removal from the river lighterage trade would decline by around 50 per cent.[120] At the time this was thought to be an overly pessimistic outlook for the industry's future.[121] However, by 1986, just three years after lighters left the river, business had fallen by around 80 per cent making all earlier predictions seem positively optimistic.[122] More than half the lighterage firms that made the move to the new facilities at Pasir Panjang closed in the same period and the remaining companies struggled to survive. Many of the trade goods typically transported on lighters in the harbour, such as pepper, rubber, coffee, maize and copra were now being handled by the PSA. The transport of animal feed which had accounted for around 30 per cent of business just a few years earlier had completely dried up as pig and poultry farms were phased out in the face of relentless urban renewal.[123] In its new location, the industry also faced a range of increased costs. There were port fees to be paid and higher maintenance outlays as lighters were exposed to the full fury of the elements all year round. For example, lighters moored in the river only needed to be slipped for cleaning every two or three years, whereas those moored at Pasir Panjang required hull cleaning every 6 to 12 months due to the rapid build up of barnacles, which could quickly double the weight of the craft.[124] Many owners, faced with business losses and increased costs, simply asked the PSA to sink their lighters at sea.[125]

The rapid decline in business was matched of course by an increase in unemployed lightermen. Younger men moved quickly to find other employment, but many of those displaced were older men with few options open to them. In the decade leading up to the removal from the river, younger workers had not wanted to join the industry, rightly fearing that it had no future.[126] In 1983 the majority of lightermen were over 55 years of age.[127] Unemployment came as a blow even though many had braced themselves for such an outcome and were nearing the end of their working lives. In spite of official assurances that the industry would do well in its new location older lightermen sensed that, just like trishaws,[128] lighters were now 'out of date', and unwelcome in the modern city state.[129] Some lightermen had family to fall back on for support and others had to rely on welfare provided by the government and the support of community and clan associations.[130] Ong Ah Cheng remembers that at the time of the move to Pasir Panjang most lightermen had resigned themselves to the change and accepted that they were possibly the last generation of men to earn a living this way.[131]

Not only did the decline of trade affect the immediate outlook of lightermen but also the new location could never ecologically match that of the river. The distantly remote wharves at Pasir Panjang were unlike the river quays and the way work was conducted was quite different.[132] Along the river, lightermen could sit aboard their lighter and be part of the river community even when there was no work to be done. In the confines of the river, nestled in the heart of the city, lighter craft formed a virtual blanket over the water linking the river, quays, town and river men. At Pasir Panjang craft were moored off the beach in the open sea and separated by some distance from each other making it impossible for communication between lighters to occur. In addition, the wharves were several kilometres from where lighters were stationed.[133] Therefore, when not in use, the lighters sat isolated and empty, away from what remained of the trade and community of lightermen. The cost of moving men from the wharves to their lighters as required was estimated to be an additional expense of S$1,000 a year per lighter.[134] As time passed, many men simply disappeared from the scene[135] no longer drawn to the changed occupational and social landscape that the industry occupied.

> Everything seemed to work against the old way of doing things at Pasir Panjang. There was less work as traditional cargoes began being handled by the PSA and at Pasir Panjang there were no lighters to work on and maintain, men simply sat around in the small food court waiting for some work, or to pass the time. In the past there was always some chore or other that needed taking care of on the twakow. And as the time passed there were fewer and fewer men even sitting around. Now most do not go to the wharves unless it has been arranged and they know there is work for them.[136]

As in the past, from time to time lightermen would still have to sit watch over a cargo throughout the night. Without the riverine community, this activity was a solitary vigil on the quiet wharves and viewed by the lightermen as a chore:

> The wharves here are very quiet, even on a day like today. So no one likes to be here during the night. Usually only two or three of us will be here at night for security if there is some cargo waiting to be unloaded. There is nothing to do but smoke, play cards and drink tea. It is not like it was along the river where something was always happening, even late at night. And it is much colder here at night.[137]

The extent to which fundamental change had occurred in the industry is perhaps best summed up in Ow Chin Seng's comment that, 'these days everyone wants to work office hours'.[138] Once a way of life, lighterage work had become simply a job for those still employed.

By the mid-1990s only a small number of individuals and firms were still operating lighters. Business had contracted so much that the transport of rice and replenishment of supplies on passing ships were the only regular source of income-earning activity undertaken by lighters.[139] While some 500 craft were still registered to 40 owners, less than 100 of these were active and many were waiting to be scuttled.[140] A large number of lighters still registered were simply too small to operate at the Pasir Panjang facilities. Only craft over 100 tonnes could safely work from these wharves.[141] With only seven cargo vessels loaded with rice arriving per month on average, even those lighters considered 'active' were only operating part-time.[142] The development of new container facilities which began at Pasir Panjang in 1993–94, added to the problems of the struggling industry with talk of yet another relocation. For owners and lightermen alike the new facilities were more evidence that their industry was now considered defunct by the authorities and that nothing could save it.[143] Ow Chin Seng found it incredible that although the industry continued to play a role in the port, planners gave it little consideration.[144]

Amongst the older lightermen still to be found along the wharves a decade on, there was resignation that they were literally witnessing the end of a way of life and, in spite of the fact that they themselves were elderly, they would probably see the industry disappear before they were ready to retire.[145] Teo Ah Lea smilingly commented that the type of work he was used to was no longer needed in Singapore:

> All over Singapore changes have happened, many good things have happened. Now our work is no longer required. See how big the PSA is, now they can do everything we [lightermen] used to do. Our time has passed. I will keep working as long as I can.[146]

Many lighter owners left the industry to pursue other commercial ventures. Some, like Ow Chin Seng, had invested in a diverse range of business interests and only maintained an interest in the lighterage industry for reasons other than profit. While it continued to be viable to operate lighters, Ow Chin Seng stated that he would keep the lighterage company started by his father because it provided men who would otherwise have nowhere else to go with employment.[147] His office at Pasir Panjang continued into the 1990s to be something of a magnet for a group of elderly men still employed by him in some capacity or other.

For a small group of individuals the move to Pasir Panjang opened up new doors of opportunity. Some owners sold lighters to act as ferries along the river realising a small profit.[148] Quek Thiam Kee spent a year preparing four craft, including a twakow and three motor sampans, to act as outdoor dining areas alongside Clarke Quay. Now 74, Quek, who has been a boat builder in the upper reaches of the river all his life, rescued the craft from a watery grave at Pasir Panjang. After selling them to the developers of Clarke Quay he repaired and refurbished them for their new life. He described the project as:

> Like preparing a daughter for marriage, I had to raise them and dress them well to be given to their new owners. It is easier to raise a daughter, she can look after herself! I had to look after these boats in all kinds of weather. It was only when I gave them to the new owners that my heart could rest ... I am marrying off my last daughter.[149]

A handful of lightermen secured work on the river as water taxi skippers.[150] Ong Ah Cheng who grew up around the industry and was actively involved with the lightermen's union started his own business as a result of the relocation. He negotiated with lighter owners to provide transport for their crews, via launch, between the wharves at Pasir Panjang and their moored lighters — a service he pointed out that was not required along the river:[151]

> I could see there was an opportunity when we moved to Pasir Panjang. Of course along the river no one needed transport to reach their twakow but at the Pasir Panjang mooring everyone needed transport to reach their twakow or to move between the wharves and their mooring. I hesitated to start because I was worried about the future but many people encouraged me to buy my first launch. So for me the move was good. Of course I do not know how long my good fortune will continue.[152]

From this humble beginning he expanded his business and by the mid-1990s he owned 14 craft including launches, motor sampans and cargo lighters. With an eye to the future and having a true entrepreneurial spirit, he was also involved in the establishment of a water taxi business along the Singapore River. Ong Ah Cheng is one of the few lightermen who has returned to the waters of the river to make a living from the new recreational trade to be found there and seemed rightly proud of this achievement.

The development of new entertainment and leisure facilities along the river has certainly created new employment opportunities. The growth of these new riverine activities happened too slowly to be of any benefit to the majority of men affected by the relocation of the lighterage industry to Pasir Panjang.[153] Most of the labour force were already in their 50s and 60s at the time of relocation and it would be more than a decade before any new opportunities for employment along the river emerged. Ow Chin Seng noted that the redevelopment and new business of the river was good for Singapore, but held no potential for the few remaining lightermen. The new face of the river is young with its bars, restaurants, clubs and boutiques.[154] When asked if he would return to the river Chan Hian Chuan smilingly replied:

> I am too old now. I have only visited the river a few times since I came to Pasir Panjang. It is very clean now and there will be no more lighters there. All the changes make it look good for tourists and young people but there is nothing there for someone like me. Can I work in one of the new clubs?[155]

Clearly the new work and social environment of the river had little appeal to displaced lightermen. Even if age had not been against them, the limited operations of river taxis and tour boats on such a small waterway could never offer the same employment opportunities that had been lost.

8
The River: Modernity and the Millennium

THE clean up of the Singapore River and planned development along its banks has continued unabated since the removal of lighters and support industries in 1983. The lower reaches of the river which cut through the business and administrative centre of the city and flow into Marina Bay have become a focal point for urban development. The Urban Redevelopment Authority (URA) is working towards turning the core district around Marina Bay and the river into a 'showcase' area.[1] If successful, this inner district will become the city's central location for not only business but also recreation in the twenty-first century. In the years since the lighters moved out, many modern concrete and glass towers and skyscrapers have sprung up along the river. Renovated shophouses and godowns that once supported entrepôt-trading activities are once again coming to life. Now refurbished, they house the cafés, bars, restaurants, boutiques and galleries of a new river trade as throngs of office workers and tourists daily make their way there to eat and to do what Singapore is famous for, shop. The work of rebuilding and remodelling the environment along the river banks continues unabated. As one development along the river is completed, and the fencing removed to allow public entry, another corrugated iron wall appears somewhere else, marking yet another project and face-lift under way.

The various urban development and renovation projects along the river reflect the Singapore government's vision of the city-state, as a 'tropical city of excellence', a 'gracious'[2] global city based on a knowledge economy. The new river scape is one of regulated planning, clean lines and beautiful façades that is compatible with the notion of a garden city of excellence.[3] The river, as a landscape, reflects the government's concern to maintain a strong sense of the nation's multicultural heritage through selective preservation of buildings and historical landmarks. These earmarked structures and sites are deemed to 'show Singapore's rich, multiethnic origins',[4] and their preservation is considered significant in the reclamation of the nation's heritage, fostering a sense of national place and pride amongst Singaporeans.[5] According to the URA:

> ... for our city to be truly great, we cannot rely only on modern architecture, which is restrained by the economics of efficient construction, the use of new technology, and the pervasive international architectural style of the 20th Century. It is inevitable that our new developments suffer the fate of looking

> like the new buildings in other cities of the world. The only way that gives our city a distinct personality is our historic past through the selective conservation of old districts and buildings.[6]

Along the river, two zones, South Boat Quay and Clarke Quay, were set aside for conservation with strict guidelines on what buildings could be demolished and how restoration work is to be undertaken (see Map 10). The URA produces conservation guidelines for developers based on the unique architecture of each area. Each provides a potted history of the 'Historic Area' and description of the various types of buildings and architecture to be found in the area. Robertson Quay is also treated as a special zone for redevelopment. The remainder of this chapter examines the post-lighter years and the future role of the river as its history is literally rerouted in a modern Singapore that is facing and preparing for the challenges of a new millennium.

Clean Waters

By the mid-1980s all activities likely to cause major pollution problems along the river or in its catchment area had been resolved. In 1983, the last of the street hawkers in Chinatown were also being removed as the lighters left the river.[7] The sole remaining industry of concern, vegetable wholesaling, operating at Ellenborough Market and Upper Circular Road was relocated from the river catchment to modern facilities at Pasir Panjang in early 1984. Even while the last of the street vendors and vegetable merchants plied their trade in Chinatown, a massive clean up operation was already under way along the river. With the lighters removed, dredging began in earnest and clearing of unwanted structures and obstructions along the banks was accompanied by the removal of tonnes of rubbish from the waterway itself. Between 1982 and 1984 more than 2,000 tonnes of rubbish was removed from the Singapore, Kallang, Rochore and Geylang Rivers.[8] In the first month of the initial clean up more than 260 tonnes of flotsam and garbage were removed[9] from the river and this occurred before any serious dredging work was done. Floating cranes dragged sunken boats, steel girders and all manner of materials from the muddy river bottom. Work also began on rebuilding the river walls which had begun to collapse once the lighters were no longer there to act as buffers against the ebb and flow of the tides.[10] This embankment work was absolutely necessary to allow proper dredging of the river bed to take place. While most of the flotsam and jetsam had been removed from the river, there still remained the basic problem of residual organic deposits which had built up along the waterway and which were often exposed at low tide.[11] These muddy banks were not only unattractive, from an aesthetic point of view, but they also emitted a noxious odour that could be detected along the quays. Nearly S$6 million was spent rebuilding and stabilising the walls so the foul smelling mud deposits could be removed without the banks collapsing.[12] The total amount of putrid mud cleared from the river was estimated at 41,000 cubic metres. The bulk of this contaminated mud, approximately 35,000 cubic metres, came from the much neglected stretch of river between Read Bridge and Kim Seng Bridge.[13]

By 1986, the various authorities responsible for the clean up operation claimed that 90 per cent of the 'pollution load', identified at the beginning of the project, had been eliminated.[14] For most, the clearest proof of cleaner waters has been the return of marine life to the river.[15] By this time the river remarkably boasted populations of groupers, snappers, gizzard shads, pony fish and silver bellies as well as crustaceans, including shrimp and mud crabs.[16] Nothing, of course, has been left to chance and much of the marine life in the river today is a result of a 10-year stocking programme instigated by the Primary Production Department since 1986.[17] Such was the determination to breath life back into the riverine waters that experiments were also undertaken as to whether artificial sea grasses might be used to encourage fish and other marine life to proliferate in the river.[18] The ultimate demonstration of faith in the cleanliness of the river came from participants of a 'swim across' organised by the Teluk Ayer Constituency in 1987.[19] In September 1987 a party of scuba divers also spent some time exploring the waters of the river and found an abundance of marine life.[20] Quite a crowd, young and old, gathered in their bathers to swim a lane between South Boat Quay and North Boat Quay, the widest stretch of the river. Not surprisingly, given the river's recent murky past, spectators greatly outnumbered participants.

In September 1987, the Ministry of Environment celebrated the success of the clean up operation by organising riverside festivities and a tour of the river by Prime Minister Lee.[21] In recognition of the successful effort to reach this point, Lee gave gold medals to the men responsible for implementing the river clean up. All government organisations involved were awarded a plaque, fittingly, in the form of a metal fish supporting a gold disc inscribed, 'Clean Rivers Better Life'.[22] A dazzling metal sculpture has also been erected on Marine Promenade to celebrate the return of clean water to Singapore's rivers. The ongoing cost of maintaining a clean river system in Singapore's densely populated urban environment was estimated to be $42,000 a month in 1991, a sum considered, by the government and the civil society, to be a small price to pay.[23] The Prime Minister, pleased with the success of the clean rivers campaign, publicly discussed the possibility that in the future, perhaps '20 years' hence, the technology would exist to seal off Marina Bay and convert it into a huge freshwater lake. Lee also speculated that the reborn river could be used in an 'emergency' as a reservoir.[24]

Quays Given New Life

Under the URA's revised Concept Plan[25] released in 1991, which outlines broad ranging goals for Singapore's development to beyond the year 2010, Singapore is divided into 55 separate planning areas or Development

Guide Plans (DGPs). Each of these plans provides specific proposals for development projects in designated areas to ensure that the broader goals of the Concept Plan are realised.[26] The Singapore River Planning Area encompasses a zone of 96 hectares including 10 hectares of water.[27] Three separate sub-areas are identified in the River DGP: Boat Quay, Clarke Quay and Robertson Quay, each having different roles to play in the new look river.[28] The north bank of the Boat Quay zone (North Boat Quay) has been retained for government with emphasis on open spaces and historical buildings. In September 1999 Singapore's new parliament building was opened on the north bank of the river near Elgin Bridge. The new parliament offers sweeping vistas of the river and the Central Business District.[29] By 2001 it had become a major tourist attraction in its own right with around 30,000 visitors.[30] The Boat Quay bank is set aside for commercial, residential and entertainment developments.[31] The Clarke Quay zone has been slated for similar commercial ventures but with an emphasis on a smaller scale village-type atmosphere and design. Close links with Fort Canning Park are envisaged in the future with various recreational and cultural activities complementing those at the nearby quay.[32] At Robertson Quay the focus of development is based on residential and hotel accommodation with the quay itself becoming an open landscaped pedestrian mall.[33]

Under URA supervision the river is being developed with a 'mix of residential and commercial' uses.[34] As was the case in an earlier era the development emphasis is still very much on the business and economic potential of the riverine area. Now it is not trade goods carried by lighters that generate wealth but the river itself — that is, the spectacle of the 'clean water' and riverine setting as an attraction for urban shoppers, diners and well-off home buyers. Much of the land covered by the River DGP, almost 44 per cent, is set aside for commercial purposes such as malls, offices and entertainment venues. Residential property constitutes a mere 3.5 per cent of the total land area and in spite of the recreational focus, only 10 per cent is allocated to open spaces.[35] The bulk of this recreational space comprises walkways and 'pocket parks' linking the commercial areas.[36] Most of the hotel and residential development is in the upper reaches of the river above Clemenceau Bridge in the Robertson Quay zone.[37] Development along South Boat Quay and Clarke Quay is restricted to accommodate the conservation of existing older structures. The river is designated Singapore's principal 'activity corridor' as shopping malls, restaurants and cafés are constructed along its banks next to hotels, offices and residential properties.[38] City dwellers can now walk the entire length of the river avoiding road traffic and congestion along a broad pedestrian promenade.

The restoration of the buildings along Boat Quay has been carried out under the 'Three R' guidelines laid down by the URA. This formula calls for 'maximum Retention, sensitive Restoration and careful Repair'[39] of all buildings covered by conservation orders. It encompasses all aspects of the refurbishment of the area's distinctive shophouses.[40] Despite some early set backs due to ongoing construction work[41] the potential of this riverside site to again attract commercial interest has not been lost on a new generation of entrepreneurs. In a densely populated city-state like Singapore, with few natural attractions, the restored river is perceived as having great appeal for tourists, as well as an urban citizenry looking for something different to do in a crowded environment. As one restaurateur put it 'to be able to eat out in the open air would definitely be a selling point for this place. Can you think of any other place where you can have lunch or dinner by the river.'[42]

Clarke Quay like Boat Quay is listed as a principal conservation site. This section of the river constituted at the time the largest conservation-restoration project ever undertaken in Singapore. The scheme, costing S$186 million,[43] was started in 1991 and completed in late 1993. Much consideration was given to the area's historical significance and a curator was employed to study the site's history so the architects and developers could employ 'appropriate concepts and create the right ambience for the project'.[44] Clarke Quay presented some unique challenges for the developers with its mix of old warehouses and shophouses of 'reasonable architectural interest'. A number of the buildings along this section of the river belonged to some of Singapore's better know merchants and businesses of the past including, Riley Hargreaves & Co (engineers), Paterson Simons & Co (merchants), Tan Yeok Nee (gambier planter and trader) and Low Kim Pong (trader) to mention just a few. The success of this particular project was considered crucial in the overall scheme of revitalising the river.[45] The aim was to create a carnival type atmosphere along the quay featuring, shops, restaurants, entertainment and 'cultural facilities'.[46]

What developed is one of Singapore's largest shopping malls,[47] which has been described as a 'festival village'.[48] No motor vehicles are allowed into the precinct, although ample parking is provided nearby, and the entire complex has centred around pedestrian traffic. The total area of the Clarke Quay mall is around 22,000 square metres. In maintaining the spirit of an earlier historical landscape, the Quay's management has attempted to conserve a sense of the past heritage of the area. A number of trishaws (now referred to as pedicabs) are allowed to operate in the village as well as street side cobblers, 'a barber', who carries his equipment, 'a tick-tock noodle seller, and an ice-ball man'.[49] Perhaps most interesting amongst this montage of historical occupations and characters is the gas lamp man. The Quay has a line of 80 gas lamps along its embankment, including Singapore's oldest surviving lamp, and these are lit each evening 'as in the old days' by 'an elderly man', a lamplighter, climbing a bamboo ladder.[50] Further decorative reminders used to embellish the quay's past are the three motor sampans and a twakow moored to the river bank as eating venues.[51] These have been carefully restored and brightly painted in the colours of a different era to serve a new type of river trade. The familiar eyes on their bows now face the shore confronting the commerce of tourism, recreation and development. Clarke Quay had barely opened to the public when it received a major ASEAN tourism award for conservation.[52]

The development of the river environs continues as the authorities work towards the principal goal of making the area an 'activity corridor' for the twenty-first century. Transport improvements to enable people to get to the river are being developed, including a station on the Northeast Line in the Mass Rapid Transport (MRT) system right on the quays. Bumboats or water taxis operate between the various quays with schedules designed to link passengers with bus and MRT timetables.[53] There are also plans for wine and dine cruises — an imaginative idea given the river's size.[54] Nicoll Highway now extends across Marina Bay to join Collyer Quay in front of the Fullerton Building, which itself has undergone a multimillion dollar renovation to become a luxury hotel.[55] Its redevelopment is unique because, due to its location, it is the only major hotel along the river with access to both the riverside and Marina Bay.[56] In 1998, the reinforcing of the river embankments after almost 15 years was also nearing completion. A final section of river wall in front of the Fullerton Building was completed by early 1999.[57] The three sub-zones along the river all have different historic profiles built into the refurbished river walls. Along Boat Quay steps allow pedestrians to walk down to the water's edge. At Clarke Quay there is a vertical wall which rises straight out of the water and at Robertson Quay there is a 'soft edge' with plants and grass to the water's edge giving it a 'garden-like atmosphere'. Fully strengthened, the walls are able to withstand the pressure of current and future large-scale development.[58] The river side promenade stretching from Great World City, near Kim Seng Bridge Road, to the river's entrance was also completed by the late 1990s, as were many commercial and recreational developments along Robertson Quay.[59]

While the conservation and redevelopment work continues, the river itself has already become a unique natural backdrop or stage for entertainment, stunts and cultural festivities. The Singapore River Regatta is an annual event which features dragon boat racing and other related activities.[60] Large crowds are also drawn to the river for one-off events such as occurred in May 1993 when French stuntman and tightrope artist Michel Menin rode a small motorcycle along a wire fastened between Empress Place on North Boat Quay and the seventh storey of the UOB building on South Boat Quay.[61] There is now a regular rubber duck race held on the waterway to raise money for the needy. In 2000 some 100,000 rubber ducks were dumped in the river in what was claimed to be a world record.[62] The well-publicised event brought more than 50,000 spectators out. Local river taxi operators said they welcomed events on the Singapore River such as this 'because it makes the place lively'.[63] Mid-Autumn Festival celebrations in 2000 included a competition for floating lanterns along the river. Entries included lanterns in the shape of a pagoda, a globe and a 'Batmobile'. Some of these creations stood as tall as six feet as they floated along the river.[64] More significant, the river has continued to play host to spectacular Chinese New Year celebrations. The river is an ideal picturesque location for such activities with its bridges lit up and the high-rise buildings of the Central Business District as a backdrop. In 1991, the

Singapore River *Hongbao* Special, to usher in the New Year, featured five floats from China. The same floats had been used in the opening ceremony of the 1990 Asian Games in Beijing one year earlier.[65] The floats and other decorations, when the lights were turned on by the Prime Minister, gave the area around Boat Quay a fairyland atmosphere.[66] The Finance Minister, to ensure good fortune before the celebrations got under way, also released more than 2,000 fish into the river.[67] The festivities, which included fireworks, entertainment by local and visiting celebrities, traditional Chinese Opera, dragon dances and martial arts displays, drew large crowds to the river and highlighted the significance of its new social and cultural role. The Singapore River Busker's Festival, started in 1997, has become an important annual event. Initially founded in response to the Government's call to make Singapore an 'arts and entertainment hub in the region and to bring life back to the streets of Singapore',[68] it has become an international event attracting buskers from around the world.[69] Fully supported by the Singapore Tourism Board, the event claims to have attracted some 300,000 people since its inception.[70]

The River as an Historical Resource and Heritage Anchor

Two major themes run concurrently through the official thinking and approach taken to development and conservation along the Singapore River. On the one hand, the river is perceived as an historical landscape of significant national importance, and on the other, it is constituted as a resource of considerable recreational value.[71] Riverine development and restoration reflects the government's goals of promoting national pride in the nation's multicultural heritage and making a profit at the same time. After all 'there's no business like old business'.[72] The river's historical and heritage value is only recently an officially recognised fact.[73] Had urban renewal reached the banks of the river a decade earlier all the historical buildings would have been completely obliterated. The rows of shophouses would almost certainly have been replaced with modern urban buildings. In the years immediately following independence there was little concern about heritage conservation in Singapore.[74] The most important goal was rapid economic development and the building of infrastructure, housing and amenities to improve the wellbeing of the population through full employment and better living standards.[75] This process involved the demolition of all older structures that stood in the way of the planned economic development. Historical conservation of areas such as Chinatown or stretches of the Singapore River did not enter the planners' minds until the mid-1970s[76] while the Singapore River was only given official conservation status in the mid-1980s.[77]

The speed and ruthless efficiency of urban renewal during this 'demolish-and-rebuild' phase had an enormous impact on the cityscape of Singapore. In five years between 1960 and 1965 more than 54,000 units of public housing were constructed, at least double the number provided by the old, colonial Singapore Improvement Trust in the previous 20 years.[78] This often destructive process rightly earned the city-state an international reputation for rapid and planned urban renewal and development. Singapore's 'deliberate urbanisation'[79] has lead Rem Koolhaas, a leading architectural theorist, to say of urban development in Singapore, 'if there is chaos, it is authored chaos; if it is ugly, it is designed ugly; if it is absurd, it is willed absurdity'.[80] As the destruction of anything old continued, the primary agency responsible for urban renewal, the Housing and Development Board (HDB), began to be disparagingly referred to by some as the Housing and Destruction Board.[81]

A shift in attitude and perception toward the urban landscape was brought about by a number of factors. By the late 1970s and early 1980s Singapore's economic situation had become stable, with many of the earlier fears regarding whether the tiny island state could economically survive having been allayed. Greater stability brought a sudden realisation that the scope and rate of economic change had entailed a high price with respect to the destruction of the city's unique architecture and historical heritage.[82] Urban planners and government officials also realised that Singapore was losing some of its worldwide tourism appeal. In the early 1980s, a task force set up to investigate the decline in tourist numbers concluded that it was partly due to Singapore losing its 'oriental mystique and charm'.[83] From the point of view of overseas visitors and many locals, being 'new' and modern did not necessarily mean better.[84] This sentiment was summed up in a letter to *The Straits Times* in 1983 entitled 'soulless' where the writer, referring to the removal of lighters from the river, suggested that all that would be left for Singaporeans and visitors to look at were hotels, high-rise offices and shopping centres.[85]

The government's greater focus on conservation, while important in terms of the way in which urban renewal proceeded, did not in fact signal a radical change in the overall policies and strategies of the government with respect to its national economic goals. Economic development and growth was and still is at the forefront of government thinking and planning, and any consideration of conservation issues in Singapore takes place within the context of these parameters. While the expansion of tourism in Singapore has led the government and planners to re-evaluate their long-held view that conservation equated to anti-development this has not meant an abandoning of the broader economic goals. The state has since the 1960s linked its legitimacy to its ability to promote and sustain economic growth[86] and this is not about to change. 'Economic viability and sustainability'[87] take precedence over all other considerations in the conservation debate in Singapore. There will be no conservation for conservation's sake. A reading of the *Singapore River Planning Area Report*, 1994, readily reveals the extent to which commercial and economic considerations take precedence over the area's historical significance. The report emphasises the development potential of river side properties over and above any other concerns. Nevertheless, tourism has globally become big business and the sale of local places to the foreign visitor has enormous economic value.[88]

There were other important considerations besides the perceived economic and lifestyle benefits that motivated the government's changed attitude toward conservation throughout the 1980s and 1990s. Conservation of areas like the Singapore River became entwined with debates about national and Asian identity. From the point of view of the state more is at stake than simply quality of life issues in conservation of areas like the Singapore River. The Singapore government has been at the forefront of a push to enshrine the notion of Asia's political and cultural distinctiveness from the West.[89] A view espoused clearly by then Deputy Prime Minister Goh Chok Tong when he declared in 1988,

> We are part of a long Asian civilisation and we should be proud of it. We should not be assimilated by the West and become a pseudo-Western society. We should be a nation that is uniquely multiracial and Asian, with each community proud of its traditional culture and heritage.[90]

In a modern consumer-driven society like Singapore, based largely on transnational capital and regional trade, the visible signs of this 'Asianness' are often difficult to locate amongst the MacDonald's, Starbucks, Gap, Gucci and other outlets of brand name food and department stores. Hence, the preservation of older buildings and heritage areas is seen as a strategic way to help foster a sense of place amongst Singaporeans[91] and validate the process of past-present development.[92] A Heritage Committee set up in 1988 made the link between selective conservation and generating a sense of Asian and Singaporean identity very clear. The Committee's report talks at length about the unique heritage of Singapore and how this can play a key role in 'nation building' and help balance 'Asian values' and 'Western influences'.[93] It went on to say with respect to the role of stone, wood and concrete in this process, 'conservation of buildings, structures and other districts which provide the sign posts from the past to the present is critical to the psyche of the nation'.[94]

The official literature of current planning and development is sprinkled with references to the conservation process and the vital bond between conservation, heritage and culture. 'It will be a city which retains its Asian identity by conserving its heritage', states the government's official blueprint for the future.[95] The same document's opening statement on conservation states, 'we are also very conscious of the need to give Singapore an Asian identity. Already buildings which are part of our heritage and which identify our multicultural background are being conserved and restored.'[96] This state managed heritage conservation ideology is incorporated into the URA's planning, which now preserves and restores many sites, so that Singapore's 'Asian identity' might be framed in concrete and stone.[97] Historical buildings and time honoured precincts provide an urban countermeasure to the transnational forces of consumerism and capitalism, leading to the development of ever more office complexes and shopping malls. Conservation in Singapore has, arguably, become a 'psychological defence', a buffer against global influences, which helps citizens' psyche reconnect with the preconceived image they have of their history and country.[98]

In this context, the Singapore River's role as a national historical resource will continue into the next century. This at least is the hope of those overseeing the river's historical planning and renovation. While the last of the lighters in Singapore have seen their days out at Pasir Panjang or faced a watery grave,[99] 'new life' has been breathed back into the river as various major urban developments along its banks reach completion. In the first years of the new millennium, the river no longer looks like the 'dead snake' that the lightermen described to me when they poignantly left it for the last time in 1983.[100] It remains to be seen whether or not the reconstructed landscape of the Singapore River will, as the ruling elite and planners hope, provide the envisaged economic benefits and become a place that Singaporean's identify with as being somehow uniquely theirs.

9
Conclusion

THE establishment of the British trading factory on the island of Singapore in 1819, changed forever the course of the Singapore River and laid the foundations for a modern city-state. Raffles' far-sighted vision for the island, that it become the centre of British trade and commerce in the Far East, was realised to a degree that he could not even have imagined, so-much-so that the importance of Singapore in the global trading network that has developed since 1819 continues up to the present. While Raffles' British Empire is now the subject of historical speculation, Singapore remains one of Asia's most important trading and commercial nations. The Singapore River and the lightermen who worked along it played a pivotal role in the trade and resultant commercial development of the island. The river lay at the heart of the settlement and was transformed in the space of a few years, beginning in 1819, from a quiet tidal stream into a bustling artery of trade and commerce. Its waters carried the natural commodities and goods of trade, and along its banks the commercial centre and heart of Singapore developed.

The first trade goods exchanged in Singapore passed through the river and the river's role as the main port of the island continued until the construction of wharves and facilities at New Harbour, later Keppel Harbour, in the 1850s and 1860s. However, the Singapore River continued to play a vital role in the island's economic life even after the development of modern port facilities to the west of the town's commercial centre. Whilst new technology in the form of steamships meant the facilities at New Harbour were to be constantly expanded over the ensuing decades to accommodate the growth of transnational trade, the overall growth in demand for entrepôt goods handled in Singapore meant the river trade continued to grow. Until the 1970s, almost all of the island's entrepôt trade continued to pass through the river. The 1970s witnessed another revolution in trans-oceanic trade, containerisation. The use of containers to transport goods was a major set back to the river trade and the people who depended on it. This eagerly adopted modern technology combined with new pressing political realities brought to an end the river's port role in 1983.

Ecologically, the river had been allowed to slowly die during its many years as a trading artery. By the time it was closed to commercial activity it had become little more than a rancid tidal creek. Successive administrations from Farquhar onwards failed to find a solution to the river's pollution problems created by reclamation, drainage and incessant trade activity. Repeated attempts to improve the condition of the river were hindered primarily by two factors. Firstly, there was always a lack of funds to carry out sustained substantial, long-term renovations. The island's free port status was considered unassailable and therefore suggestions to use it for raising revenue and higher taxes of any kind were always rejected by the residents. Secondly, until at least the end of colonial rule, ecologically sustainable solutions to the problems of the river were considered secondary to simply keeping it open to trade. Numerous complaints were made officially and unofficially about the poor environmental condition of the river from as early as the 1820s to as late as the 1970s, and at least five committees or commissions of inquiry were set up to find solutions over that period.

Most of these investigations started out with an agenda to find concrete ways to improve the river to further facilitate trading activities. On at least two occasions, the first in 1899 and the second, in the 1950s, sweeping improvements were recommended by commissions of inquiry to change the character of the river and enhance its trading capability. After months, even years, of false starts and deliberations by the colonial authorities and other interested parties, little more was ever done than repair work to quays and river walls and dredging to keep the waterway open to lighter traffic.

The Lightermen

The work of lightermen who made the river their home was crucial to the economic development of Singapore and their efforts should not go unnoted. It was their labour and seamanship which freighted the cargo-producing wealth of the port city. Most of the pre-war lightermen who worked on the river were sojourners seeking a better life away from the economic and social problems that plagued India and China in a period of European expansion and imperialism. Initially it was men from the Coromandel Coast of India who made the river trade possible. These hard-working, south Asian boatmen brought with them the craft and skills they had acquired over centuries of life on the Indian Ocean. They assiduously applied their seafaring abilities to the task of carrying Singapore's growing wealth. Indian tongkang and lightermen played an integral part in the life of the river until 1900. The central role of Indian lightermen declined at the beginning of the twentieth century, as they were replaced by Chinese twakow and lightermen. From the turn of the century, Hokkien and Teochew Chinese businesses and towkay began to dominate the lighterage industry in the Singapore River. These men continued to control the industry right up until the last lighters were removed in the early 1980s. The Hokkien and Teochew brought to the river their own distinctive lighter craft (twakow) and social and cultural institutions and influences, and like the Indian boatmen before them, played a key role in Singapore's economic development.

The one thing that remained constant whoever was hauling the trade in and out of the river was the strenuous and often dangerous nature of the work. Lightermen were at the hard end of Singapore's stunning emergence onto the world stage of transnational commerce and regional trade. They risked their lives daily to load, unload and convey the commodified wealth that made a 'great' empire, and later, island state, a tropical city of excellence. They also lived in a social and recreational world along the river that culturally reflected their origins but in some respects was unique to the particular social and ecological environment created by the forces of colonialism and demography.

The Future

The history of the river, as a new millennium begins, is still unfolding. The waterway now plays a new social and economic role in Singapore with its clean waters, theme-park like restorations, cafés and boutiques, but questions remain about its place in a tropical city of excellence. From a purely technical point of view the restoration of buildings along the various Quays has been meticulously carried out in such a way as to maintain the authenticity of the original structures. There is little, however, that links these renovated and brightly painted structures with their clean lines to the river and riverine community of old. The preservation and restoration of buildings does not of itself ensure that the river will act as cultural anchor that links, in a meaningful way, the present with people and events of the past. There seems to be an ever present tension between economic goals and conservation efforts. The river's contribution to the economic and social wellbeing of Singapore will continue to be significant, if the expectations of government planners, futurists and developers are fully realised. It remains to be seen, however, whether or not younger Singaporeans will find along the river a connection between the past and present.

Appendix 1
Lighter Craft of the Singapore River

MANY different types of indigenous Asian craft were seen at one time or another in the Singapore River. Everything from small Chinese sampans ferrying people around, to large sailing prows, carrying trade goods and supplies, from Singapore's neighbours. Between 1819 and 1983, the type and design of cargo-carrying lighter craft employed on the river varied little. Throughout this period two types of lighters dominated the river scape, tongkang and twakow. As the volume of trade goods increased, the size of lighters similarly grew, but there was no significant modification in the design of the boats themselves. Certainly, the most important changes were to occur firstly, around 1900, with the displacement of tongkang and Indian lightermen by twakow and Chinese lightermen; and secondly, in the 1930s, with the introduction of motor powered lighters. But even then, the design of the craft was not radically altered, merely adapted to the new technology which also allowed for the building of larger boats.

Cargo carrying tongkang crewed by Indians held sway on the river until the latter years of the nineteenth century, and were still a part of the river flotilla into the twentieth century. By the early 1900s, Chinese twakow were the principal cargo carriers in the river and continued as such until the removal of lighters in the early 1980s. The following discussion is a summary of the origins and design of these two types of lighter craft.

Figure 1: 1900 Tongkang on Singapore River (post-card).

Tongkang

Tongkang is a Malay term used to describe a number of cargo-carrying craft in the Malay Archipelago.[1] From before the establishment of modern Singapore a variety of sturdily built tongkang plied the waters of the region carrying various cargoes such as timber and granite. The design of cargo-carrying lighters, commonly called tongkang on the Singapore River, is similar to that of craft found along the Madras coast of India, with some European influences noticeable to the trained eye.[2] The first lightermen in Singapore originated from South India and naturally brought with them the style of craft with which they were most familiar on the Coromandel Coast. These boats might more accurately be called *dhonis*[3] given their Indian design and origins.

The proceeding photographs show a flotilla of tongkang at Boat Quay in 1900 and two larger craft alongside the wharf at Pasir Panjang in 1993. Tongkang are easily distinguishable by their rounded hull and double-ended bow appearance. At a glance it is difficult to tell the bow from the stern. The rudder attached to the stern is all that distinguishes it from the bow of the craft. In the photographs taken in 1993, it can be seen that this large type of lighter, 200–250 tonne burthen, also has a small accommodation structure on the bow. Tongkang of this size were rarely seen in the Singapore River and were based largely in Teluk Ayer Basin.[4] The earliest tongkang used in the river were considerably smaller than those shown here, being 20 tonne burthen or less, and they were propelled by 8–12 rowers and guided by a steersman.[5] Long punt poles were also used to manoeuvre these smaller tongkang in shallow water and even outside the river, where the water depth permitted, they would be propelled in this fashion. By the 1860s, the size of these lighters had increased and

Figure 2: Tongkang 1993 (Dobbs).

Figure 3: Twakow, Pasir Panjang (Dobbs 1993).

they were powered by sail using a rig of southern Indian design.[6] In the post-card of Boat Quay, featured above where the sturdy mast and rigging of these tongkang can be discerned, fastened down the centre of each boat. Nearly a century later, the two large tongkang photographed at Pasir Panjang had no means to propel themselves and relied on being towed by a motorised launch.

Twakow

The twakow is a lighter vessel indigenous to Singapore. Twakow crewed by Chinese first appeared on the river in the second half of the nineteenth century and rapidly displaced the tongkang and Indian lightermen. In spite of some concerns expressed by certain European trading houses as to their seaworthiness they were, by 1900, the principal lighter vessel in use on the river.

The hull of the twakow is clearly Chinese in design and looks similar to that of a junk or sampan. It has an almost flat bottom with a narrow V-shaped transom bow and a broad transom stern to which the rudder is attached.[7] The twakow is a squat looking craft originally designed by local Chinese shipwrights to carry heavy cargoes such as sand, granite, tin ore and firewood between Johore and Singapore and the outer islands. Its construction allows for as much cargo as possible to be carried for its displacement.[8] When fully loaded twakow lie low in the water, often with less than a metre of freeboard, which means they can only operate effectively in relatively sheltered waters or they run the risk of being swamped.

Twakow were, like tongkang, originally propelled by punt poles and sail. Various rigs and combinations were deployed including lugsails and from

Figure 4: Twakow Beached for Repairs (Dobbs 1993).

the 1920s 'traditional Chinese batten sails'.[9] During the 1930s engines began being put into twakow, and from that time on increasing numbers of motorised craft appeared on the river. Some twakow continued to use sails into the 1950s, however, their use declined as non-motorised twakow began to be towed by motor powered launches.[10] One motor launch could tow two large twakow up to 200 tonnes each, or three smaller craft, at a time.[11]

Figure 5: Loaded Twakow (Dobbs 1993).

Figure 6: Twakow Under Tow (Dobbs 1993).

Whilst I have used the term twakow to refer to all craft of this particular design, lightermen distinguish between motorised and non-motorised twakow in a more specific way. Collectively lighters are referred to as *bochuan* by the lightermen — a Chinese term which means 'boats used for linking or joining'.[12] Craft fitted with engines are called *tian chun* or motor lighters/sampans and only those without engines are actually called twakow. Colloquially, however, twakow is used with reference to either type of craft. Gibson-Hill noted in 1952 that it was common to call these motorised twakow 'motor tongkangs' a term he rejected in favour of the more accurate 'motor twakow'.[13] There is little visually to distinguish twakow with motors from those without. With motors fitted there is less room in the hold for cargo and this would seem to be the major difference.

Another notable feature of twakow are the eyes painted on the bow. The eyes are there to help the craft see where it is going and must be above the water at all times. Though some now say they were for decorative purposes more than anything else, Ow Chin Seng claimed few lightermen would venture out to sea on a lighter if it did not have the eyes in place.[14]

In the absence of load lines the eyes also serve the practical purpose of indicating when the lighter is fully laden. It should be noted as well that some twakow have the area around the eyes coloured green while others are red. This difference indicates whether the lighter is owned by Teochew or Hokkien Chinese. Teochew-owned twakow are always painted red around the eyes whilst Hokkien twakow are coloured green.

Figure 7: Photographs Show Eyes Painted on Bows (Dobbs).

Appendix 2

TABLE 1

Various measures used throughout the sources and equivalents in metric system.

1 Tahil	=	1.3 oz. / 36.8 grams
1 Kati (16 Tahil)	=	1.3 lb. / 589.6 grams
1 Picul (100 Kati)	=	133.3 lb. / 60.4 kilograms
1 Coyan (40 Picul)	=	5,333,3 lb. / 2.416 tonne

Note: Conversions based on Avoirdupois Weight System.

TABLE 2

Value of trade through Singapore 1819–69.

Year	*Total Imports/Exports (Spanish dollars)*	*Year*	*Total Imports/Exports (Spanish dollars)*
1819–21	8,000,000	1845–46	23,394,656
1822–23	8,568,171	1846–47	23,637,871
1823–24	11,417,036	1847–48	23,489,768
1824–25	12,351,643	1848–49	23,432,347
1825–26	11,627,800	1849–50	23,772,090
1826–27	13,067,426	1850–51	25,110,417
1827–28	13,667,645	1851–52	26,142,194
1828–29	17,892,351	1852–53	29,018,627
1829–30	18,892,357	1853–54	36,660,999
1830–31	17,589,246	1854–55	32,848,829
1831–32	15,898,570	1855–56	42,601,666
1832–33	16,693,731	1856–57	44,891,148
1833–34	18,118,716	1857–58	55,446,113
1834–35	14,443,934	1858–59	48,140,494
1835–36	14,329,414	1859–60	46,197,338
1836–37	16,052,977	1860–61	44,545,936
1837–38	16,853,448	1861–62	46,922,330
1838–39	15,872,890	1862–63	52,445,787
1839–40	19,955,089	1863–64	52,315,141
1840–41	26,066,484	1864–65	59,029,734
1841–42	25,334,168	1865–66	64,554,435
1842–43	24,712,982	1866–67	66,884,630
1843–44	24,451,856	1867–68	58,250,915
1844–45	22,258,134	1868–69	58,944,141

Sources: Figures for the years 1819–23 taken from SSR, L2, No. 2, 1823, p. 3. Also, Sir Stamford Raffles, *Statement of the Services* [To the Court of Directors of the East-India Company], 1824, p. 56. All other figures from Wong Lin Ken, 'The Trade of Singapore, 1819–69', p. 254.

TABLE 3
Tonnage of shipping to arrive and depart Singapore from 1819–20 to 1865–66

Year	*Tonnage*
1819	9,567
1820–21	97,568
1821–22	184,127*
1822–23	139,362*
1823–24	157,170*
1824–25	200,387*
1825–26	187,089*
1826–27	240,423*
1827–28	257,854*
1828–29	251,696*
1829–30	307,791+
1832–33	299,160+
1835–36	402,748+
1838–39	442,633+
1841–42	593,558+
1844–45	629,572+
1847–48	660,529+
1850–51	761,100+
1853–54	858,346+
1856–57	1,127,671+
1862–63	1,025,044+
1865–66	1,530,092+

Notes: * square-rigged vessels only.
+ all vessels.

Sources: Figures for 1819–29, *The Straits Times*, 27/8/1850; 1830–65, Wong Lin Ken, 'The Trade of Singapore, 1819–69', p. 295.

TABLE 4
Principal goods traded at Singapore 1819–69

- Alum
- Anchors
- Antimony Ore
- Arrack
- Bees' Wax
- Betel Nut
- Brandy
- Beef
- Beer
- Brass Wire
- Camphor
- Canes
- *Cassia Lignea*
- *Cassia Vera*
- Chains
- China
- Cloves
- Coals
- Coffee
- Copper
- Copper Nails
- Copper Sheathing
- Cordage
- Cotton
- Cubebs
- Cutch
- Dragon's Blood
- Ebony
- Earthenware
- Elephant Tusks
- Flint Stone
- Flour
- Gambier
- Gambouge
- Gram
- Gum Dummar
- Gum Benjamin
- Gunnies
- Gutta-percha
- Guns
- Glassware
- Gunpowder
- Hides
- Horns
- Hemp
- Iron
- Indian Rubber
- Lead
- Muskets
- Mother-of-pearl
- Mace
- Nutmegs
- Oil Coco
- Oil Linseed
- Opium
- Pitch
- Piece Goods
    - Drills
    - Camlets
    - Twists
    - Col'd do
    - Canvas
- Paint
- Pepper
    - Black
    - White
    - Long
- Pork
- Rattans
- Rice
- Rosin
- Sago
    - Flour
    - Pearl
- Saltpetre
- Sandalwood
- Sapanwood
- Segars
- Silk
- Sticklac
- Sugar
- Sugar Candy
- Steel
- Sulphur
- Tar
- Tea
- Treasure
- Tallow
- Tapioca
- Teel Seed
- Tin
- Tin Plates
- Tobacco
- Tortoiseshell
- Wheat
- Window Glass
- Wine

Sources: List of lighterage charges on various goods approved by the Singapore Chamber of Commerce in 1858. It matches closely other tables and trade returns that list the variety of goods handled in Singapore during the period 1819–69. Cited in, *The Straits Calender and Directory*, 1865, pp. 29–31.

TABLE 5
Chinese population of Singapore, 1824–1947

Year	*Total Chinese*	*% Female Chinese*	*Population of Singapore*	*% of Chinese*
1824	3,317	9.1	10,683	31.0
1834	10,767	7.6	26,329	40.8
1849	27,988	7.9	52,891	52.9
1860	50,043	6.4	81,743	61.2
1871	50,098	14.9	97,111	51.5
1881	86,766	16.3	139,208	62.3
1891	121,098	17.7	184,554	65.6
1901	164,041	20.1	228,555	71.7
1911	219,577	26.3	303,321	72.3
1921	317,491	31.9	425,912	74.5
1931	421,821	37.6	567,453	74.3
1947	730,133	46.8	940,824	77.6

Source: Data provided in Joyce Ee, 'Chinese Migration to Singapore, 1896–1941', *Journal of Southeast Asian History* 2 (1961): 50.

TABLE 6
Non-governmental and governmental income 1947–50
(monthly income in Straits Dollars[1])

Year / Occupation	*Non-government* 1946	1947	1948	1950
Lightermen	70–150	48–200	48–200	40–80
Driver (Lorry)	80–120	120–140	120–140	80–100
Moulders	40–110	100–180	100–160	110–140
Stevedore (Roads)	60–70	–	–	–
Welders	60–100	100–160	100–200	80–92
Rubber/Millers	40–60	76–196	100–160	96–140
Driers/Packers (Sago)	80–120	–	–	–
General Labourer (Sago)	–	140–152	80–120	40–44
Stone Breakers (Quarry)	160–180	96–240	100–180	90–110
Sweeper	30–60	–	–	–
Casual Labourer	60–120	–	–	–
Labourer (Rubber)	–	100–132	96–120	70–100
Rattan Labourer	–	60–84	60–80	–
Glass Labourer	–	–	–	34–60

Year / Occupation	*Government* 1947	1948	1949	1950
Unskilled Labourer	20.6–22	–	–	20.6–22
Specialist Labourer	22–26	–	–	22–26
Semi-skilled Labourer	23–31	–	–	23–31

Notes: 1. Figures are based on Labour Department Annual Reports. In some cases the reports have monthly figures and in others they provide daily rates. Where daily rates have been cited, a 20-day working month has been used to arrive at the figures in the table.

2. There were at least 41 occupations covered by these categories of labourers.

Notes

Chapter 1

1. This earlier period in Singapore's history is covered quite comprehensively by Malcolm H Murfett, *et al.*, *Between Two Oceans: A Military History of Singapore From First Settlement to Final British Withdrawal* (Singapore: Oxford University Press, 1999), pp. 1–34.
2. There are some notable exceptions. See James Warren, *Rickshaw Coolie: A People's History of Singapore 1880–1940* (Singapore: Oxford University Press, 1986); James Warren, *Ah Ku and Karayuki-San: Prostitution in Singapore 1870–1940* (Singapore: Oxford University Press, 1993); Katherine Yeo, *Hawkers and the State in Colonial Singapore: Mid-nineteenth Century to 1939* (Melbourne: Monash University Microfilms, Master's thesis, 1989); Peter J Rimmer and Lisa M Allen (eds.), *The Underside of Malaysian History: Pullers, Prostitutes, Plantation Workers...* (Singapore: Singapore University Press, 1990).
3. *The Asiatic Journal for British India and its Dependencies* (hereafter *The Asiatic Journal*) 9 (April 1820): 402–403.
4. George Bennett, *Wanderings in New South Wales, Batavia, Pedir Coast, Singapore, and China: Being the Journal of a Naturalist in those Countries, During 1832, 1833 and 1834*, Vol. 1 (London: R Bentley, 1834), p. 140.
5. *Straits Settlements Records* (hereafter SSR), L10, 1/3/1819, p. 24; *The Asiatic Journal* 10 (September 1820): 293.
6. SSR, L10, 8/4/1819, p. 35; 13/5/1820, pp. 381–82.
7. SSR, K6, 16/2/1819, p. 10.
8. CE Wurtzburg, *Raffles of the Eastern Isles*, edited for publication by C Witting (Singapore: Oxford University Press, 1990), pp. 475–524.
9. SSR, L9, 13/1/1822, p. 166.
10. SSR, M2, No. 23, 13/10/1823.
11. *The Asiatic Journal* 14 (September 1822): 308.
12. CM Turnbull, *A History of Singapore 1819–1988* (Singapore: Oxford University Press, 1989), pp. 27–28.
13. SSR, L20, No. 21, 6/6/1823.
14. Turnbull, *A History of Singapore 1819–1988*, p. 33.
15. SSR, L4, 17/4/1821, pp. 327–28.
16. Wurtzburg, *Raffles of the Eastern Isles*, p. 519.
17. The word *kampung* is spelt with a number of variations (*campong*, *kampong*) throughout the sources for this study. Except when quoting directly from sources the current spelling convention, i.e. kampung, will be used.
18. This system of reference is in accordance with the way in which roads were named, i.e. North and South Bridge Roads. In much of the literature there is some confusion in regards to this matter with south and west, north and east being used to describe the same banks of the river.
19. Wurtzburg, *Raffles of the Eastern Isles*, pp. 522–23; SSR, L10, 5/6/1819, pp. 71–75; L10, 25/6/1819, pp. 71–75.

20. SSR, L10, 5/7/1819, pp. 82–83.
21. SSR, L7, 13/4/1822. Collection of letters from European merchants concerning the suitability of the river for trading purposes.
22. See SSR, L7, letters from leading European merchants dated April 1822.
23. SSR, L9, 12/11/1822, p. 192.
24. Turnbull, *A History of Singapore 1819–1988*, p. 15.
25. Wurtzburg, *Raffles of the Eastern Isles*. This account is perhaps the most detailed in regards to this dispute. Much of the actual correspondence between the two men, relating to this matter, is contained in the following record: SSR, L9.
26. SSR, L9, 23/10/1822, pp. 62–66.
27. SSR, L6, 2/12/1822, p. 6.
28. See for example, Bennett, *Journal of a Naturalist*, Vols. 1 and 2, 1834; Albert Bickmore, *Travels in the East Indian Archipelago* (London: J Murray, 1868).
29. This observation is based on viewing old maps and Municipal Reports.
30. For a discussion of the impact of technology on civilisation, see Michael Adas, *Machines as the Measure of Man: Science, Technology, and Ideologies of Western Dominance* (Ithaca: Cornell University Press, 1989); Arnold Pacey, *Technology in World Civilisation: A Thousand-Year History* (Oxford: Basil Blackwell, 1990); Arnold Pacey, *The Maze of Ingenuity Ideas and Idealism in the Development of Technology* (London: Lane, 1974).
31. The effect of opening the Suez Canal on Singapore is analysed in George Bogaars, 'The Effect of the Opening of the Suez Canal on the Trade and Development of Singapore', *Journal of the Malayan Branch of the Royal Asiatic Society* 23, no. 1 (1955). For a study of the development of Singapore as a port, see KG Tregonning, *Home Port Singapore: A History of the Straits Steamship Company Limited 1890–1965* (Singapore: Oxford University Press, 1967).
32. Bogaars, 'The Effect of the Opening of the Suez Canal on the Trade and Development of Singapore', p. 106.
33. Turnbull, *A History of Singapore 1819–1988*, p. 83.
34. Bogaars, 'The Effect of the Opening of the Suez Canal on the Trade and Development of Singapore', pp. 101–102.
35. *The Straits Times*, Overland Edition, 4/1/1870.
36. *Singapore Daily Times*, 11/6/1870.
37. *Singapore Daily Times*, 3/3/1870.
38. Bogaars, 'The Effect of the Opening of the Suez Canal on the Trade and Development of Singapore', p. 104.
39. *Marine Department Annual Report*, 1881, p. 117.
40. Some ambiguity surrounds the discovery of New Harbour, in so far as who it was that first realised its potential. Farquhar in his initial report on the settlement to Raffles, on 2 September 1819, seems to be the first person, officially at least, to mention the area's potential as a harbour.
41. *Marine Department Annual Reports*, 1880–1939.
42. Singapore Legislative Assembly, Part I of First Session, Volume 11, Monday 14/12/1959, Columns 1174–1176.
43. SSR, A60, 13/10/1829, pp. 306–312.
44. *Report of the Singapore River Commission*, laid before the Legislative Council, 13/6/1899.
45. *Report of the Singapore River Commission*, evidence by Alexander Gunn, secretary to the Chamber of Commerce, 24/2/1899, p. C201.

46. *Report of the Singapore River Commission*, p. C148.
47. River Improvement Schemes, No. 22, Legislative Council, 14/4/1905; *River Committee* 1919, Legislative Council, 10/3/1919, No. 6.
48. Also called *Singapore River Working Committee.*
49. *Final Report of the Singapore River Working Party*, 1955, pp. 5–6.
50. Along with containerisation another threat to the work of lighters on the river was 'Lash Ships'. These vessels did not prove to be as popular as container ships, however they were for some time a matter of concern to the lighterage industry. They actually carried their own lighters onto which they could off load cargo to be transferred to the wharves. For a time they were popular with shippers, as they were capable, of transporting both containerised and non-containerised cargoes.
51. *The Straits Times*, 6/8/1970.
52. *The Straits Times*, 24/6/1972.
53. *The Straits Times*, 23/6/1972.
54. *The Straits Times*, 21/4/1979.
55. *The Straits Times*, 13/10/1971.
56. *The Straits Times*, 4/9/1975.
57. *The Straits Times*, 22/4/1973.
58. Chang Ham Chwee, chairman of the Lighter Owners Association, Ow Chin Seng, treasurer of the Lighter Owners Association, also present Xavier Samy, PSA Senior Operations Executive, interview by author, assisted by Ng Hwee Poh, Pasir Panjang, 17/8/93.

    Chang Ham Chwee is a Teochew Chinese. Chang was born in 1938 and grew up along the Singapore River. His family lived in premises at Boat Quay but moved during the Second World War to live near Hallpike Street. Chang was a third generation lighter owner. He took over the running of his family's business at the age of 14 after an explosion on a tongkang in the river claimed his father's life. He was the last Teochew lighter owner left in Singapore in 1993/94. Chang had been Chairman of the Lighter Owners Association since 1967. He was married.

    Ow Chin Seng is a Hokkien Chinese. Born 1946 in Singapore. He was a second-generation lighter owner. He operated the largest remaining lighterage company in Singapore in 1993/94. His fleet was made up of 14 lighters and two tugs. The last eight Indian tongkangs still operating in the harbour were owned by Ow. They were still manned by Indian crews. He was Treasurer of the Lighter Owners Association (1994). Ow was an entrepreneur with a diverse range of business interests and property investments in Singapore and abroad. He was married with two children.
59. *The Straits Times*, 4/9/1975.
60. *The Straits Times*, 1/10/1970.
61. Ibid.
62. Ibid.
63. *The Straits Times*, 12/6/1971.
64. Address by Prime Minister Lee Kuan Yew at the opening of Upper Peirce Reservoir on 27 February 1977.
65. Figures taken from Tan Way Tong, 'The HDB Resettlement Department and its Role in the Cleaning-up Program of Singapore River and Kallang Basin Catchments', *Action Plan for the Seas of East Asia: COBSEA Workshop on Cleaning Up of Urban Rivers*, 14–16 January 1986, Singapore, Annex 10E, pp. 4–5. See also Dr Ahmad Mattar, Minister for the Environment,

Forward to Joan Hon, *Tidal Fortunes, a Story of Change: The Singapore River and Kallang Basin* (Singapore: Landmark Books, n.d.). There were 3,959 squatters relocated from along the Singapore River.

66. *The Straits Times*, 9/8/1980.
67. *The Sunday Times*, 6/4/1986.
68. *The Straits Times*, 1/9/1983.
69. Ibid.
70. Tan Hong Chuan, Administrative Officer Marine Division, Port of Singapore Authority, interview by author, Pasir Panjang, 11/8/93.

    Tan Hong Chuan was responsible for liaising between the Port of Singapore Authority and concerned parties in the lighterage industry.

Chapter 2

1. Daniel Ross, Captain Bombay Marine, Report on Singapore Harbour, SSR, L10, 16/2/1819. Report actually dated 7/2/1819.
2. Farquhar to Raffles, SSR, L4, 17/4/1821, pp. 327–28. Sophia Raffles (Lady), *Memoir of the Life and Public Services of Sir Thomas Stamford Raffles*, 1830; reprint, Oxford in Asia Hardback (Singapore: Oxford University Press, 1991); Wurtzburg, *Raffles of the Eastern Isles*.
3. SSR, L4, 17/4/1821, pp. 327–28.
4. 'Land Allotment Committee Report', SSR, L9, 23/10/1822. This report matches the portrayal given by Munshi Abdullah in his account of 1819 (see note 7).
5. SSR, L9, 5/11/1822, p. 109.
6. Ibid., pp. 105–114.
7. Munshi Abdullah, 'The Hikayat Abdullah', trans. AH Hill, *Journal of the Malayan Branch of the Royal Asiatic Society* 28, no. 3 (June 1955): 142.
8. Letter to Colonel Addenbrooke (10/6/1819), cited in Sophia (Lady), *Sir Thomas Stamford Raffles*, p. 379.
9. Letters to Marsden (31/1/1819) and the Duchess of Somerset (22/2/1819), cited in Sophia (Lady), *Sir Thomas Stamford Raffles*, pp. 376–79.
10. Wurtzburg, *Raffles of the Eastern Isles*, pp. 482–83.
11. Raffles to Farquhar, SSR, L10, 25/6/1819, pp. 71–75.
12. Farquhar to Raffles, SSR, L9, 13/11/1822, p. 167.
13. A Guthrie to Farquhar, SSR, L7, 13/4/1822, p. 183.
14. Johnston to Farquhar, SSR, L7, 13/4/1822, p. 181.
15. Turnbull, *A History of Singapore 1819–1988*, p. 16. See also, Farquhar to Raffles, SSR, L9, 13/11/1822, p. 164.
16. Johnston to Farquhar, SSR, L7, 13/4/1822, p. 181.
17. Farquhar to Raffles, SSR, L4, 17/4/1821, p. 334.
18. Napier to Farquhar, SSR, L7, 13/4/1822, p. 182.
19. See petitions by various merchants in respects to the suitability of the river in SSR, L7, 13/4/1822. See also, Farquhar to Lieut. N Hull, SSR, L9, 5/11/1822, pp. 105–106 and SSR, L9, 13/11/1822.
20. *The Asiatic Journal* 18 (October 1824): 428.
21. Stamford Raffles, *Statement of the Services* [To the Court of Directors of the East-India Company] (London: Cox & Baylis, 1824).
22. See letters from A Guthrie, AL Johnston, DS Napier and G Mackenzie regarding the prohibitive cost of building on the south bank of the river in SSR, L7, 13/4/1822.

23. See Farquhar to Lieut. N Hull, SSR, L9, 5/11/1822, pp. 111–12.
24. Raffles to Farquhar, SSR, L10, 25/6/1819, pp. 71–75.
25. C Buckley, *An Anecdotal History of Old Times in Singapore 1819–1867*, 1902; reprint (Singapore: Oxford University Press, 1984), p.75.
26. Farquhar to Lieut. N Hull, SSR, L9, 13/11/1822, pp. 162–84.
27. 'Report of the Land Allotment Committee', SSR, L9, 23/10/1822. Raffles' instructions to the Land Allotment Committee are reproduced in full, in JR Logan, 'Notices of Singapore', *The Journal of the Indian Archipelago and Eastern Seas* 8 (1854): 405–407.
28. Instructions to the Town Committee quoted in full in, Logan, 'Notices of Singapore', pp. 99–109. See SSR, L17, 25/2/1823.
29. Frank Broeze, 'The External Dynamics of Port City Morphology: Bombay 1815–1914'. Unpublished conference paper, p. 2.
30. Logan, 'Notices of Singapore', p. 102.
31. Ibid.
32. Logan, 'Notices of Singapore', pp. 103–104.
33. See SSR, L10, 25/6/1819, pp. 71–75.
34. 'Advertisement' detailing the sites chosen by the Sultan and Temenggong for their new compounds, signed by Lieut. N Hull, SSR, L17, 14/3/1823.
35. Church to the Governor of the Straits Settlements, SSR, AA12, 2/9/1841.
36. Secretary to the Government of India to Governor of the Straits Settlements, SSR, U9, No. 240, 1843, p. 38.
37. Logan, 'Notices of Singapore', pp. 103–104.
38. 'Report of the Land Allotment Committee', SSR, L9, 23/10/1822, pp. 64–65.
39. Ibid., p. 66.
40. See George Windsor Earl, *The Eastern Seas or Voyages and Adventures in the Indian Archipelago, in 1832–33–34* (London: Wm. H. Allen and Col, 1837), pp. 347–48. See also, John Cameron, *Our Tropical Possessions In Malayan India*, 1865; reprint, Oxford in Asia Historical Reprints (Kuala Lumpur: Oxford University Press, 1965), p. 54.
41. *Singapore Sixty Years Ago; Including Journal by Mr Walter Scott Duncan*, Journal covers the period February–June 1824, National Library of Singapore, microfilm, n.p., n.d., p. 22.
42. Letter from the leading European and Chinese merchants to Crawfurd, SSR, BB1, 30/6/1823, pp. 117–19.
43. Logan, 'Notices of Singapore', pp. 105–107.
44. Ibid., p. 105.
45. Ibid.
46. Ibid.
47. Ibid., p. 102.
48. Ibid., p. 106
49. Logan, 'Notices of Singapore', p. 108.
50. Ibid. See also, comments on the number of Indian boatmen by, Earl, *The Eastern Seas*, p. 392.
51. B Hodder, 'Racial Groupings in Singapore', *The Malayan Journal of Tropical Geography* 1 (October 1953): 27.
52. Logan, 'Notices of Singapore', p. 108.
53. Turnbull, *A History of Singapore 1819–1988*, p. 21.
54. Raffles' instructions to the Town Committee in, Logan, 'Notices of Singapore', p. 106. See also, Turnbull, *A History of Singapore 1819–1988*, p. 21.

55. Hodder, 'Racial Groupings in Singapore', p. 27.
56. Wong Lin Ken, 'The Trade of Singapore, 1819–69', *Journal of the Malayan Branch of the Royal Asiatic Society* 33, no. 4 (December 1960): 163; J Phipps, *A Practical Treatise on the China and Eastern Trade: Comprising the Commerce of Great Britain and India, Particularly Bengal and Singapore, With China and the Eastern Seas* (Calcutta: Thacker, 1835), p. 269.
57. Ibid., pp. 406–407, see also 'Report of the Land Allotment Committee', SSR, L9, 23/10/1822.
58. 'Report of the Land Allotment Committee', SSR, L9, 23/10/1822, p. 64.
59. Munshi Abdullah, 'The Hikayat Abdullah', p. 146.
60. Logan, 'Notices of Singapore', p. 108.
61. Ibid.
62. So called by John Crawfurd, SSR, L19, 15/7/1823, pp. 155–56.
63. *The Asiatic Journal* 14 (September 1822): 308.
64. Crawfurd to Swinton, SSR, L19, 9/10/1823, p. 286.
65. Crawfurd to Swinton, SSR, L19, 15/7/1823, pp. 154–59. See also SSR, BB1, 30/6/1823, pp. 117–19.
66. Crawfurd to Swinton, SSR, L19, 15/7/1823, pp. 154–55.
67. *The Asiatic Journal* 18 (October 1824): 429.
68. Ibid.: 428
69. *The Asiatic Journal* 16 (September 1823): 246.
70. Hodder, 'Racial Groupings in Singapore', p. 27.
71. Garling to Farquhar, SSR, L10, 5/7/1819, pp. 82–83, and Farquhar to Bernard, SSR, L10, 10/7/1819, p. 91.
72. *The Asiatic Journal* 14 (September 1822): 308.
73. Captain Daniel Ross, 'Report on Singapore Harbour 7/2/1819', SSR, L10, 16/2/1819.
74. Ibid.
75. Cameron, *Our Tropical Possessions*, p. 45.
76. Bennett, *Journal of a Naturalist*, Vol. 1, p. 131.
77. Guido Weigend, 'Some Elements in the Study of Port Geography', *The Geographical Review* 48 (1958): 186. On the functioning of ports see, Frank Broeze (ed.), *Brides of the Sea: Port Cities of Asia from the 16th–20th Centuries* (Honolulu: University of Hawaii Press, 1989); Frank Broeze (ed.), *Gateways of Asia: Port Cities of Asia in the 13th–20th Centuries* (New York: Kegan Paul International, 1997); Dilip Basu (ed.), *The Rise and Growth of the Colonial Port Cities in Asia* (Lanham: University Press of America, 1985); J Kathirithamby-Wells and John Villiers (eds.), *The Southeast Asian Port and Polity: Rise and Demise* (Singapore: Singapore University Press, 1990); Malcolm Murfett, *et al.*, *Between Two Oceans: A Military History of Singapore From First Settlement to Final British Withdrawal* (Singapore: Oxford University Press, 1999).
78. Weigend, 'River Ports and Outports: Matadi and Banana', *The Geographical Review* 44, no. 3 (1954): 430.
79. TJ Newbold, *British Settlements in the Straits of Malacca*, Vols. I and II, reprint (Singapore: Oxford University Press, 1971), p. 352.
80. 'Historical Sketch Of Singapore', *The Asiatic Journal* 16 (July 1823): 27. See also, comments by Paul Wheatley, 'Land Use in the Vicinity of Singapore in the Eighteen-Thirties', *The Malaysian Journal of Tropical Geography* 2 (March 1954): 64.

81. CM Turnbull, *The Straits Settlements 1826–67: Indian Presidency to Crown Colony* (London: Athlone Press, 1972), p. 140.
82. Bennett, *Journal of a Naturalist*, Vol. 1, pp. 199–200.
83. Turnbull describes the 'story of agriculture' in Singapore as one of 'almost unrelieved gloom'. See Turnbull, *A History of Singapore 1819–1988*, pp. 43–45. An important source on agriculture, its development and prospects, in Singapore is the *Journal of the Indian Archipelago and Eastern Asia between 1849 and 1854.* See articles by JT Thomson, Government Surveyor. Also, James Jackson, 'Chinese Agricultural Pioneering in Singapore and Johor 1800–1917', *Journal of the Malayan Branch of the Royal Asiatic Society* 38, no. 1 (1965); Lee Poh Ping, *Chinese Society in Nineteenth Century Singapore* (Kuala Lumpur: Oxford University Press, 1978); CA Trocki, 'The Origins of the Kangchu System 1740–1860', *Journal of the Malaysian Branch of the Royal Asiatic Society* 49, no. 2 (1976).
84. Jackson, 'Chinese Agricultural Pioneering in Singapore and Johor 1800–1917', pp. 80–81.
85. Broeze, 'The External Dynamics of Port City Morphology', pp. 3–4.
86. Weigend, 'Some Elements in the Study of Port Geography', p. 185.
87. Wong, 'The Trade of Singapore, 1819–69', p. 195.
88. For a detailed discussion of the trade of Singapore focussing on the volume and countries involved during the period 1819–1869, see Wong, 'The Trade of Singapore, 1819–69'.
89. Cameron, *Our Tropical Possessions*, p. 58.
90. Ibid., p. 57.
91. Appendix 2, Table 4 is a table of goods that were transported by lighters based on a list of lighterage charges passed by the Singapore Chamber of Commerce in 1858.
92. Turnbull, *A History of Singapore 1819–1988*, p. 89.
93. Ibid.
94. Ibid.
95. *Singapore Chronicle*, 15/2/1827.
96. Dr. Yvan, physician to the scientific mission sent by France to China. In, James Blackwood, *Six Months Among the Malays and a Year in China* (London: Paternoster Row, 1855), p. 59.
97. Turnbull, *The Straits Settlements 1826–67*, p. 183.
98. Wong, 'The Trade of Singapore, 1819–69', pp. 110–11.
99. Earl, *The Eastern Seas*, pp. 365–67.
100. Ibid.
101. 80,000 Spanish dollars would have been equal to approximately £16,000.
102. *The Asiatic Journal* 18 (September 1824): 326.
103. *Singapore Chronicle*, 28/4/1831.
104. *Singapore Chronicle*, 23/4/1829. The value of goods is in Spanish dollars.
105. *Singapore Chronicle*, 28/4/1831.
106. Wong, 'Singapore its Growth as an Entrepot Port, 1819–1994', *Journal of Southeast Asian Studies* 9, no. 1 (1978): 51.
107. Wong, 'The Trade of Singapore, 1819–69', pp. 108–109.
108. *Singapore Chronicle*, 28/4/1831. See also, *The Asiatic Journal* 18 (October 1824): 429–30.
109. SSR, L4, 18/11/1820, pp. 205–206.
110. *The Asiatic Journal* 19 (May 1825): 710. For a more detailed account of the significance of the Bugis in the intra-island trade and politics of the region see, Christian Pelras, *The Bugis* (Oxford: Blackwell Publishers,

1996); C Trocki, *Prince of Pirates: The Temenggongs and the Development of Johor and Singapore, 1784–1885* (Singapore: Singapore University Press, 1979). See also Wong, 'The Trade of Singapore, 1819–69', pp. 74–77.

111. *Singapore Chronicle*, 1/2/1824.
112. JH Moor, *Notices of the Indian Archipelago and Adjacent Countries*, 1837; reprint (Great Britain: Frank Cass & Co. Ltd, 1968), pp. 101–102.
113. *Singapore Chronicle*, 17/2/1825.
114. Bennett, *Journal of a Naturalist*, Vol. 2, p. 210.
115. GF Davidson, *Trade and Travel in the Far East or Recollections of Twenty-one Years Passed in Java, Singapore, Australia, and China* (London: P Madden and Malcolm, 1846), pp. 62–63.
116. Wong, 'The Trade of Singapore, 1819–69', pp. 78–82.
117. Ibid.
118. Calculation based on figures provided in Wong, 'The Trade of Singapore, 1819–69', Appendix C, Table IVB and VB, pp. 278–79.
119. *Singapore Chronicle*, 1/2/1824.
120. Ibid.
121. Wong, 'The Trade of Singapore, 1819–69', pp. 255–56.
122. Cameron, *Our Tropical Possessions*, pp. 57–58.
123. This list is based on various and numerous trade reports in the *Singapore Chronicle* and *Singapore Free Press*. See for example, *Singapore Chronicle*, 29/12/1831; *Singapore Free Press*, 5/11/1835 and 26/11/1835.
124. *Singapore Chronicle*, 29/12/1831.
125. Wong, 'The Trade of Singapore, 1819–69', pp. 27–29.
126. Turnbull, *The Straits Settlements 1826–67*, p. 179.
127. Regulation No. 11 of 1823, SSR, L17, p. 295.
128. SSR, W21, 9/3/1855, pp. 31–32. See also, SSR, U29, 14/3/1855, p. 19, and 16/3/1855, p. 22.
129. Cameron, *Our Tropical Possessions*, p. 67.
130. Bennett, *Journal of a Naturalist*, Vol. 1, p. 59.
131. Raffles to Farquhar, SSR, L10, 25/6/1819, pp. 71–75.
132. Ibid.
133. Bennett, *Journal of a Naturalist*, Vol. 1, pp. 199–200.
134. Farquhar to Raffles on the reservoir and aqueduct, SSR, L10, 2/9/1819, pp. 103–104.
135. Ibid.
136. 'Provisional Regulations For the Port of Singapore', SSR, A31, 1826, p. 81.
137. Bonham to the Secretary to the Government, SSR, R6, 2/10/1840, p. 190.
138. 'Report on the Proposed Singapore Water Works', SSR, AA26, 1852.
139. Crawfurd to the Secretary to the Government, SSR, L19, 15/8/1823, p. 284.
140. Ibid.
141. Flint to Crawfurd, SSR, BB1, 1/12/1823 and 18/12/1823. See also, SSR, BB2, No. 20, February 1824; SSR, R3, 23/6/1835, p. 180; also SSR, R6, 2/10/1840, p. 190.
142. Ibid.
143. See *The Straits Times Almanac, Calender and Directory*, and also various advertisements run in the settlement's newspapers.
144. *The Asiatic Journal* 21 (January 1826): 94.
145. *Singapore Chamber of Commerce Annual Report*, 1962, p. 21.
146. See *The Straits Times Almanac, Calender and Directory*, 1846–52: *The Singapore Almanack and Directory*, 1853–58: *The Royal Almanack and Directory*, 1859–60: *The Straits Calender and Directory, Including Sarawak and Labuan*, 1861–72.

147. Ibid.
148. Walter Makepeace, *et al., One Hundred Years of Singapore*, Vol. 2 (London: John Murray, 1921), pp. 485–86.
149. *Singapore Free Press*, 2/10/1856 and 21/10/1856.
150. Makepeace, *et al., One Hundred Years of Singapore*, Vol. 2, pp. 485–86. See George Norris, 'Singapore Thirty Years Ago: A Paper Read at a Meeting of the Mutual Improvement Society, 15 July 1878', *Straits Times Press*, 1878, p. 9.
151. Cameron, *Our Tropical Possessions*, p. 59.
152. See maps: 'Singapore 1847', *Singapore Annual Reports 1947*; 'A General Plan of the Town of Singapore', Calcutta, September 1857; 'Singapore Residency 1860s', cited at Singapore National Library and Geography Department, National University of Singapore.
153. Turnbull, *A History of Singapore 1819–1988*, p. 43.
154. Ibid. See also, Logan, 'Manufacture of Pearl Sago in Singapore by Chinese', *Journal of the Indian Archipelago and Eastern Asia* 3, series 1 (1849): 302–311.
155. Logan, 'Manufacture of Pearl Sago in Singapore by Chinese', p. 306.
156. Ibid., p. 302.
157. Ibid.
158. Turnbull, *The Straits Settlements 1826–67*, p. 219.
159. Earl, *The Eastern Seas*, p. 145.

Chapter 3

1. James Warren, *At the Edge of Southeast Asian History* (Quezon City: New Day Publishers, 1987), p. 83.
2. Turnbull, *A History of Singapore 1819–1988*, p. 5. See also, Saw Swee-Hock, 'Population Trends in Singapore, 1819–1967', *Journal of Southeast Asian History* 10, no. 1 (1969): 39.
3. Kernial Singh Sandhu, 'Some Aspects of Indian Settlement in Singapore, 1819–1969', *Journal of Southeast Asian History* 10, no. 2 (1969): 193; *Indians in Malaya: Some Aspects of their Immigration and Settlement 1786–1957* (London: Cambridge University Press, 1969); Paul Wheatley, *The Kings of the Mountain: An Indian Contribution to Statecraft in Southeast Asia* (Kuala Lumpur: University of Malaya, 1980); Oliver Wolters, *Early Indonesian Commerce: A Study of the Origins of Srivijaya* (Ithaca: Cornell University Press, 1967); Kenneth Hall, *Explorations in Early Southeast Asian History*, Center for South and Southeast Asian Studies (Ann Arbor: University of Michigan, 1976).
4. Ibid.
5. Sandhu, *Indians in Malaya*, pp. 31–32.
6. Sandhu, 'Some Aspects of Indian Settlement in Singapore, 1819–1969', p. 199.
7. Ibid., p. 193.
8. Turnbull, *The Straits Settlements 1826–67*, p. 47.
9. Sandhu, *Indians in Malaya*, p. 174.
10. Turnbull, *A History of Singapore 1819–1988*, p. 45.
11. Turnbull, *The Straits Settlements 1826–67*, p. 47.

12. *The Straits Times*, 19/8/1845.
13. *Singapore Free Press*, 25/7/1851.
14. JF McNair and WD Bayliss, *Prisoners their Own Warders* (Westminster: A. Constable, 1899).
15. Sandhu, 'Some Aspects Of Indian Settlement In Singapore, 1819–1969', p. 195.
16. Turnbull, *The Straits Settlements 1826–67*, p. 50.
17. *Singapore Free Press*, 16/2/1860 and 1/3/1860.
18. 'Receipts and Disbursements of the Assessment of Singapore' between 1840 and 1856, reported in the *Singapore Free Press*, 14/1/1841, 5/2/1846, 24/1/1851, 31/1/1856.
19. *Singapore Free Press*, 14/5/1846 and 16/7/1846.
20. SSR, U35, 6/4/1858, Governor Blundell to the Resident Councillor at Singapore.
21. *Singapore Free Press*, 16/7/1846.
22. SSR, AA21, 1850.
23. Governor to Resident Councillor of Singapore, SSR, U31, 29/3/1856.
24. Petition from the 'Hindoos [sic] of Singapore', SSR, A34, May 1827, p. 37.
25. Ibid.
26. Ibid.
27. SSR, L6, 2/12/1822.
28. Helen Fujimoto, *The South Indian Muslim Community and the Evolution of the Jawi Peranakan in Penang up to 1948* (Tokyo: Institute for Languages and Cultures of Asia and Africa, Tokyo Gaikokugo Daigaku, 1988), pp. 29–31.
29. Ibid., p. 31. See also, Sandhu, 'Some Aspects of Indian Settlement in Singapore, 1819–1969', p. 196.
30. Fujimoto, *The South Indian Muslim Community and the Evolution of the Jawi Peranakan in Penang up to 1948*, pp. 30–31.
31. Ibid., pp. 4–5.
32. Ibid., p. 5.
33. Ibid.
34. See P Prabhakaran Nair, *Indian Labour in the Singapore Lighterage Industry*, Master's dissertation, Department of Social Studies, University of Malaya, Singapore, 1958, p. 9.
35. CA Gibson-Hill, 'Tongkang and Lighter Matters', *Journal of the Malayan Branch of the Royal Asiatic Society* 25, no. 1 (1952): 96.
36. Captain William Flint, Raffles' brother-in-law, was Master Attendant at Singapore between 1820 and 1828.
37. Chang Ham Chwee, chairman of the Lighter Owners Association; Ow Chin Seng, treasurer of the Lighter Owners Association; interview by author, assisted by Ng Hwee Poh, Pasir Panjang, 17/8/93.
38. *The Asiatic Journal* 20 (October 1825): 469.
39. SSR, A45, Statistical Report on the Island of Singapore 1827–28, pp. 41–58.
40. George Windsor Earl, *The Eastern Seas or Voyages and Adventures in the Indian Archipelago, in 1832–33–34*, 1837; reprint (Singapore: Oxford University Press, 1990), p. 392. See Makepeace, *et al.*, *One Hundred Years of Singapore*, Vol. 1, p. 356. See also, Gibson-Hill, 'Tongkang and Lighter Matters', p. 98.
41. Earl, *The Eastern Seas*, p. 392.

42. GF Davidson, *Trade and Travel in the Far East: Or Recollections of Twenty-one Years Passed in Java, Singapore, Australia, and China* (London: Madden and Malcolm, 1846), pp. 47–48.
43. John Cameron, *Our Tropical Possessions in Malayan India*, 1865; reprint, Oxford in Asia Historical Reprints (Kuala Lumpur: Oxford University Press, 1965), pp. 56–57.
44. Ibid.
45. *Singapore Free Press*, 14/9/1910, 21/4/1911.
46. Gibson-Hill, 'Tongkang and Lighter Matters', p. 100.
47. Ibid.
48. George Bogaars, 'The Effect of the Opening of the Suez Canal on the Trade and Development of Singapore', *Journal of the Malayan Branch of the Royal Asiatic Society* 23, no. 1 (1955).
49. Wong Lin Ken, 'Singapore its Growth as an Entrepôt Port, 1819–1994', *Journal of Southeast Asian Studies* 9, no. 1 (1978): 60–69.
50. *Singapore Free Press*, 31/5/1884.
51. *Report of the Singapore River Commission.* Laid before the Legislative Council, Tuesday, 13 June 1899.
52. Evidence by Alexander Earle for Gilfillan, Wood & Co, given 14/12/1898, *Report of the Singapore River Commission*, p. C156.
53. Ibid.
54. Ibid.
55. Evidence by Captain Joseph Gray, Head of the Tanjong Pagar Lighterage Department, given 13/6/1899, *Report of the Singapore River Commission*, p. C163.
56. Evidence by Alexander Gentle, President of the Municipal Commissioners, given 4/2/1899, *Report of the Singapore River Commission*, p. C190.
57. Evidence by William Cuscader, Chief Police Officer, *Report of the Singapore River Commission*, p. C190.
58. Straits Settlements Legislative Council Proceedings, 13/6/1899, p. C148.
59. Evidence by Yeo Tuah, twakow owner, given 4/1/1899, *Report of the Singapore River Commission*, p. C169.
60. Evidence by Alexander Earle for Gilfillan, Wood & Co, given 14/12/1898, *Report of the Singapore River Commission*, p. C151.
61. For example, see, Evidence by Frederick Darke, for Boustead and Co, given 23/1/1899, *Report of the Singapore River Commission*, p. C177.
62. Turnbull, *A History of Singapore 1819–1988*, p. 5. See also, James C Jackson, 'Chinese Agricultural Pioneering in Singapore and Johor 1800–1917', *Journal of the Malayan Branch of the Royal Asiatic Society* 38, no. 1 (1965): 78; and W Bartley, 'The Population of Singapore in 1819', *Journal of the Malayan Branch of the Royal Asiatic Society* 9, no. 2 (1933).
63. Saw Swee-Hock, 'Population Trends in Singapore, 1819–1967', p. 41.
64. Lea Williams, 'Chinese Leadership in Early British Singapore', *Asian Studies* 2, no. 2 (1964): 172. For a summary of the more successful Chinese, see Song Ong Siang, *One Hundred Years, History of the Chinese in Singapore* (London: John Murray, 1902), pp. 6–7.
65. *Nanyang* is the Chinese term for Southeast Asia and means South Seas.
66. Turnbull, *A History of Singapore 1819–1988*, p. 13.
67. Williams, 'Chinese Leadership in Early British Singapore', p. 171.
68. Maurice Freedman, 'Immigrants and Associations: Chinese in Nineteenth-Century Singapore', *Comparative Studies in Society and History* 3 (1960–61): 26.

69. See Marjorie Topley, 'The Emergence And Social Function Of Chinese Religious Associations In Singapore', *Comparative Studies in Society and History* 3 (1960–61); Ta Chen, *Emigrant Communities in South China: A Study of Overseas Migration and its Influence on Standards of Living and Social Change*, Secretariat, Institute of Pacific Relations, 1939; Lee Poh Ping, *Chinese Society in Nineteenth Century Singapore* (Kuala Lumpur: Oxford University Press, 1978).
70. Siah U Chin, 'The Chinese in Singapore: General Sketch of the Numbers, Tribes, and Vocations of the Chinese in Singapore', *Journal of the Indian Archipelago and Eastern Asia* 2 (1848): 284.
71. Ta Chen, *Emigrant Communities in South China*, p. 260.
72. Pit Kuan Wah, 'Chinese Coolie Immigrants in Nineteenth Century Singapore', *Review of Asian Studies* 14 (June 1984): 31.
73. Joyce Ee, 'Chinese Migration to Singapore, 1896–1941', *Journal of Southeast Asian History* 2 (1961): 33.
74. Ibid., p. 35.
75. Pit Kuan Wah, 'Chinese Coolie Immigrants in Nineteenth Century Singapore', p. 33.
76. Ta Chen, *Emigrant Communities in South China*, p. 260.
77. Warren, *Rickshaw Coolie*, p. 16; Freedman, *The Study of Chinese Society. Essays by Maurice Freedman* (Stanford: Stanford University Press, 1979), pp. 73, 82.
78. Ibid. See also, *Report of the Commissioners Appointed to Enquire into the State of Labour in the Straits Settlements and Protected Native States with Appendices and Papers in Continuation* (Singapore: Government Printing Office, 1891), Chapter II.
79. Warren, *Rickshaw Coolie*, p. 16.
80. Ibid., p. 17.
81. Saw Swee-Hock, 'Population Trends in Singapore, 1819–1967', p. 41. See Table 3.IV.
82. Farquhar to Raffles, SSR, L10, 2/9/1819, pp. 103–105.
83. Raffles to the Duchess of Somerset, in, Sophia Raffles (Lady), *Memoir of the Life and Public Services of Sir Thomas Stamford Raffles*, 1830; Reprint, Oxford in Asia Hardback Reprints (Singapore: Oxford University Press, 1991), p. 383.
84. It seems Raffles rather overstated the population in his correspondence. Saw Swee-Hock, 'Population Trends in Singapore, 1819–1967', p. 38.
85. Munshi Abdullah, 'The Hikayat Abdullah', trans. AH Hill, *Journal of the Malayan Branch of the Royal Asiatic Society* 28, Part 3 (June 1955): 146.
86. Murchison to the Acting Secretary to the Government, Prince of Wales Island, SSR, LAA1, 15/1/1829, pp. 34–35.
87. For an example see, *Singapore Free Press*, 7/12/1848.
88. Ibid.
89. Saw Swee-Hock, 'Population Trends in Singapore, 1819–1967', p. 44.
90. Ibid.
91. Joyce Ee, 'Chinese Migration to Singapore, 1896–1941', p. 48.
92. WL Blythe, 'Historical Sketch Of Chinese Labour In Malaya', *Journal of the Malayan Branch of the Royal Asiatic Society* 20, no. 1 (1947): 103.
93. Cameron, *Our Tropical Possessions*, pp. 56–57. See also, Earl, *The Eastern Seas*, pp. 144–46; Charles Carleton Coffin, *Our New Way Around the World* (London: Sampson Low, Son and Marston, 1869), pp. 235–38.

94. Bennett, *Journal of a Naturalist*, Vol. 2, p. 131.
95. Ibid.
96. Evidence by Duncan MacDougal for Paterson, Simons and Co, given, 21/12/1898, *Report of the Singapore River Commission*, p. C159.
97. Chang Ham Chwee, interview by author, assisted by Ng Hwee Poh, Pasir Panjang, 17/8/93; Chan Hian Chuan, lighterman, interview by author, assisted by Ng Hwee Poh, Pasir Panjang, 6/12/93 [*Chan Hian Chuan* is a Teochew Chinese. Born 1923 in a house at Boat Quay, his father worked in a godown along the Quay so Chan grew up in the shadow of the lighterage industry. He began working as a lighterman at the age of 24 after the Second World War and had worked as a taikong ever since (1994) for various lighterage companies. Chan was married with 5 children]; Lim Kwang Hee, cited in, *Singapore Lifeline: The River and its People* (Singapore: Times Books International, 1986), p. 72.
98. Chang Ham Chwee, interview by author, assisted by Ng Hwee Poh, Pasir Panjang 17/8/93.
99. Ow Hin Kok, interview by author, assisted by Ng Hwee Poh, Singapore, 24/1/94 [*Ow Hin Kok* is a Hokkien Chinese. Born in China in 1921, at the age of 20 he travelled to Singapore in search of work. A relative already working on lighters helped him secure his first job as a lighterman. For a time he also owned a sampan which he used to transport people around the Singapore harbour. During the Second World War he smuggled fish between Singapore and Indonesia. With the money earned he was able to build his first lighter at the war's end. He went on to own more than 30 lighters ranging from 100 to 250 tonnes burden. Ow Hin Kok passed control of his business interests over to his son in 1978]; Chang Ham Chwee, interview by author, assisted by Ng Hwee Poh, Pasir Panjang, 7/10/93.

Chapter 4

1. Tan Hong Chuan, Administrative Officer, Marine Division, Port of Singapore Authority, interview by author, Pasir Panjang, 11/8/93.
2. Raffles to Farquhar, 6/2/1819, quoted in, Buckley, *An Anecdotal History of Old Times in Singapore 1819–1867*, p. 42.
3. Ibid., pp. 41–43.
4. SSR, L19, 4/9/1823, p. 220.
5. Report to Resident Farquhar by the Committee appointed to look into the question of trade restrictions at the port, SSR, L10, 19/4/1820, pp. 336–37.
6. SSR, L19, 4/9/1823, pp. 218–22.
7. CA Gibson-Hill, 'The Master Attendants (Harbour Masters) at Singapore, 1819–67', *Journal of the Malayan Branch of the Royal Asiatic Society* 33, no. 1 (1960). See section on Captain Flint, pp. 16–32.
8. Flint to Farquhar, SSR, L7, 5/1/1822, p. 31. For information on Flint's activities, see also, Assistant Secretary to the Lieutenant Governor to Captain Flint; SSR, L19, 1/5/1823, p. 6. 'Regulation No. 11 of 1823, A Regulation for the Port of Singapore'; SSR, L17, pp. 293–96, and 'The Singapore Emporium', *Singapore Chamber of Commerce Annual Report*, 1962, p. 21.
9. Crawfurd to Captain Flint, SSR, L19, 4/9/1823, pp. 218–22.

10. Crawfurd to the Secretary to the Government at Fort Williams, SSR, L19, 15/9/1823, pp. 235–43.
11. See also, Turnbull, *A History of Singapore 1819–1988*, pp. 18–19.
12. Crawfurd to the Secretary to the Government at Fort Williams, SSR, L19, 15/9/1823, pp. 235–43.
13. Gibson-Hill, 'The Master Attendants (Harbour Masters) at Singapore, 1819–67', pp. 19–21. See also, Wurtzburg, *Raffles of the Eastern Isles*, pp. 675–76.
14. 'Regulation No. 11 of 1823, A Regulation for the Port of Singapore', SSR, L17, pp. 293–96. Also published in full in *The Asiatic Journal* 16 (October 1823): 360–61.
15. Ibid.
16. Ibid.
17. Ibid.
18. Provisional Regulations for the Port of Singapore, SSR, L19, 29/8/1823.
19. SSR, L19, 30/8/1823, pp. 215–16.
20. Crawfurd to Flint, SSR, L19, 4/9/1823, pp. 218–22.
21. SSR, BB2, 15/7/1824, No. 106.
22. Provisional Regulation for the Port of Singapore, SSR, A31, 29/8/1823, pp. 77–81.
23. Ibid., pp. 79–80.
24. Secretary to the Government of India to Governor Blundell, SSR, S23, 5/9/1856, p. 185.
25. *Straits Settlements Legislative Council Proceedings*, 7 October 1929, p. C260.
26. See for example, *Singapore Free Press*, 30/11/1849 and *Singapore Daily Times*, 28/11/1866.
27. Secretary to the Government of India to Governor Blundell, SSR, S23, 5/9/1856, p. 185.
28. See various amendments in, *Straits Settlements Legislative Council Proceedings*, 2 September 1918 and 7 October 1929, p. 270.
29. Ibid.
30. Evidence presented to the Commission, in, *Report of the Singapore River Commission,* laid before the Legislative Council, Tuesday, 13 June 1899.
31. *Singapore Free Press*, 10/8/1920.
32. Tanjong Pagar Dock Board. Minutes of meeting held on the 29/1/1907.
33. *Singapore Free Press*, 20/10/1917.
34. *Report of the Singapore Chamber of Commerce for the year 1926*, p. 42.
35. *Singapore Free Press*, 6/5/1926.
36. *Singapore Free Press*, 10/2/1927.
37. *Singapore Free Press*, 24/3/1927. See also, *Report of the Singapore Chamber of Commerce for the year 1926*, p. 42; and *Singapore Free Press*, 21/12/1923.
38. *Report of the Singapore Chamber of Commerce for the year 1927*, p. 32.
39. 'Merchant Shipping Ordinance No. 125', Straits Settlements Legislative Council Proceedings, 7 October 1929, pp. C118–140.
40. Petition by boatmen and owners in, *Report of the Singapore Chamber of Commerce for the year 1901*, Appendix E, pp. 24–26.
41. Ibid.
42. Ibid.
43. *Report of the Singapore Chamber of Commerce for the year 1901*, p. xxi.
44. Ibid., Appendix O, pp. 73–75. Letter from Boustead & Co; Behn, Meyer & Co and Paterson & Co.

45. Chang Ham Chwee, chairman of the Lighter Owners Association; Ow Chin Seng, treasurer of the Lighter Owners Association; interview by author, assisted by Ng Hwee Poh, Pasir Panjang, 17/8/93.
46. Letter from the leading merchants of the settlement to Crawfurd, SSR, BB1, 30/6/1823, pp. 117–19.
47. Ibid.
48. Crawfurd to the Government at Fort Williams, SSR, L19, 15/7/1823, pp. 154–59.
49. Ibid.
50. Letter from (River Committee) to Raffles, SSR, L9, 11/11/1822, pp. 185–86.
51. Ibid.
52. Detailed in a letter to Flint from Crawfurd, SSR, BB1, 24/12/1823, p. 125.
53. Crawfurd to the Secretary to the Government, G Swinton, SSR, L19, 9/10/1823, pp. 284–87.
54. Ibid.
55. *Singapore Free Press*, 10/5/1855.
56. See for example, Resident's Diary, SSR, N5, 25/2/1829, pp. 186–87; *Singapore Free Press*, 19/4/1850; letter from Governor Butterworth to the Government of India, SSR, R26, 7/3/1854, pp. 37–38.
57. *Singapore Free Press*, 19/4/1850.
58. Statement of works carried out by convicts in Singapore, SSR, AA21, January–December 1850. See also Statements of Receipts and Disbursements published in the newspapers of Singapore in January or February each year for much of the nineteenth century.
59. *Singapore Free Press*, 6/4/1843.
60. Ibid.
61. *Singapore Free Press*, 19/4/1849; *Singapore Free Press*, 5/10/1849.
62. Butterworth to the Government of India, SSR, R22, June 1851, pp. 47–48.
63. Letter to Resident Councillor Church from Tivendale and Co, SSR, AA26, 14/3/1853.
64. Governor Blundell to the Superintendent of Marine Department Calcutta, SSR, R22, 21/5/1855, pp. 264–65.
65. *Singapore Free Press*, 20/3/1856.
66. Governor's Diary, Marine 1859–60, SSR, X47, 24/9/1859.
67. Governor to the Resident Councillor at Singapore, SSR, U39, 1/10/1859, pp. 86–87.
68. Ibid.
69. Governor's Letters from Bengal, SSR, S25, November 1857, p. 301.
70. Reverend AD Nicolson to Governor, SSR, W39, 1/8/1861, p. 85. Governor to Resident Councillor at Singapore, SSR, U43, 2/8/1861, p. 151.
71. *Singapore Daily Times*, 7/4/1870.
72. Letter from the Colonial Secretary to Mr Bayliss (Master Attendant), 28/2/1877, reprinted in Straits Settlements Legislative Council Proceedings, Tuesday, 16 April 1878.
73. Letter from the Colonial Secretary to Captain EM Smith, 28/2/1877, reprinted in Straits Settlement Legislative Council Proceedings, Tuesday, 16 April 1878.
74. Report of committee appointed to investigate 'the best means of cleansing and deepening the Singapore River', 19/2/1878. Reprinted in Straits Settlements Legislative Council Proceedings, Tuesday, 16 April 1878.

75. Ibid.
76. Graham, 'Debate on Supply Bill for 1882', Straits Settlements Legislative Council Proceedings, Tuesday, 15 November 1881, pp. 96–97.
77. McCallum, Acting Colonial Engineer, 'Debate on Supply Bill for 1882', Straits Settlements Legislative Council Proceedings, Tuesday, 15 November 1881, p. 102.
78. Report of committee appointed to investigate 'the best means of cleansing and deepening the Singapore River', 19/2/1878.
79. Acting Colonial Engineer to Colonial Secretary, Colonial Office Records (CO), 273/110, 15 December 1881, p.125.
80. Acting Colonial Engineer to Colonial Secretary, CO, 273/110, 15 December 1881, p. 127.
81. Colonial Engineer to Colonial Secretary, CO, 273/126, 26 January 1884, pp. 313–14.
82. Colonial Engineer to Colonial Secretary, CO, 273/126, 26 January 1884, p. 314.
83. Straits Settlements Legislative Council Proceedings, Tuesday, 8 May 1900.
84. Straits Settlements Legislative Council Proceedings, Friday, 9 February 1912, p. B7.
85. Straits Settlements Legislative Council Proceedings, Tuesday, 24 July 1900, pp. B129–30.
86. Straits Settlements Legislative Council Proceedings, Friday, 15 May 1903, No. 17.
87. Straits Settlements Legislative Council Proceedings, Friday, 9 February 1912, p. B7.
88. See various sessions of the Straits Settlement Legislative Council Proceedings between 1880 and 1912.
89. Straits Settlements Legislative Council Proceedings, Friday, 9 February 1912, p. B7.
90. *Report of the Singapore River Commission*, p. 149.
91. *Singapore Free Press*, 22/6/1905.
92. *Report of the Singapore River Commission*, p. C150.
93. Ibid.
94. In fact at least two more inquiries were held into ways of improving the river for trade between 1900 and 1953. River Committee, 1905, Legislative Council Proceedings, 14/4/1905 and River Committee, 1919, Legislative Council Proceedings, 10/3/1919.
95. Report on Singapore's Dredging Fleet 1942–49, Public Works Department (PWD), 279/47, 12/4/1947.
96. Ow Hin Kok, former lighterman and owner, interview by author, assisted by Ng Hwee Poh, Pasir Panjang, 24/1/94.
97. *Report of Enquiry into the Working of the Ports of Singapore, Penang and Port Swettenham*, September 1946, p. 5.
98. Ibid.
99. Director of Public works to Colonial Secretary, PWD, 223/53, 10/3/1953.
100. *Singapore River Working Committee*, 1955, PWD, 223/53, p. 5.
101. (L.W.O.S.T.) Low Water on Spring Tides; (H.W.O.S.T.) High Water on Spring Tides.
102. *Singapore River Working Committee*, 1955, PWD, 223/53, pp. 6–7.
103. Ibid., p. 10.

104. Ibid., pp. 7–8. See also Foreshores Ordinance, Chapter 22 and Municipal Ordinance, Chapter 133.
105. Ibid.
106. Development Planning Committee Secretary to PWD Chief Planner, PWD, 223/53, 20/6/1964, p. 37.
107. Executive Engineer Marine (PWD) to Chief Engineer (PWD), PWD, 122/57, 11/2/1957, pp. 1–2.
108. Development Planning Committee Secretary to PWD Chief Planner, PWD, 223/53, 20/6/1964, p. 37.
109. Letter to Wong Chooi Sen (PWD) from Prime Minister, PWD, 223/53, 26/3/1969.
110. Tan Way Tong, 'The HDB Resettlement Department and its Role in the Cleaning-up Program of Singapore River and Kallang Basin Catchments', *Action Plan for the Seas of East Asia: COBSEA Workshop on Cleaning Up of Urban Rivers*, 14–16 January 1986, Singapore, Annex 10E, p. 5.

Chapter 5

1. Lim Chwee Pin, lighterman, interview by Ms Tan Beng Luan, Oral History Department, National Archives of Singapore, Acc. A 000723/008, Reel 1, 1986.
2. *Singapore River Commission*, Tabled in the Legislative Council Proceedings, Tuesday, 13 June 1899, p. C172.
3. Bennett, *Journal of a Naturalist*, Vol. 2, 1834, p. 331.
4. Cameron, *Our Tropical Possessions*, pp. 56–57. For further examples see, Dr Yvan, physician to the scientific mission sent by France to China, in James Blackwood, *Six Months Among the Malays and a Year in China* (London: Paternoster Row, 1855), pp. 61–75; Charles Carleton Coffin, *Our New Way Around the World* (London: Sampson Low, Son and Marston, 1869), pp. 235–38; Verner Helms Ludvig, *Pioneering in the Far East* (London: WH Allen & Co, 1882), p. 9.
5. *Singapore Free Press*, 14/12/10.
6. Teo Ah Lea, lighterman, interview by author, Pasir Panjang, 18/11/93. (*Teo Ah Lea* is a Hokkien Chinese. He was born in Singapore in 1930. A friend helped him to secure work in the lighterage industry. For more than 30 years he had worked as a lighterman. Mr Teo was married. In 1993, at the age of 63, he was still working on lighters when work was available.) See also Tan Chee Soon, lighterman, interview by Ms Tan Beng Luan, Oral History Department, National Archives of Singapore, Acc. A 000269/008, Reel 4, 1986.
7. The term *chor coolie* was used most commonly by all lightermen.
8. Lim Kim Boi, lighterman, interview by Ms Tan Beng Luan, Oral History Department, National Archives of Singapore, Acc. A 000717/006, Reel 3, 1986.
9. Ibid.
10. Chang Ham Chwee, lighter owner, chairman of the Lighter Owners Association; Ow Chin Seng, lighter owner, treasurer of the Lighter Owners Association; interview by author, assisted by Ng Hwee Poh, Pasir Panjang, 8/9/93. See also Lim Chwee Pin, interview by Ms Tan Beng Luan, Oral History Department, National Archives of Singapore, Acc. A 000717/006, Reel 4, 1986.

11. Lee Sek Keong, lighter owner, interview by Ms Tan Beng Luan, Oral History Department, National Archives of Singapore, Acc. A 000712/005, Reel 5, 1986.
12. Kwek Ah Lam, lighterman, quoted in *The Straits Times*, 29/9/1974.
13. Old Man Tan quoted in *The Straits Times*, 3/8/1982.
14. *Tiao chin* a Hokkien term used by lightermen for mobile cranes.
15. Chang Ham Chwee, Ow Chin Seng, interview by author, assisted by Ng Hwee Poh, Pasir Panjang, 8/9/93.
16. Tan Chee Soon, lighterman, interview by Ms Tan Beng Luan, Acc. A 000269/008, Reel 4, 1986. Teo Ah Lea, lighterman, interview assisted by Ng Hwee Poh, Pasir Panjang, 18/11/93.
17. Chang Ham Chwee, Ow Chin Seng, interview by author, assisted by Ng Hwee Poh, Pasir Panjang, 8/9/93.
18. Ow Hin Kok, former lighterman and owner, interview by author, assisted by Ng Hwee Poh, Singapore, 24/1/94.
19. Industrial Arbitration Court, *Case No. 26 of 1980*, p. 8.
20. Ow Hin Kok, interview by author, assisted by Ng Hwee Poh, Singapore, 24/1/94. See also Chang Ham Chwee, Ow Chin Seng, interview by author, assisted by Ng Hwee Poh, Pasir Panjang, 8/9/1993. Several of the people interviewed for this study expressed a similar view.
21. Ibid.
22. Evidence by Alexander Gentle, *The Straits Settlements and the Federated Malay States Opium Commission*, Vol. II, 1908, p. 322.
23. Chang Ham Chwee, Ow Chin Seng, interview by author, assisted by Ng Hwee Poh, Pasir Panjang, 8/9/1993.
24. Ibid.
25. Ibid.
26. Chan Hian Chuan, lighterman, interview by author, assisted by Ng Hwee Poh, Pasir Panjang, 6/12/93.
27. Ibid.
28. Chang Ham Chwee, Ow Chin Seng, interview by author, assisted by Ng Hwee Poh, Pasir Panjang, 8/9/93.
29. Ong Geok Seng, president of the Lighter Owners Association, quoted in *The Straits Times*, 29/9/74.
30. Chang Ham Chwee, Ow Chin Seng, interview by author, assisted by Ng Hwee Poh, Pasir Panjang, 8/9/93.
31. Sunday, 3 October 1993, on the freighter *Sang Thai Fortune*.
32. Lim Chwee Pin, interview by Ms Tan Beng Luan, Oral History Department, National Archives of Singapore,Acc. A 000717/006, Reel 4, 1986.
33. See also, Ong Geok Seng, quoted in *The Straits Times*, 29/9/1974.
34. Chang Ham Chwee, interview by author, 8/9/93.
35. Chan Hian Chuan, interview by author, assisted by Ng Hwee Poh, Pasir Panjang, 6/12/93.
36. Kwek Ah Lam, quoted in *The Straits Times*, 29/9/1974.
37. Ibid.
38. Ibid.
39. Chang Ham Chwee, Ow Chin Seng, interview by author, assisted by Ng Hwee Poh, Pasir Panjang, 8/9/93.
40. Ibid.
41. Ow Hin Kok, interview by author, assisted by Ng Hwee Poh, Singapore, 24/1/94.

42. Ibid.
43. Yap Aik Kun, *The Singapore River: Economic Landscape in Retrospect*, Academic Exercise, Department of Geography, National University of Singapore, 1983/84, p. 68.
44. Teo Ah Lea, interview by author, assisted by Ng Hwee Poh, Pasir Panjang, 18/11/93.
45. Tan Pung Hun, lighterman, interview by author, assisted by Ng Hwee Poh, Pasir Panjang, 6/12/93.

    Tan Pung Hun is a Hylam Chinese. Born 1924, he arrived in Singapore at the age of 13, in 1937, to join an uncle already residing in the colony. Tan's main reason for leaving China was the Sino-Japanese war. After working on a rubber plantation for a period he was helped by friends to get job as a lighterman. He had been in the industry ever since working for various companies. Tan was married with seven children.
46. Ow Hin Kok, interview by author, assisted by Ng Hwee Poh, Singapore, 24/1/94.
47. Ibid.
48. Ibid. See also Chang Ham Chwee, Ow Chin Seng, interview by author, assisted by Ng Hwee Poh, Pasir Panjang, 8/9/93.
49. Ibid.
50. See *The Straits Calender and Directory*, 1865, p. 33, for a schedule of fees set in 1858 including for demurrage.
51. Ow Hin Kok, interview by author, assisted by Ng Hwee Poh, Singapore, 24/1/94.
52. Ibid. See also Teo Ah Lea, interview by author, Pasir Panjang, 18/11/93.
53. Ong Ah Cheng, lighterman and owner, formerly a chairman of the Transport Vessel Workers Association, interview by author, Singapore, 4/1/94.

    Ong Ah Cheng is a Hokkien Chinese. Born in 1943 at Geylang, Singapore, his father worked as a lighterman. As a child he travelled to China with his father where they lived for a number of years. Later Ong returned to Singapore to work on lighters with his father. Concerns over the working conditions of lightermen led him to become involved with the Lightermen's Union in 1960. Between 1964 and 1984 Ong was the union's chairman. In 1993 he owned 14 vessels of his own, including motor launches, motor sampans and cargo lighters. Ong was married with two children.
54. *Report of the Singapore River Commission*, 1899.
55. J. Wong Geok Lin, comp., *Investigation Report on Unemployment of Lightermen in Relation to Unseaworthy and Idle Lighters in the Port of Singapore in General and in Singapore River in Particular*, Special Projects Section, Department of Statistics, Singapore, 1960, p. 2.
56. Ow Hin Kok, interview by author, assisted by Ng Hwee Poh, Singapore, 24/1/94.
57. Tan Ah Poh, lighterman, quoted in, *Singapore Lifeline: The River and its People* (Singapore: Times Books International, 1986), p. 83.
58. *Singapore Free Press*, 5/8/1847.
59. Ow Hin Kok, interview by author, assisted by Ng Hwee Poh, Singapore, 24/1/94.
60. Ibid. See also, *Investigation Report on Unemployment of Lightermen*, p. 2.
61. Chang Ham Chwee, Ow Chin Seng, interview by author, assisted by Ng Hwee Poh, Pasir Panjang, 17/8/93.

62. Chan Hian Chuan, interview by author, assisted by Ng Hwee Poh, Pasir Panjang, 6/12/93.
63. Ibid.
64. Ibid.
65. Tan Pung Hun, interview by author, assisted by Ng Hwee Poh, Pasir Panjang, 7/12/93; Chang Ham Chwee, Ow Chin Seng, interview by author, assisted by Ng Hwee Poh, Pasir Panjang, 17/8/93.
66. Tan Chee Soon, interview by Ms Tan Beng Luan, Oral History Department, National Archives of Singapore, Acc. A 000269/008, Reel 5, 1986.
67. *Tian chun* is a Hokkien term for motorised lighters or motor sampan.
68. Lim Chwee Pin, interview by Ms Tan Beng Luan, Singapore, Acc. A 000723/008, Reel 5, 1986. See also, Yap, *The Singapore River: Economic Landscape in Retrospect*, p. 63.
69. Ibid.
70. Chang Ham Chwee, Ow Chin Seng, interview by author, assisted by Ng Hwee Poh, Pasir Panjang, 17/8/93. Indian lightermen were recruited in exactly the same way. See P Prabhakaran Nair, *Indian Labour in the Singapore Lighterage Industry*, PhD dissertation for the Department of Social Studies, University of Malaya, Singapore, 1958, p. 16. This is a fine study of Indian involvement in the lighterage industry of Singapore in the late 1950s. At this time Indian lighters were largely stationed in the Kallang River and at Teluk Ayer Basin.
71. Chang Ham Chwee, 17/8/93.
72. Ibid.
73. Chang Ham Chwee, interview by author, assisted by Ng Hwee Poh, Pasir Panjang, 7/10/1993.
74. Tan Chee Soon, lighterman, interview by Ms Tan Beng Luan, Oral History Department, National Archives of Singapore, Reel 4, 1986.
75. Ow Chin Seng, interview by author assisted by Ng Hwee Poh, Pasir Panjang, 14/2/94.
76. Yap, *The Singapore River: Economic Landscape in Retrospect*, p. 56.
77. Ibid.
78. Chang Ham Chwee, Ow Chin Seng, interview by author, assisted by Ng Hwee Poh, Pasir Panjang, 17/8/93.
79. Ibid.
80. Ibid.
81. Ibid. Also Ow Hin Kok, interview by author, assisted by Ng Hwee Poh, Pasir Panjang, 24/1/94.
82. Ibid.
83. Ibid.
84. Wang Aik Mong, former lighter owner, interview by author, assisted by Ng Hwee Poh, Pasir Panjang, 1/12/93. In 1993/94 Wang was employed as a clerk for Chang Ham Chwee, chairman of the Lighter Owners Association.

    Wang Aik Mong is a Teochew Chinese. Born 1928, Wang came with his family, including his grandfather, to Singapore when he was one year old. His family lived at number 76 Boat Quay. His father and grandfather established a lighterage business (Meng Loon Co) and this is how Wang became involved in the industry. After the Second World War Wang began supervising the business which had 32 lighters. He was married and has 12 children from two wives.

85. Chang Ham Chwee, interview by author, assisted by Ng Hwee Poh, Pasir Panjang, 7/10/93. This same point was restated by Ow Chin Seng, interview by author, assisted by Ng Hwee Poh, Pasir Panjang, 18/11/93.
86. Ibid.
87. Wang Aik Mong, interview by author, assisted by Ng Hwee Poh, Pasir Panjang, 1/12/93.
88. Ibid.
89. Chang Ham Chwee, Ow Chin Seng, interview by author, assisted by Ng Hwee Poh, Pasir Panjang, 8/9/93.
90. Ibid., 17/8/93. See also, Yap, *The Singapore River: Economic Landscape in Retrospect*, p. 55.
91. Ibid.
92. Ibid.
93. Ibid. See also, Yap, *The Singapore River: Economic Landscape in Retrospect*, p. 55.
94. Teo Ah Lea, interview by author, assisted by Ng Hwee Poh, Pasir Panjang, 18/11/93.
95. Chan Hian Chuan, interview by author, assisted by Ng Hwee Poh, Pasir Panjang, 6/12/93.
96. Ibid.
97. For studies on the importance of these ties to Chinese immigrants see Hugh DR Baker, *Chinese Family and Kinship* (London: Macmillan Press, 1979); Yen Ching-Hwang, 'Early Chinese Clan Organisations in Singapore and Malaya, 1819–1911', *Journal of Southeast Asian Studies* 12, no. 1 (1981); Maurice Freedman, *The Study of Chinese Society. Essays by Maurice Freedman* (Stanford: Stanford University Press, 1979).
98. Chang Ham Chwee, Ow Chin Seng, interview by author, assisted by Ng Hwee Poh, Pasir Panjang, 17/8/93.
99. Ibid.
100. Tan Chee Soon, lighterman, interview by Ms Tan Beng Luan, Oral History Department, National Archives of Singapore, Acc. A 000269/008, Reel 3, 1986.
101. Chang Ham Chwee, Ow Chin Seng, interview by author, assisted by Ng Hwee Poh, Pasir Panjang, 8/9/93.
102. Ibid.
103. Ibid.
104. Ow Chin Seng, interview by author, assisted by Ng Hwee Poh, Pasir Panjang, 3/12/93.
105. Tong Dow Ngiam, *Chinese Labour and Tongkang Trade in Singapore 1958*, Graduation Exercise, History Department, University of Malaya, Singapore, 1958–59.
106. Chang Ham Chwee, interview by author, assisted by Ng Hwee Poh, 8/9/93.
107. Lim Chwee Pin, lighterman, interview by Ms Tan Beng Luan, Acc. A 000723/008, Reel 2, 1986.
108. Chan Hian Chuan, interview by author, assisted by Ng Hwee Poh, Pasir Panjang, 6/12/93.
109. In the 1950s through government and union involvement this became the standard.
110. Ong Ah Cheng, interview by author, assisted by CP Wong, 12/2/94.
111. Ibid.

112. Ong Ah Cheng, interview by author, assisted by CP Wong, Pasir Panjang, 4/1/94.
113. Ibid.
114. Figures in this range were quoted by all the interviewees for this study.
115. Tan Chee Soon, lighterman, interview by Ms Tan Beng Luan, Reel 4, 1986.
116. *Annual Report of the Labour Department 1946*, Singapore, p. 59.
117. *Investigation Report on Unemployment of Lightermen*, p. 7.
118. Ong Ah Cheng, interview by author, assisted by CP Wong, Pasir Panjang, 4/1/94.
119. Yap, *The Singapore River: Economic Landscape in Retrospect*, p. 67.
120. Ow Chin Seng, interview by author, assisted by Ng Hwee Poh, Pasir Panjang, 18/11/93.
121. Teo Ah Lea, interview by author, assisted by Ng Hwee Poh, Pasir Panjang, 18/11/93.
122. Ow Chin Seng, interview by author, assisted by Ng Hwee Poh, Pasir Panjang, 18/11/93.
123. Ibid.
124. *Chendera Mata Perayaan Ulang Tahun Yang Ke-22 Kesatuan Pekerja² Kapal Pengangkut Singapura*, Transport Vessel Workers Association, 1960. (A copy of this Journal/Newsletter was given to me by Ng Hwee Poh, English secretary for the Lighter Owners Association.)
125. *Singapore Free Press*, 26/5/1842. See also, C Buckley, *An Anecdotal History of Old Times in Singapore 1819–1867* (Kuala Lumpur: University of Malaya Press, 1965), p. 375.
126. *Singapore Free Press*, 8/1/1857.
127. The union was not registered until 24/5/1939. It had offices at 115 Cecil Street. *Annual Report of the Labour Department*, Singapore, 1946, p. 48. The following studies examine in detail the development of the labour movement and militancy in Malaya and Singapore. MR Stenson, *Industrial Conflict in Malaya: Prelude to the Communist Revolt* (Singapore: Oxford University Press, 1970); R Clutterbuck, *Riot and Revolution in Singapore and Malaya, 1945–1963* (London: Faber and Faber, 1973); C Gamba, *The Origins of Trade Unionism in Malaya: A Study of Colonial Labour Unrest* (Singapore: D Moore for Eastern Universities Press, 1962); V Thompson, *Labor Problems in Southeast Asia* (New Haven: Yale University Press, 1947); Alex Josey, *Trade Unionism in Malaya* (Singapore: D. Moore, 1958).
128. Ong Ah Cheng, interview by author, assisted by Ng Hwee Poh, Pasir Panjang, 4/1/94. Tan Ah Poh, interview by Ms Tan Beng Luan, Oral History Department, National Archives of Singapore, Reels 4 and 5, 1986.
129. Ibid.
130. Ibid.
131. Ibid.
132. CP Wong, former organiser and secretary for the Transport Vessel Workers Association, interview by author, Singapore, 13/2/94.

    CP Wong was born in Cameron Highlands, Malaysia. His father was a fighter in the Malayan People's Anti-Japanese Army (MPAJA) and a member of the Malayan Communist Party. In 1956 he went to Singapore for schooling. Later Wong returned to Malaysia and worked in the accounts department of Sime Darby. When Singapore and Malaysia split in 1965 he moved to Singapore in order to obtain citizenship there and became involved in the union movement around 1967. He worked as secretary and organiser for a number of unions, The Singapore Catering Services Staff and Workers' Trade Union, Singapore Motor Workshop Employees' Union, and Film Industrial Employees of Singapore Union, before taking up the position of English Secretary for the Transport Vessel Workers Association in 1969–70. Wong was actively involved between 1970 and 1983 in efforts to improve the wages and working conditions of lightermen. In 1994 he was still involved with the union movement in Singapore as well as being a partner in several businesses with Ong Ah Cheng.

133. Tan Ah Poh, interview by Ms Tan Beng Luan, Oral History Department, National Archives of Singapore, Acc. A 000655/005, Reel 3, 1986.
134. Lim Chwee Pin, interview by Ms Tan Beng Luan, Singapore, Acc. A 000723/008, Reel 7, 1986. See also *The Straits Times*, 3/8/1982. Lighter owners I interviewed, such as, Chang Ham Chwee and Ow Chin Seng, agreed that 'some' towkay did deliberately cheat on the figures to increase their own share.
135. Ibid. Ong Ah Cheng, interview by author, assisted by C P Wong, Singapore, 12/2/94.
136. Tan Ah Poh, interview by Ms Tan Beng Luan, Singapore, Acc. A 000655/005, Reel 3, 1986.
137. CP Wong, interview by author, Pasir Panjang, 20/1/94.
138. The Transport Vessel Workers Association was the second union to seek registration after the Second World War. *Report of Singapore Labour Department 1948*, p. 101.
139. P Prabhakaran Nair, *Indian Labour in the Singapore Lighterage Industry*, p. 76.
140. First appears as registered in the *Report of Singapore Labour Department 1948*, p. 105.
141. Ibid., pp. 76–81.
142. Ong Ah Cheng, interview by author, assisted by Ng Hwee Poh, Singapore, 12/2/94.
143. Tan Ah Poh, interview by Ms Tan Beng Luan, Singapore, Acc. A 000655/005, Reel 3, 1986.
144. Ong Ah Cheng, interview by author, assisted by CP Wong, Singapore, 12/2/94.
145. Tan Ah Poh, interview by Ms Tan Beng Luan, Singapore, Acc. A 000655/005, Reel 3, 1986.
146. Ibid.
147. Ong Ah Cheng, interview by author, assisted by CP Wong, Singapore, 20/1/94.
148. Tan Chee Soon quoted in, *Singapore Lifeline: The River and its People*, p. 78.
149. Lim Chwee Pin, interview by Ms Tan Beng Luan, Singapore, Acc. A 000723/008, Reel 8, 1986.
150. Ong Ah Cheng, interview by author, assisted by CP Wong, Singapore, 12/2/94.
151. Ibid. See also, Ow Chin Seng, interview by author, assisted by Ng Hwee Poh, Pasir Panjang, 18/11/93.
152. Chang Ham Chwee, Ow Chin Seng, interview by author, assisted by Ng Hwee Poh, Pasir Panjang, 17/8/93.
153. Ong Ah Cheng, interview by author, assisted by CP Wong, Singapore, 4/1/94.
154. Ibid.
155. Chang Ham Chwee, Ow Chin Seng, interview by author, assisted by Ng Hwee Poh, Pasir Panjang, 17/8/93.

156. Ibid.
157. Ong Ah Cheng, interview by author, assisted by CP Wong, Singapore, 4/1/94.
158. Ibid. This sentiment was also supported by the Owners interviewed, Chang Ham Chwee and Ow Chin Seng.
159. Lee Ting Hui, *The Communist Organisation In Singapore: Its Techniques Of Manpower Mobilization And Management, 1948–66*, Field Report Series No. 12 (Singapore: Institute of Southeast Asian Studies, August 1976), p. 122.
160. CP Wong, interview by author, Pasir Panjang, 20/1/94.
161. CP Wong, interview by author, Pasir Panjang, 13/2/94.
162. Also known as the Joint Consultative Committee.
163. *Memorandum of Agreement*, Joint Committee 9/5/55. A copy of this memorandum was given to me by Ow Chin Seng.
164. Ibid.
165. CP Wong, interview by author, Pasir Panjang, 13/2/94.
166. Ong Ah Cheng, interview by author, assisted by Ng Hwee Poh, Singapore, 12/2/94. Also interviews with Ow Chin Seng and Chang Ham Chwee.
167. Ibid.
168. Ow Chin Seng, interview by author, assisted by Ng Hwee Poh, Pasir Panjang, 18/11/93.
169. Ibid.
170. Ow Chin Seng, interview by author, assisted by Ng Hwee Poh, Pasir Panjang, 18/11/93.
171. Ibid. Also Lim Chwee Pin, interview by Ms Tan Beng Luan, Singapore, Acc. A 000723/008, Reel 8, 1986.
172. Ow Chin Seng, interview by author, assisted by Ng Hwee Poh, Pasir Panjang, 18/11/93.
173. Ong Ah Cheng, interview by author, assisted by CP Wong, Singapore, 12/2/94. Also interviews with Ow Chin Seng and Chang Ham Chwee.
174. CP Wong, interview by author, Pasir Panjang, 13/2/94. A similar assessment was made by Chang Ham Chwee.
175. Chang Ham Chwee, Ow Chin Seng, interview by author, assisted by Ng Hwee Poh, Pasir Panjang, 8/9/93. Also interview with CP Wong, Pasir Panjang, 20/1/94.
176. Ibid.
177. Ibid.
178. *The Straits Times*, 1/10/1970, 12/6/1971, 7/9/1979. Ow Chin Seng, interview by author, assisted by Ng Hwee Poh, Pasir Panjang, 18/11/93.
179. *The Straits Times*, 5/4/1974, 8/4/1974.
180. *The Straits Times*, 21/4/1975.
181. CP Wong, interview by author, Pasir Panjang, 13/2/94. A similar assessment was made by Chang Ham Chwee.

Chapter 6

1. Warren, *Rickshaw Coolie*, p. 236.
2. Ow Hin Kok, former lighterman and owner, interview by author, assisted by Ng Hwee Poh, Singapore, 24/1/94.
3. Ibid.
4. The lighter wharves at Pasir Panjang served a similar function for the few remaining lightermen in 1993–94.

5. For a general discussion of the importance of maintaining this contact see Yen Ching-hwang, *A Social History of the Chinese in Singapore and Malaya 1800–1911* (Singapore: Oxford University Press, 1986), p. 73.
6. Ow Hin Kok, interview by author, assisted by Ng Hwee Poh, Singapore, 24/1/94.
7. Ibid.
8. Ibid.
9. Ibid.
10. Ibid.
11. Ibid.
12. Pek Sin Choon, quoted in, *Singapore Lifeline: The River and its People* (Singapore: Times Books International, 1986), p. 101. The situation was similar for all men of the labouring class in Singapore. See Warren, *Ah Ku and Karayuki-San*, pp. 259–60.
13. Ow Chin Seng, lighter owner, treasurer of the Lighter Owners Association, interview by author, Pasir Panjang, 18/11/93.
14. Ibid.
15. Chan Hian Chuan, lighterman, interview by author, assisted by Ng Hwee Poh, Pasir Panjang, 6/12/93.
16. Ow Hin Kok, interview by author, assisted by Ng Hwee Poh, Singapore, 24/1/94.
17. Wang Aik Mong, former lighter owner, interview by author, assisted by Ng Hwee Poh, Pasir Panjang, 1/12/93.
18. Tan Ah Poh, lighterman, interview by Ms Tan Beng Luan, Oral History Department, National Archives of Singapore, Acc. A 000655/005, Reel 3, 1986.
19. For a detailed summary of housing conditions, see *Proceedings and Report of the Commission Appointed to Inquire into the Cause of the Present Housing Difficulties in Singapore, and the Steps which should be taken to Remedy such Difficulties*, Vols. 1 and 2 (Singapore: Government Printing Office, 1918); also *Report of the Housing Committee Singapore* (Singapore: Government Printing Office, 1947). An important study of Singapore's urban development under British colonialism is Brenda Yeoh's, *Contesting Space: Power Relations and the Urban Built Environment in Colonial Singapore* (Kuala Lumpur: Oxford University Press, 1996).
20. Wang Aik Mong, interview by author, assisted by Ng Hwee Poh, Pasir Panjang, 1/12/93.
21. Chang Ham Chwee, lighter owner, chairman of the Lighter Owners Association; Ow Chin Seng, lighter owner, treasurer of the Lighter Owners Association, interview by author, assisted by Ng Hwee Poh, Pasir Panjang, 17/8/93.
22. Wang Aik Mong, interview by author, assisted by Ng Hwee Poh, Pasir Panjang, 1/12/93.
23. Tan Pung Hun, lighterman, interview by author, assisted by Ng Hwee Poh, Pasir Panjang, 7/12/93.
24. Mr Tan, quoted in *The Straits Times*, Section 3, p. 1, 3/8/1982.
25. Ow Chin Seng, interview by author, assisted by Ng Hwee Poh, Pasir Panjang, 18/11/93.
26. Tan Ah Poh, lighterman, quoted in, *Singapore Lifeline: The River and Its People*, p. 90. Also interview with Wang Aik Mong, interview by author, assisted by Ng Hwee Poh, Pasir Panjang, 1/12/93.

27. Ibid.
28. Chang Ham Chwee, Ow Chin Seng, interview by author, assisted by Ng Hwee Poh, Pasir Panjang, 17/8/93.
29. Ibid.
30. Turnbull, *A History of Singapore 1819–1988*, p. 86.
31. See *Census Report*, 1891, 1901, 1911.
32. Ee Joyce, 'Chinese Migration to Singapore, 1896–1941', *Journal of Southeast Asian History* 2 (1961): 48.
33. JD Vaughan, *The Manners and Customs of the Chinese of the Straits Settlements*, 1879; reprint, Oxford in Asia Paperbacks (Kuala Lumpur: Oxford University Press, 1977), p. 6.
34. Ow Hin Kok, interview by author, assisted by Ng Hwee Poh, Pasir Panjang, 24/1/94.
35. Yen, *A Social History of the Chinese in Singapore and Malaya 1800–1911*, p. 224.
36. Ibid.
37. Ibid., p. 248.
38. Ow Hin Kok, interview by author, assisted by Ng Hwee Poh, Singapore, 24/1/94. During interviews with lightermen there was understandably a reluctance to discuss this issue. However, when queried regarding the recreational pursuits of lightermen all those interviewed, without exception, put 'womanising' at or near the top of their list. Other interviewees such as Ow Hin Kok were clear in stating that 'womanising' was a reference to liaisons with prostitutes.
39. Ong Ah Cheng, former chairman of the Transport Vessel Workers Association, interview by author, assisted by CP Wong, Singapore, 12/2/94.
40. A number of important studies on the role of prostitution and opium in Singapore's history have been written. See Warren, *Ah Ku and Karayuki-San*; Carl Trocki, *Opium and Empire Chinese Society in Colonial Singapore, 1800–1910* (Ithaca: Cornell University Press, 1990).
41. 'Social Conditions In Singapore', *Report of Venereal Diseases Committee, 1923*, Vol. 1, pp. 2–3.
42. Turnbull, *A History of Singapore 1819–1988*, p. 86.
43. Warren, *Ah Ku and Karayuki-San*, p. 100.
44. See Warren, 'Prostitution and the Politics of Venereal Disease, 1870–1898', *Journal of Southeast Asian Studies* 21, no. 2 (September 1990).
45. Ow Hin Kok, interview by author, assisted by Ng Hwee Poh, Singapore, 24/1/94. See also Wang Aik Mong, interview by author, assisted by Ng Hwee Poh, Singapore, 6/12/93.
46. Ibid.
47. Ow Hin Kok, interview by author, assisted by Ng Hwee Poh, Singapore, 24/1/94.
48. Leong Chee Sang, quoted in *The Straits Times*, Section 3, p. 1, 7/9/1982.
49. Ibid.
50. Ow Hin Kok, interview by author, assisted by Ng Hwee Poh, Singapore, 24/1/94.
51. Wang Aik Mong, interview by author, assisted by Ng Hwee Poh, Singapore, 1/12/93.
52. Senior Inspector SM Farooq and Senior Sergeant Yunos Bin Salleh, interview by author, Singapore, 9/9/93.

    At the time of the interview Senior Inspector SM Farooq and Senior Sergeant

Yunos Bin Salleh had more than 25 years experience with the Marine Police in Singapore and had intimate knowledge of policing the Singapore River.

53. Jack Flowers, the somewhat dubious central character of Paul Theroux's novel, *Saint Jack*, earns notoriety by transporting twakow loads of women to ships in the harbour.
54. Senior Inspector SM Farooq and Senior Sergeant Yunos Bin Salleh, interview by author, 9/9/93.
55. *The Straits Settlements and the Federated Malay States Opium Commission*, Vol. 1, Section 4, 1908, p. 2.
56. Ibid.
57. *The Straits Times*, Section 3, p. 2, 14/9/1982.
58. Gentle, evidence to *The Straits Settlements and the Federated Malay States Opium Commission*, Vol. II, 1908, p. 322.
59. Ibid.
60. R Little, 'On the Habitual use of Opium in Singapore', *The Journal of the Indian Archipelago and Eastern Asia* 2, series 1 (1848): 2 and 66.
61. Gentle, evidence to *The Straits Settlements and the Federated Malay States Opium Commission*, Vol. 2, 1908, p. 20.
62. Ibid., p. 318.
63. Chang Ham Chwee, Ow Chin Seng, interview by author, assisted by Ng Hwee Poh, Pasir Panjang, 17/8/93.
64. Ibid.
65. Lim Buck Chua, quoted in *The Straits Times*, Section 2, p. 2. 14/9/1982.
66. Gentle, evidence to *The Straits Settlements and the Federated Malay States Opium Commission*, Vol. 2, 1908, p. 322.
67. Tan Pung Hun, interview by author, assisted by Ng Hwee Poh, Pasir Panjang, 7/12/93.
68. Ow Hin Kok, interview by author, assisted by Ng Hwee Poh, Singapore, 24/1/94.
69. Little, 'On the Habitual Use of Opium in Singapore', p. 20; see also CJ Saunders, evidence to *The Straits Settlements and the Federated Malay States Opium Commission*, Vol. 2, 1908, p. 95.
70. An excellent analysis of the role of opium in colonial Singapore is contained in, Trocki, *Opium and Empire*.
71. Between 1898 and 1906 the percentage of total government revenue raised through opium was never less than 44 per cent and as much as 59 per cent. See *The Straits Settlements and the Federated Malay States Opium Commission*, Vol. 1, Section 16, 1908, p. 42; see also Turnbull, *A History of Singapore 1819–1988*, p. 114.
72. *The Straits Times*, Section 2, p. 2, 14/9/1982.
73. *Singapore Daily Times*, Vol. 7, No. 10,020, 30/8/1866.
74. Chang Ham Chwee, Ow Chin Seng, interview by author, assisted by Ng Hwee Poh, Pasir Panjang, 17/8/93.
75. Ibid.
76. Ibid.
77. Ibid.
78. Ow Hin Kok, interview by author, assisted by Ng Hwee Poh, Singapore, 24/1/94. Many such 'accidents' were reported in the island's newspapers. See *Singapore Daily Times*, 14/2/1867, *Singapore Free Press*, 13/6/1889, 23/6/1890, 12/1/1912.
79. Yen, *A Social History of the Chinese in Singapore and Malaya 1800–1911*, p. 225.

80. Gentle, evidence to *The Straits Settlements and the Federated Malay States Opium Commission*, Vol. II, 1908, p. 318.
81. Lim, quoted in *The Straits Times*, Section 2, p. 2, 14/9/1982.
82. Ow Hin Kok, interview by author, assisted by Ng Hwee Poh, Singapore, 24/1/94.
83. *The Straits Settlements and the Federated Malay States Opium Commission*, Vol. 1, Section 17, 1908, p. 44.
84. Certificate of Coroners' Views Singapore (CCVS), No. 298, 14/6/27.
85. CCVS, No. 220, 10/5/26.
86. Ow Hin Kok, interview by author, assisted by Ng Hwee Poh, Singapore, 24/1/94.
87. Chang Ham Chwee, interview by author, assisted by Ng Hwee Poh, Singapore, 8/9/93.
88. Ibid.
89. Teo Ah Lea, lighterman, interview by author, assisted by Ng Hwee Poh, Pasir Panjang, 18/11/93.
90. Ibid. Also Lock Heng Huat, stevedore, in, *Singapore Lifeline: The River and its People*, p. 95.
91. Ow Hin Kok, interview by author, assisted by Ng Hwee Poh, Singapore, 24/1/94.
92. *The Straits Times*, Section 2, p. 1, 7/9/1982.
93. Ow Hin Kok, interview by author, assisted by Ng Hwee Poh, Singapore, 24/1/94.
94. Ibid.
95. Ibid.
96. Teo Ah Lea, interview by author, assisted by Ng Hwee Poh, Singapore, 18/11/93.
97. Ong Ah Cheng, interview by author, assisted by CP Wong, 12/2/94.
98. *Singapore Free Press*, Vol. 14, No. 52, 28/12/1849.
99. Teo Ah Lea, interview by author, assisted by Ng Hwee Poh, Pasir Panjang, 18/11/93.
100. Ong Ah Cheng, interview by author, assisted by CP Wong, 12/2/94.
101. Ibid.
102. Ibid.
103. Ibid.
104. Teo Ah Lea, interview by author, assisted by Ng Hwee Poh, Singapore, 18/11/93.
105. *Singapore Lifeline: The River and its People*, p. 97.
106. Ong Ah Cheng, interview by author, assisted by CP Wong, Singapore, 12/2/94. See also, Joan Hon, *Tidal Fortunes, a Story of Change: The Singapore River and Kallang Basin* (Singapore: Landmark Books, n.d.), p. 151.
107. Ibid.
108. Ibid.
109. Tan Pung Hun, interview by author, assisted by Ng Hwee Poh, Singapore, 7/12/93.
110. Chang Ham Chwee, interview by author, assisted by Ng Hwee Poh, Pasir Panjang, 7/10/93.
111. Ibid.
112. Ibid. See also, Hon, *Tidal Fortunes, a Story of Change*, pp. 153–54.
113. Chang Ham Chwee, interview by author, assisted by Ng Hwee Poh, Pasir Panjang, 7/10/93.

114. Ow Hin Kok, interview by author, assisted by Ng Hwee Poh, Singapore, 24/1/94.
115. Chang Ham Chwee, interview by author, assisted by Ng Hwee Poh, Pasir Panjang, 7/10/93.
116. Ow Hin Kok, interview by author, assisted by Ng Hwee Poh, Singapore, 24/1/94.
117. Ibid. See also Yap Aik Kun, *The Singapore River: Economic Landscape in Retrospect*, Academic Exercise, Department of Geography, National University of Singapore, 1983/84, pp. 47–48.
118. Datok Pek Kong's (Da Bo Gong) origins are explained differently by the various Chinese communities but he is generally held to be a local variation of the Chinese God of the Land. See *The Straits Times*, Section 3, p.1, 21/9/1982.
119. Chang Ham Chwee, interview by author, assisted by Ng Hwee Poh, Pasir Panjang, 7/10/93.
120. Ibid.
121. *The Straits Times*, Section 3, p. 1, 21/9/1982. See also Chang Ham Chwee, interview by author, assisted by Ng Hwee Poh, Singapore, 7/10/93.
122. Chang Ham Chwee, interview by author, assisted by Ng Hwee Poh, 7/10/93.

Chapter 7

1. Hon, *Tidal Fortunes, a Story of Change*, p. 41.
2. See British Military Administration (BMA), 159/45.
3. Ibid. See also, Turnbull, *A History of Singapore 1819–1988*, p. 220.
4. *Report on the dredging fleet of Singapore*, PWD 279/47, 12/4/47.
5. Ibid.
6. Ibid.
7. Colonial Secretary's Office (CSO) 2013/48, Ministry of Finance (MF 056). See also, PWD 175/48; 249/49; 372/070.
8. *The Sunday Times*, 6/3/1949.
9. PWD 175/48, p. 13.
10. There is no shortage of records relating to the condition of the river in this period. See for example, PWD 538/50, 27/9/50, 8/11/50; PWD 136/52, 23/1/52; PWD 741/54, 28/8/54.
11. Ow Hin Kok, interview by author, assisted by Ng Hwee Poh, Singapore, 24/1/94.
12. Ibid. See also, *Report of the Singapore River Commission*, 1899; *Singapore River Working Committee*, 1955.
13. Copy of official 'Press Release', CSO, 1163/53/30, 10A, September 1953.
14. *Singapore River Working Committee, Final Report*, CSO, 2792/29, September 1955, p.4.
15. Ibid., p.17. See also, 'Comments on the Singapore River Working Committee Report and recommendations for a five year programme of reconstruction work', DPW, 223/53, Vol. II, pp. 4–5.
16. Singapore Legislative Assembly, Part I of First Session, Volume 11, Monday 14/12/1959. Columns 1174–1176.
17. See correspondence and related documents in PWD file 223/53. The early volumes of this file contain much discussion of the Committee's report, its merits and cost.

18. *Singapore Free Press*, 22/11/1960.
19. *Malay Mail*, 6/3/1962.
20. Confidential memo, from the Development Planning Committee to the Director of Public Works, PWD 223/53, Vol. IV, 25/9/64, p. 43.
21. *Malay Mail*, 26/4/1963.
22. See for example, PWD 223/53; PWD 122/57, 28/1/57; PWD 122/57, Vol. II, 1/3/58.
23. For a full discussion of the 1957 *Census Report* see R Neville, 'The Areal Distribution of Population in Singapore', *The Journal of Tropical Geography* 20 (June 1965).
24. R Wikkramatileke, 'Focus on Singapore', *The Journal of Tropical Geography* 20 (June 1965): 79.
25. The Housing Development Board was set up in 1960 and in 1962 the Urban Renewal Department was organised as a unit within it.
26. Wikkramatileke, 'Focus on Singapore', p. 80.
27. Chia Lin Sien, *et al.*, *The Coastal Environmental Profile of Singapore*, Technical Publications Series 3, Association of Southeast Asian Nations/United States Coastal Resources Management Project, Manila, 1988, pp. 33, 40–44.
28. Brenda Yeoh and Shirlena Huang, 'The Conservation–redevelopment Dilemma in Singapore', *Cities* 13, no. 6 (1996): 412.
29. Robert Gamer, *The Politics of Urban Development in Singapore* (Ithaca: Cornell University Press, 1972), p. 47.
30. Urban Redevelopment Authority, *Living the Next Lap: Towards a Tropical City of Excellence*, 1991, p. 8.
31. Ibid., p. 9.
32. Sim Kee Boon was on an advisory board to the government.
33. Letter to Howe Yoon Chong, Permanent Secretary, Ministry of National Development, PWD 223/53, Vol. IV, p. 44.
34. Ibid.
35. PWD 223/53, Vol. IV, p. 45.
36. Ibid. See also letter dated 8/6/1969.
37. See PWD 223/53, pp. 84, 86, 89, 90. There is a large volume of material contained in this file relating to efforts undertaken.
38. Copy of minute from the Prime Minister to Wong Chooi Sen, PWD 223/53, Vol. V, 26/3/69.
39. Ibid.
40. PWD 223/53, Vol. V, 7/4/69, p. 103.
41. Minutes of meetings held on 1/10/1969; 7/10/1969; 17/10/1969, PWD 223/53, p. 178A.
42. David Chow (Drainage and Marine), 'Improvement to Canals and Rivers', notes of a meeting held on 7/4/69, PWD 223/53, Vol. III, p. 3.
43. 'Preliminary Survey of Atmospheric and Effluent Pollution in Singapore', PWD 223/53, Vol. IV, pp. 2–5; 'Report on Hydrogen Sulphide Content Just Above the Surface of the Singapore River at Various Points', Department of Chemistry, PWD 223/53, 15/7/69, Vol. IV, pp. 134–35.
44. 'Report on the River Pollution of Singapore River', Atmospheric and Effluent Pollution Study Group, PWD 223/53, Vol. IV, 23/7/69, p. 143A.
45. Ibid.
46. Minutes of meeting held on 4/6/69, Atmospheric and Effluent Pollution Study Group, PWD 223/53, p. 2; see also, Letter from Chief Chemist, Department of Chemistry, to the Director of Public Works, attached document

details tests done with chemicals along the river, PWD 223/53, p. 134.

47. 'Improvement to Canals and Rivers', minutes of meeting held on 16/10/1969, PWD 223/53, p. 178A.
48. 'Interim Report on Improvement to Rivers and Canals in Singapore', PWD 223/53, Vol. V, pp. 2–3.
49. PWD (Drainage and Marine) 450/3, 17/8/1970.
50. 'Interim Report on Improvement to Rivers and Canals in Singapore', PWD 223/53, Vol. V.
51. Removal of 'illegal' structures and squatters was actively under way all along the river. See PWD (Drainage and Marine) 434/5, Vol. 2, pp. 21, 26; PWD 223/53, Vol. V, p. 99.
52. 'Interim Report on Improvement to Rivers and Canals in Singapore', PWD 223/53, Vol. V.
53. See PWD 223/53, Vol. V, p. 108.
54. Chang Ham Chwee, lighter owner, chairman of the Lighter Owners Association, interview by author, assisted by Ng Hwee Poh, Pasir Panjang, 7/10/93.
55. PWD 223/53, Vol. V, p. 121.
56. *The Straits Times*, 14/10/1970.
57. PWD 223/53, Vol. V, p. 99A.
58. Both these were filled by late 1970. ENV(D) 3/65, p. 148.
59. PWD (Drainage and Marine) 434/6, p. 6; PWD 223/53, Vol. V, p. 39.
60. 'The Vanishing Singapore River', *Malay Mail*, 28/8/69.
61. PWD (Drainage and Marine) 434/5, Vol. 2, 28/1/70.
62. Ibid.
63. PWD (Drainage and Marine) 434/5, 27/11/1969.
64. PWD 223/53, Vol. V, p. 16A.
65. Ibid., p. 17.
66. PWD(Drainage and Marine) 434/5, 27/10/70.
67. Ibid.
68. PWD 223/53, Vol. V, p. 100.
69. *The Sunday Times*, 13/9/1970.
70. Ibid.
71. 'Republic of Singapore Master Plan Third Review, 1975', Planning Department, Ministry of National Development, September 1975, p. 82.
72. 'Lighter Owners Want Singapore River Godowns to Remain', *The Straits Times*, 1/10/1970.
73. *The Straits Times*, 2/3/1970.
74. Chang Ham Chwee, interview by author, Pasir Panjang, 7/10/93.
75. 'Lighter Sites at River to Stay', *The Straits Times*, 12/6/1971.
76. Ow Chin Seng, lighter owner, treasurer of the Lighter Owners Association, interview by author, assisted by Ng Hwee Poh, Pasir Panjang, 3/12/1993.
77. Loy Wei Sun, 'Phasing Out of Pig and Open Range Duck Farms in Water Catchments', *Action Plan for the Seas of East Asia: COBSEA Workshop on Cleaning Up of Urban Rivers*, 14–16 January 1986, Singapore, pp. 2–3.
78. Hon, *Tidal Fortunes, a Story of Change*, p. 41.
79. Chiang Kok Meng, 'Cleaning Up of Singapore River and Kallang Basin Catchments', *Action Plan for the Seas of East Asia*, pp. 3–4.
80. For a detailed examination of hawking in Singapore, see Katherine Yeo, *Hawkers and the State in Colonial Singapore: Mid-nineteenth Century to 1939*, Master's thesis (Melbourne: Monash University Microfilms, 1989).

81. Tan Way Tong, 'The HDB Resettlement Department and its Role in the Cleaning-up Program of Singapore River and Kallang Basin Catchments', *Action Plan for the Seas of East Asia,* p. 4.
82. Ibid.
83. Teo Boo Teck, 'Cleaning Up of Singapore and Kallang Basin Catchments – Role of Environmental Health Department in the Clean Up Program', *Action Plan for the Seas of East Asia,* Annex 1.
84. Ibid.
85. Tan Way Tong, 'The HDB Resettlement Department and its Role in the Cleaning-up Program of Singapore River and Kallang Basin Catchments', p. 7.
86. Ibid., p. 9.
87. Ibid., p. 8.
88. Ibid., p. 4.
89. Chiang Kok Meng, 'Cleaning Up of Singapore River and Kallang Basin Catchments', p. 7.
90. 'Cleaning up of Singapore River/Kallang Basin Catchment and all Water Catchments (1977–March 1982)', Progress Report, Ministry of the Environment, May 1982, p. 5.
91. Teo Boo Teck, 'Cleaning Up of Singapore and Kallang Basin Catchments — Role of Environmental Health Department in the Clean Up Program', p. 3.
92. Ibid.
93. Chang Ham Chwee, interview by author, assisted by Ng Hwee Poh, Pasir Panjang, 7/10/93.
94. *The Straits Times,* 18/2/1972.
95. For a comprehensive discussion of these developments in Southeast Asia, see Keith Trace, 'ASEAN Ports Since 1945: Maritime Change and Port Rivalry', in Frank Broeze (ed.), *Gateways of Asia: Port Cities of Asia in the 13th–20th Centuries* (New York: Kegan Paul International, 1997).
96. *The Straits Times,* 21/4/1979.
97. 'The Dying Lighters Down by the Riverside', *The Straits Times,* 14/5/1975.
98. Ibid.
99. *The Straits Times,* 10/7/1975; 22/10/1975.
100. *The Straits Times,* 21/4/1975.
101. *The Straits Times,* 19/5/1975.
102. CP Wong, interview by author, Clarke Quay, 13/2/94. This opinion was confirmed by lighter owners Chang Ham Chwee and Ow Chin Seng.
103. Ibid.
104. Ibid.
105. *The Straits Times,* 7/9/1979.
106. Ibid.
107. *The Straits Times,* 27/7/1980.
108. Ibid.
109. *The Straits Times,* 9/8/1980.
110. *The Straits Times,* 6/4/1978.
111. Poon Im Hung, 'PSA's Role in the Cleaning up Programme', in *Action Plan for the Seas of East Asia* (Annex 10E). See also, *The Straits Times,* 5/8/1982.
112. Ibid.
113. *Singapore Business Times,* 24/5/1983.

114. Ow Chin Seng, interview by author, assisted by Ng Hwee Poh, Pasir Panjang, 3/12/93.
115. *The Straits Times*, 1/9/1983.
116. Ibid.
117. The removal of the lighterage industry had caused some to describe the river as 'soulless'. *The Straits Times*, 10/9/1983.
118. Ong Ah Cheng, former chairman of the Transport Vessel Workers Association, interview by author, assisted by CP Wong, Singapore, 12/2/1994.
119. In this section I refer to the state of the industry as it was in 1993–94 when I carried out fieldwork in Singapore.
120. Chang Ham Chwee, interview by author, assisted by Ng Hwee Poh, Pasir Panjang, 17/8/93.
121. Ibid.
122. *The Sunday Times*, 6/4/86.
123. Ibid.
124. Ibid. Also, Ow Chin Seng, interview by author, assisted by Ng Hwee Poh, Pasir Panjang, 17/8/93.
125. *The Sunday Times*, 6/4/1986. Also, Tan Hong Chuan, Administrative Officer, Marine Division, Port of Singapore Authority, interview by author, Pasir Panjang, 11/8/93.
126. Chang Ham Chwee, interview by author, assisted by Ng Hwee Poh, Pasir Panjang, 17/8/93.
127. Yap Aik Kun, *The Singapore River: Economic Landscape in Retrospect*, Academic Exercise, Department of Geography, National University of Singapore, 1983/84, p. 72.
128. An important recent study of the trishaws is Jason Lim's *'Sor Leng Ngia': The Rise and Demise of the Trishaw Industry in Singapore 1945–1983*, Honours Thesis, Murdoch University, 1995.
129. Lim Chong Teet cited in, Linda Berry, *Singapore River: a Living Legacy* (Singapore: Eastern Universities Press, 1982), p. 49.
130. Ong Ah Cheng, interview by author, assisted by CP Wong, 12/2/94. See also, *Memories by the River*, a video documentary by Oral History Department, National Archives of Singapore, 1998.
131. Ong Ah Cheng, interview by author, assisted by CP Wong, 12/2/94. See also, *The Straits Times*, 10/8/1982.
132. CP Wong, interview by author, Singapore River, 20/1/94.
133. Ibid.
134. *The Straits Times*, 10/9/1983.
135. CP Wong, interview by author, Singapore River, 20/1/94.
136. Ibid.
137. Teo Ah Lea, lighterman, interview by author, Pasir Panjang, 18/11/93.
138. Ow Chin Seng, interview by author, Pasir Panjang, 17/3/93.
139. Chang Ham Chwee, interview by author, assisted by Ng Hwee Poh, Pasir Panjang, 17/8/93.
140. Chang Ham Chwee, interview by author, Pasir Panjang, 17/8/93. Tan Hong Chuan, Administrative Officer, Marine Division, Port of Singapore Authority, interview by author, Pasir Panjang, 11/8/93.
141. *The Straits Times*, 19/10/1982.
142. Chang Ham Chwee, interview by author, assisted by Ng Hwee Poh, Pasir Panjang, 17/8/93.

143. Ow Chin Seng, interview by author, assisted by Ng Hwee Poh, Pasir Panjang, 3/12/93.
144. Ibid.
145. Teo Ah Lea, interview by author, assisted by Ng Hwee Poh, Pasir Panjang, 18/11/93. Tan Pung Hun, interview by author, assisted by Ng Hwee Poh, Singapore, 7/12/93.
146. Teo Ah Lea, interview by author, assisted by Ng Hwee Poh, Pasir Panjang, 18/11/93.
147. Ow Chin Seng, interview by author, assisted by Ng Hwee Poh, Pasir Panjang, 3/12/1993.
148. Ibid.
149. *The Sunday Times*, 9/1/1994.
150. Ong Ah Cheng, interview by author, assisted by Ng Hwee Poh, Pasir Panjang, 4/1/94.
151. Ibid.
152. Ibid.
153. Ow Chin Seng, interview by author, Pasir Panjang, 17/3/93.
154. Ibid.
155. Chan Hian Chuan, lighterman, interview by author, Pasir Panjang, 6/12/93.

Chapter 8

1. Alison Harvey, 'The Skyline of the Future', *Silver Kris*, February 1993, p. 46.
2. *The Straits Times*, 10/6/1999.
3. Victor Savage, 'Singapore's Garden City: Reality, Symbol, Ideal', *Solidarity* 131–32 (July–December 1991).
4. Urban Redevelopment Authority, *Living the Next Lap: Towards a Tropical City of Excellence*, Singapore, 1991, p. 25.
5. Brenda Yeoh and Lily Kong, 'Reading Landscape Meanings: State Construction and Lived Experiences in Singapore's Chinatown', *Habitat International* 18, no. 4 (1994): 29.
6. *Annual Report*, Urban Redevelopment Authority, 1985, p.1.
7. *The Straits Times*, 12/10/1983.
8. Poon Im Hung, 'PSA's Role in the Cleaning up Programme', *Action Plan for the Seas of East Asia: COBSEA Workshop on Cleaning Up of Urban Rivers*, 14–16 January 1986, Singapore, Annex 10E.
9. Teo Boo Teck, 'Cleaning Up of Singapore and Kallang Basin Catchments — Role of Environmental Health Department in the Clean Up Programme', *Action Plan for the Seas of East Asia*, Annex 1.
10. Chang Ham Chwee, chairman of the Lighter Owners Association, interview by author, assisted by Ng Hwee Poh, Pasir Panjang, 7/10/93. See also, Hon, *Tidal Fortunes, a Story of Change*, p. 93.
11. Yap Kheng Guan, 'Physical Improvement Works to the Singapore River and Kallang Basin', *Action Plan for the Seas of East Asia*, p. 1.
12. Ibid.
13. Ibid.
14. Chiang Kok Meng, 'Cleaning Up of Singapore River and Kallang Basin Catchments', *Action Plan for the Seas of East Asia*, Annex 10A.

15. Ibid., p. 10.
16. Chia Lin Sien and Chou Loke Ming (eds.), *Urban CoastalArea Management: The Experience of Singapore*, Conference Proceedings 7, Association of Southeast Asian Nations/United States Coastal Resources Management Project, 1991, p. 21.
17. Ibid.
18. Ibid.
19. Hon, *Tidal Fortunes, a Story of Change*, p. 101.
20. *The Straits Times*, 4/9/87.
21. *The Straits Times*, 3/9/87. See also, Hon, *Tidal Fortunes A Story of Change*, p. 96.
22. Ibid., p. 99.
23. Victor Savage, 'Singapore's Garden City: Reality, Symbol, Ideal', *Solidarity* 131–32 (July–December 1991): 68–69.
24. *River Reborn*, television documentary produced by the Singapore Broadcasting Corporation in conjunction with the Ministry of the Environment, 29/8/87.
25. 'Year X' is how the period beyond 2010 is described in the document, when the nation's population is expected to reach 4 million. The goals of the plan are detailed in, Urban Redevelopment Authority, *Living the Next Lap*, 1991.
26. Preface to *Singapore River Planning Report 1994*, Urban Redevelopment Authority. Document cited at <http://www.ura.gov.sg/dgp_reports/sinriver/main.html> (official website of the Urban Redevelopment Authority).
27. Introduction to *Singapore River Planning Report 1994*.
28. Tan Mong Hong, 'Planning for the Singapore River', *Action Plan for the Seas of East Asia*, Annex 10H, p. 3.
29. *The Straits Times*, 29/8/1999.
30. *The Straits Times*, 20/2/2002.
31. Tan Mong Hong, 'Planning for the Singapore River', p. 4.
32. Ibid., pp. 4–5.
33. Ibid., pp. 6–7.
34. 'Planning Strategies', *Singapore River Planning Report 1994*, Urban Redevelopment Authority.
35. 'Land Use', *Singapore River Planning Report 1994*, Urban Redevelopment Authority.
36. 'Open Space', *Singapore River Planning Report 1994*, Urban Redevelopment Authority.
37. 'Special and Detailed Controls', *Singapore River Planning Report 1994*, Urban Redevelopment Authority. See also, *The Straits Times*, 26/7/1990.
38. *Living the Next Lap*, p. 25.
39. *Conservation Principle and Approaches*, Urban Redevelopment Authority, Module 3. Document cited at <http://www.ura.gov.sg/conservation/mod3.htm>.
40. *Conservation Guidelines for Boat Quay Conservation Area*, Urban Redevelopment Authority, November 1991, p. 5.
41. *The Straits Times*, 20/4/1993.
42. *The Straits Times*, 5/2/1993.
43. *The Straits Times*, 5/2/1993 and 22/3/1993.
44. *The Straits Times*, 23/1/1990.
45. Ibid.

46. Ibid.
47. *The Straits Times*, 22/3/1993.
48. *The Straits Times*, 20/4/1993.
49. *The Straits Times*, 22/3/1993.
50. Ibid.
51. *The Sunday Times*, 9/1/1994.
52. *New Paper*, 10/1/1994.
53. *The Straits Times*, 15/1/1993, 27/3/2001.
54. *The Straits Times*, 16/3/2001.
55. *Award of Tender for Fullerton Square*, Press Release, Urban Redevelopment Authority, 2/10/97, document cited at <http://www.ura.gov.sg/pr/text/pr97-58.html>.
56. Ibid.
57. *Reconstructed River Wall adds to Revitalisation of Singapore River*, Press Release, Urban Redevelopment Authority, 9/9/97, document cited at <http://www.ura.gov.sg/pr/text/pr97-53.html>.
58. Ibid.
59. *URA to Build a Continuous Riverside Promenade*, Press Release, Urban Redevelopment Authority, 15/7/97, document cited at <http://www.ura.gov.sg/pr/text/pr97-41.html>.
60. *The Straits Times*, 17/12/1991.
61. *The Straits Times*, 8/5/1993.
62. *The Straits Times*, 11/12/2000.
63. *The Straits Times*, 11/9/2000.
64. *The Straits Times*, 9/11/2000.
65. *The Straits Times*, 7/2/1991.
66. *The Straits Times*, 9/2/1991.
67. Ibid.
68. <http://www.singapore-buskers.com/Background.htm> [30 July 2001].
69. *The Straits Times*, 22/11/1999.
70. <http://www.singapore-buskers.com/Background.htm> [30 July 2001].
71. Tan Mong Hong, 'Physical Improvement Works to the Singapore River and Kallang Basin', *Action Plan for the Seas of East Asia*, Annex 10B, p. 2.
72. *Punch* 29/11/1972, p. 777, cited in, David Lowenthal, *The Past is a Foreign Country* (Great Britain: Cambridge University Press, 1990), p. 4.
73. Of course Singapore is not alone in this respect. See Lowenthal, *The Past is a Foreign Country*, pp. 384–89.
74. Lily Kong and Brenda Yeoh, 'Urban Conservation in Singapore: A Survey of State Policies and Popular Attitudes', *Urban Studies* 31, no. 2 (1994): 248–49.
75. Ibid. See also, *First Decade in Public Housing 1960–1969*, Housing and Development Board, Singapore, 1969, p. 6.
76. Kong and Yeoh, 'Urban Conservation in Singapore', p. 249.
77. *Annual Report*, Urban Redevelopment Authority, 1984/85.
78. Robert Gamer, *The Politics of Urban Development in Singapore* (Ithaca: Cornell University Press, 1972), p. 47.
79. TG McGee, 'Beach-heads and Enclaves: The Urban Debate and Urbanisation Process in South-East Asia Since 1945', in YM Yeung and CP Lo (eds.), *Changing Southeast Asian Cities: Readings in Urbanisation* (Singapore: Oxford University Press, 1972).

80. Quoted in William Lim, *Asian New Urbanism and Other Papers* (Singapore: Select Books, 1998), p. 17.
81. Ronald Hill, *Southeast Asia People, Land and Economy* (Australia: Allen and Unwin, 2002), p. 256.
82. Kong and Yeoh, 'Urban Conservation in Singapore', p. 251.
83. KC Wong, *et al.*, *Report of the Tourism Task Force,* Ministry of Trade and Industry, 1984, p. 6.
84. For an interesting study of why tourists go to Singapore, and what they do there, see Alan Lew, 'English Speaking Tourists and the Attractions of Singapore', *Singapore Journal of Tropical Geography* 8, no. 1 (1987).
85. *The Straits Times,* 10/9/1983.
86. M Castells, 'Four Asian Tigers with a Dragon Head: A Pacific Rim', in R Appelbaum and J Henderson (eds.), *State and Development in the Asian Pacific Rim* (Newbury Park: Sage, 1992), p. 56.
87. Peggy Teo and Shirlena Huang, 'Tourism and Heritage Conservation in Singapore', *Annals of Tourism Research* 22, no. 3 (1995): 593.
88. R Sharpley, *Tourism, Tourists and Society* (Huntingdon: ELM Publications, 1994), p.156.
89. For an insight into Lee Kuan Yew's views, see Fareed Zakaria, 'Culture is Destiny: A Conversation with Lee Kuan Yew', *Foreign Affairs* 73, no. 2 (March/April 1994); see also, Joseph Tamney, *The Struggle Over Singapore's Soul: Western Modernisation and Asian Culture* (New York: Walter de Gruyter, 1996). The economic crisis that struck in 1997 has resulted in some new twists occurring in this debate.
90. Goh Chok Tong, 'Our national ethic', *Speeches: A Bimonthly Selection of Ministerial Speeches* 12, no. 5 (1988), Ministry of Communications and Information.
91. Brenda Yeoh and Lily Kong, 'The Notion of Place in the Construction of History, Nostalgia and Heritage in Singapore', *Singapore Journal of Tropical Geography* 17, no. 1 (June 1996): 60.
92. Lowenthal, *The Past is a Foreign Country,* p. 369.
93. *The Committee on Heritage Report,* Singapore, 1988.
94. Ibid., p. 46.
95. *Living the Next Lap,* p. 5.
96. Ibid., p. 25.
97. *Annual Report,* Urban Redevelopment Authority, 1988/89, p. 21.
98. *The Straits Times,* 16/12/1988, cited in, Yeoh and Kong, 'The Notion of Place in the Construction of History, Nostalgia and Heritage in Singapore', p. 61.
99. *The Sunday Times,* 6/4/1986.
100. Ow Chin Seng, treasurer of the Lighter Owners Association, interview by author, assisted by Ng Hwee Poh, Pasir Panjang, 17/8/93.

Appendix 1

1. CA Gibson-Hill, 'Tongkang and Lighter Matters', *Journal of the Malayan Branch of the Royal Asiatic Society* 25, no. 1 (1952): 84.
2. Ibid., p. 97.
3. Erick R Alfred, 'The Ubiquitous Twakow', *Port View* 1, no. 9 (September 1980): 2.

4. Ow Chin Seng, lighter owner, treasurer of the Lighter Owners Association, interview by author, assisted by Ng Hwee Poh, Pasir Panjang, 10/9/93. Mr Ow owned the last eight lighter tongkangs in Singapore — all of which were crewed by Indians.
5. Gibson-Hill, 'Tongkang and Lighter Matters', p. 97.
6. Ibid., p. 98.
7. Alfred, 'The Ubiquitous Twakow', p. 2.
8. Ibid.
9. Ibid.
10. Gibson-Hill, 'Tongkang and Lighter Matters', p. 89.
11. Ow Chin Seng, interview by author, assisted by Ng Hwee Poh, Pasir Panjang, 10/9/93.
12. Yap Aik Kun, *The Singapore River: Economic Landscape in Retrospective*, Academic Exercise, Department of Geography, National University of Singapore, 1983/84, p. 45. Ow Chin Seng, interview by author, assisted by Ng Hwee Poh, Pasir Panjang, 10/9/93.
13. Gibson-Hill, 'Tongkang and Lighter Matters', p. 89.
14. Ow Chin Seng, interview by author, assisted by Ng Hwee Poh, Pasir Panjang, 10/9/93.

Glossary of Terms

Campong, kampong, kampung	Village or town
Chandu	Prepared opium
Chor coolies or **Lau ah hia**	Rough labourers or stevedores
Bochuan	Chinese term for lighters
Duffadar	Petty Officer in the 'native police'
Godown	Warehouse
Jemador	Police officer, equal to Lieutenant
Nanyang	Chinese term for Southeast Asia meaning South Seas
Peon	Policeman
Singkeh	New arrival from China
Swaylo	Ordinary crewman
Taikong	Helmsmen/person responsible for the lighter
Tian Chun	Motor sampan/lighters
Tongkang	Lighter craft used primarily by Indian lightermen
Towkay	Chinese businessman
Twakow	Type of lighter craft used along river, of Chinese origin
Twalow	Helmsmen/person responsible for the lighter

Bibliography

Oral History Interviews — National Archives of Singapore

Lim Chwee Pin, Lighterman. Interview by Ms Tan Beng Luan. Oral History Department, Acc. A 000723/008, 1986. Lim spoke about the situation which led to migration to Singapore; wages and working conditions; classes of lightermen and their responsibilities; role of the union in settling disputes.

Lim Kim Boi, Lighterman. Interview by Ms Tan Beng Luan. Oral History Department, Acc. A 000717/006, 1986. Lim spoke about reasons for migrating; living conditions and routine of life as a twakow man in Singapore; goods carried on lighters and the organisation of jetties along the river; wage rates of lightermen and their responsibilities; crew sizes on lighters of different tonnage; and conflicts between lightermen.

Lee Sek Keong, Lighter Owner. Interview by Ms Tan Beng Luan. Oral History Department, Acc. A 000712/005, 1986. Lee spoke about his family background and reasons for migrating to Singapore; the role of motor sampans in the lighterage industry; the Motor Sampan Association; cooperation between lighter owners to protect each others business interests; and the Lightermen's Union.

Tan Ah Poh, Lighterman. Interview by Ms Tan Beng Luan. Oral History Department, Acc. A 000655/005, 1986. Tan spoke about distribution of jetties along Boat Quay; coolie accommodation and costs; causes of disputes between lightermen; factors which led to the formation of the Lightermen's Union; role of the union in uniting lightermen to improve working and pay conditions.

Tan Chee Soon, Lighterman. Interview by Ms Tan Beng Luan. Oral History Department, Acc. A 000269/008, 1986. Tan spoke on his family background in China; living on the lighter; crew sizes and responsibilities; cargo rates; profit-sharing arrangements between owners and lightermen; conflicts and division of jetties; and the role of the Lightermen's Union.

Oral History Interviews — Conducted by the Author

Chan Hian Chuan, Lighterman. Interview by author, assisted by Ng Hwee Poh, English Secretary for the Lighter Owners Association, 6/12/93.

Chang Ham Chwee, Lighter owner and Chairman of the Lighter Owners Association. Interview by author, assisted by Ng Hwee Poh, 17/8/93, 8/9/93, 7/10/93.

Senior Inspector Farooq SM and Senior Sergeant Yunos Bin Salleh. Interview by author. Marine Police Headquarters, Kallang, 9/9/93.

Ong Ah Cheng, former Chairman of the Transport Vessel Workers Association. Interview by author, assisted by Ng Hwee Poh, 4/1/94; assisted by CP Wong, 20/1/94, 12/2/94.

Ow Chin Seng, Lighter owner, treasurer of the Lighter Owners Association. Interview by author, 17/8/93, 10/9/93, 18/11/93, 3/12/93, 14/2/94.

Ow Hin Kok, former Lighterman and owner. Interview by author, assisted by Ng Hwee Poh, 24/1/94.
Tan Hong Chuan, Administrative Officer, Marine Division, Port of Singapore Authority. Interview by author, 11/8/93.
Tan Pung Hun, Lighterman. Interview by author, assisted by Ng Hwee Poh, 7/12/93.
Teo Ah Lea, Lighterman. Interview by author, assisted by Ng Hwee Poh, 18/11/93.
Wang Aik Mong, former lighter owner. Interview by author, assisted by Ng Hwee Poh, 1/12/93.
Wong CP, former Secretary and Organiser for the Transport Vessel Workers Association. Interview by author, 20/1/94, 13/2/94.

Films

Oral History Department. *Memories by the River.* Ministry of Community Development, Singapore, 1989.
Perera, Ananda. *The Lightermen.* Singapore Broadcasting Corporation, Singapore, 1976.

Newspapers

New Paper
Singapore Chronicle
Singapore Chronicle and Commercial Register
Singapore Daily Times
Singapore Free Press
The Straits Times
The Sunday Times

Unpublished Official Records — National Archives of Singapore

Straits Settlements Records (SSR), 1819–67.
Straits Settlements Annual Reports, 1861–1941.
Colonial Office Records Singapore 1867–1941. CO 273, Various.
Straits Settlements Legislative Council Proceedings, 1867–1941.
Singapore Coroners Inquests and Inquiries, 1882–1939.
Administration Reports of the Singapore Municipality, 1888–1939.
Certificate of Coroners Views, 1906–1940.
Public Works Department (PWD) 223/53, Various.

Government Reports and Commissions

Committee on Heritage, Singapore. *The Committee on Heritage Report.* 1988.
Department of Statistics, Singapore. *Investigation Report on Unemployment of Lightermen in Relation to Unseaworthy and Idle Lighters in the Port of Singapore in General and in Singapore River in Particular.* Compiled by J. Wong Geok Lin, Supervisor, Special Projects Section. 1960.

Government Printing Office, Singapore. *Proceedings and Report of the Commission Appointed to Inquire into the Cause of the Present Housing Difficulties in Singapore, and the Steps which should be taken to Remedy such Difficulties.* Vols. 1 and 2. 1918.

Government Printing Office, Singapore. *Report of the Commissioners Appointed to Enquire into the State of Labour in the Straits Settlements and Protected Native States with Appendices and Papers in Continuation.* 1891.

Government Printing Office, Singapore. *Report of the Housing Committee Singapore, 1947.* 1947.

Government Printing Office, Singapore. *Report of Venereal Diseases Committee, 1923.* 1923.

Legislative Council. *Report of the Singapore River Commission.* 13/6/1899.

Legislative Council. *Straits Settlements Report of the Police Commission.* 1879.

Ministry of Trade and Industry, Singapore. *Report of the Tourism Task Force.* 1984.

Report of the Commission of Inquiry into the Port of Singapore. August–September 1957.

The Straits Settlements and the Federated Malay States Opium Commission. Vols. I–III. 1908.

Singapore: Committee Appointed to Inquire into and Report on the Singapore New Harbour Railway. 1866.

Singapore's National Report for the 1992 UN Conference on Environment and Development Preparatory Committee.

Urban Redevelopment Authority, Singapore. *Singapore River Planning Area.* Planning Report 1994.

Reference, Government Departments and Private Publications

Action Plan for the Seas of East Asia: Coordinating Body for Seas of East Asia (COBSEA) Workshop on Cleaning Up of Urban Rivers. Singapore, 14–16 January 1986.

A Gazetter of Southern India with the Tenasserim Provinces and Singapore (Madras: Pharoah and Co., 1855).

Archives and Oral History Department. *Pioneers of Singapore a Catalogue of Oral History Interviews.* Singapore, 1984.

Archives and Oral History Department. *Singapore Retrospect through Postcards: 1900–1930.* Singapore,1982.

A Short History of the Port of Singapore. Raffles Library. Singapore, 1924.

Braddell,Thomas and Matthew Gregory. *The General Municipal and Straits Municipal Acts Nos. XXV and XVII of 1856.* With full analytical index. Penang, 1857.

Colony of Singapore Master Plan Report of Survey. Written July–December 1954.

Committee of the Singapore Chamber of Commerce *Memorandum on the Proposed Singapore Harbour Improvement Scheme.* Drawn up by a member of the Committee. Singapore, 1904.

Drafts of the Assessment, Municipal and Police Acts for the Straits Settlements (Singapore: Mission Press, 1854).

Housing and Development Board. *First Decade in Public Housing 1960–1969.* Singapore,1969.

Industrial Resources Study Group. *Master Plan Reports of Study Groups and Working Parties.* Report. July–August, Singapore, 1954.

Institute of Southeast Asian Studies. *Singapore, Malaysian and Brunei Newspapers and International Union List.* Compiled by P. Lim Pui Huen with the assistance of Marion Southerwood and Katherine Hui. Library Studies No. 19. Singapore, 1992.

Lee Ting Hui. *The Communist Organisation In Singapore: Its Techniques Of Manpower Mobilization And Management, 1948–66*. Field Report Series No.12 (Singapore: Institute of Southeast Asian Studies, August 1976).
Oral History Department. *Recollections People and Places*. Singapore, 1990.
Oral History Department. *Singapore Lifeline: The River and its People* (Singapore: Times Books International, 1986).
Planning Department Ministry of Development. *Republic of Singapore Master Plan Third Review, 1975, Report of Survey*. Singapore, September 1975.
Planning Department Ministry of Development. *Republic of Singapore Master Plan Third Review, 1980, Report of Survey*. Singapore, October 1980.
Port of Singapore Authority. *Singapore Port History*. Compiled by the Maritime Museum. Singapore.
Port of Singapore Authority. *Singapore: Portrait of a Port*. Singapore, 1984.
Raffles, Sir Stamford. *Statement of the Services* [To the Court of Directors of the East–India Company] (London: Cox & Baylis, 1824).
Rotary Club and the Municipal Commissioners of the town of Singapore. *Singapore*. A book of information. Singapore, 1933.
Singapore International Chamber of Commerce. *Annual Reports*. Singapore, 1885–1990.
Singapore Free Press Office. *Rules and Regulations for the Guidance of the Singapore Police Force*. Made and passed in the Quarter Session, 2/10/1846 (Singapore: SM Frederick, 1846).
Singapore International Chamber of Commerce. *Annual Reports*, Singapore, 1885–1986.
Singapore Local Laws and Institutions 1823 (London: Cox and Baylis, 1824).
Singapore National Trades Union Congress. 'Towards Tomorrow: Essays on Development and Social Transformation in Singapore'. Chapter 10. *The Port of Singapore*. Singapore, 1973.
Singapore Transport Vessel Workers Association. *Chendera Mata Perayaan Ulang Tahun Yang Ke–22 Kesatuan Pekerja² Kapal Pengangkut Singapura*. 1960. (A copy of this Journal/Newsletter was given to the author by Ng Hwee Poh, English Secretary for the Lighter Owners Association.)
Tanjong Pagar Constituency. *Tanjong Pagar Singapore's Cradle of Development* (Singapore: Landmark Books, 1989).
The Committee on Heritage. Report. Singapore, November 1988.
The Colonial Directory of the Straits Settlements, Including Sarawak, Labuan, Bangkok and Saigon.1873–76.
The Government of Singapore. *Singapore the Next Lap*. Singapore, 1991.
The Municipal Ordinance of 1913. Ordinance No. VIII of 1913 (Singapore: Government Printer, 1913).
The Municipal Ordinance of 1896 No. XV of 1896 (as amended by Ordinance X of 1900, III of 1903, VIII of 1904, I of 1905, XII of 1906 and XXXVII of 1907) (Singapore: Government Printing Office, 1909).
The Rise and Progress of the Tanjong Pagar Docks. Reprint (Singapore: Singapore Free Press, 1896).
The Royal Almanack and Directory. Singapore, 1859–60.
The Singapore Almanack and Directory. Singapore, 1853–58.
The Singapore Directory for the Straits Settlements, 1877–79.
The Straits Times Almanac, Calender and Directory. Singapore, 1846–52.
The Straits Calender and Directory, Including Sarawak and Labuan. Singapore, 1861–72.

Urban Redevelopment Authority. *Clarke Quay Develop Your Own Corner of Historic Singapore*. Singapore, 1989.

Urban Redevelopment Authority. *Living the Next Lap towards a Tropical City of Excellence*. Singapore, 1991.

Articles

'150 Years of Progress Singapore National Day August 9, 1969'. *The Straits Times*, August 1969.

Alfred, Erick R. 'The Ubiquitous Twakow'. *Port View* I, No. 9 (September 1980), PSA.

Barr, Flinders. 'How Singapore was Founded'. Five articles in *The Straits Times*, 4, 11, 18, 25 of October and 1 November 1937.

Blake, DJ. 'Patterns of Singapore's Trade 1961–1966'. *Malayan Economic Review* 12 (1967).

Drysdale, John. *In the Service of Our Nation*. 1984. Provided by the Police Department, Singapore.

Norris, George. 'Singapore Thirty Years Ago: A Paper Read at a Meeting of the Mutual Improvement Society, 15 July 1878'. *Straits Time Press*, 1878.

Duncan, Walter Scott. Journal. *Singapore Sixty Years Ago*. Journal covers the period February–June 1824. N.p., n.d. (Singapore: National Library of Singapore Microfilms).

Conference Papers

Broeze, Frank, *et al.* 'Port Cities in the Indian Ocean Region 1815–1939: Functional and Methodological Issues'. Conference paper. *International Conference on Indian Ocean Studies*. Perth W.A., Australia, 5–12 December 1984.

____. 'The External Dynamics of Port City Morphology: Bombay 1815–1914'. Unpublished conference paper.

Hoyle, BS. 'The Port-City Interface: Some Geographical Perspectives'. Conference paper. *Waterfront Redevelopment and the Cityport*. Southampton, England, 1987.

Academic Exercise and Theses

Cheng Hui Cheng. *Singapore: Early Town Development 1819–36*. Academic Exercise, Department of History, National University of Singapore, 1981/82.

Chong Kie Cheong. *The Ship Building and Ship Repairing Industry in Singapore*. Academic Exercise, Department of Economics, University of Malaya, Singapore, 1968/69.

Iau Kuo Kwong, Robert. *Labour and Aspects of Trade in the Singapore Chinese Lighterage Industry (Within Port Limits)*. Graduation Exercise, Economics Department, University of Malaya, Singapore, 1958/59.

Khoo Kay Kim. *The Municipal Department of Singapore 1887–1940*. Academic Exercise, History Department, University of Malaya, Singapore, 1961.

Da Silva, Henry Lawrence. *Singapore's Entrepot Trade in Sago*. Academic Exercise, Department of Economics, University of Malaya, Singapore, 1961.

Lim, Jason. *'Sor Leng Ngia' The Rise and Demise of the Trishaw Industry in Singapore 1945–1983*. Honours Thesis, Murdoch University, 1995.

Loh Wen Fong. *Singapore Agency Houses, 1819–1900.* Honours Thesis, University of Malaya, Singapore, 1958.

Menon, Vila-sini. *The Singapore Houses of Agency, 1900–1940.* Honours Thesis, University of Malaya, Singapore, 1958.

Nair, P Prabhakaran. *Indian Labour in the Singapore Lighterage Industry.* Dissertation, Department of Social Studies, University of Malaya, Singapore, 1958.

Ngiam Tong Dow. *Chinese Labour and Tongkang Trade in Singapore 1958.* Graduation Exercise, History Department, University of Malaya, Singapore, 1958/59.

Niva, Dutt. *A Study of the Entrepot Trade in Rice and Rice Products.* Dissertation, Faculty of Arts, University of Malaya, Singapore, 1961.

Ong Tion-Whatt. *Farquhar's Administration of Singapore, 1819–1823.* Honours Thesis, University of Malaya, Singapore, 1959.

Rajah Thavamani Devi. *John Crawfurd, Resident of Singapore, 1823–1826.* Honours Thesis, University of Malaya, Singapore, 1959.

Tan Bee Choo. *Street Names in Selected Areas of Singapore: A Study in Historical Geography.* Academic Exercise, Department of Geography, University of Singapore, Singapore, 1976/77.

Tay Seow-huah. *The History of the Singapore Police Force, 1819–1889.* Honours Thesis, University of Malaya, Singapore, 1956.

Tiwary, Ram Avadh. *Raffles at Singapore.* Honours Thesis, University of Malaya, Singapore, 1952.

Yap Aik Kun. *The Singapore River: Economic Landscape in Retrospect.* Academic Exercise, Department of Geography, National University of Singapore, 1983/84.

Yeo, Katherine. *Hawkers and the State in Colonial Singapore: Mid-nineteenth Century to 1939.* Master's Thesis, Melbourne: Monash University, 1989.

Journals

Abdullah, Munshi. 'The Hikayat Abdullah'. Trans. AH Hill. *Journal of the Malayan Branch of the Royal Asiatic Society* 28, no. 3 (June 1955).

Alfred, Eric. 'Boats of Singapore'. *Journal of the Malayan Branch of the Royal Asiatic Society* 60, no. 2 (1987).

Barnes, Warren. 'Singapore Old Straits and New Harbour'. *Journal of the Straits Branch of the Royal Asiatic Society* 60 (1911).

Bartley, W. 'The Population of Singapore in 1819'. *Journal of the Malayan Branch of the Royal Asiatic Society* 11, no. 2 (1933).

Bellett, J. 'Singapore's Central Area Retail Pattern in Transition'. *The Journal of Tropical Geography* 28 (June 1969).

Birch, E. 'The Vernacular Press in the Straits'. *Journal of the Straits Branch of the Royal Asiatic Society* no. 4 (December 1879).

Bogaars, George. 'The Effect of the Opening of the Suez Canal on the Trade and Development of Singapore'. *Journal of the Malayan Branch of the Royal Asiatic Society* 23, no. 1 (1955).

Blythe, WL. 'Historical Sketch of Chinese Labour in Malaya'. *Journal of the Malayan Branch of the Royal Asiatic Society* 20, no. 1 (1947).

Braddell, Ronald. 'Lung-Ya-Men and Tan Ma Hsi'. *Journal of the Malaysian Branch of the Royal Asiatic Society* 23, no. 1 (February 1950).

Braddell, Thomas. 'Resident's Report — Notices of Singapore 1819'. *Journal of the Indian Archipelago and Eastern Asia* 8, series 1 (1854).

____. 'Resident's Report — Notices of Singapore 1819'. *Journal of the Indian Archipelago and Eastern Asia* 9, series 1 (1855).

Braudel, Fernand. 'Personal Testimony'. *Journal of Modern History* 44, no. 1 (1972).

Broeze, Frank. 'Port Cities the Search for an Identity'. *Journal of Urban History* 11, no. 2 (1985).

____ *et al.* 'Imperial Ports and the Modern World Economy: The Case of the Indian Ocean'. *The Journal of Transport History* 7, no. 3 (1986).

Brown, CC, trans. 'Temasek and Singapura: An Extract from the Malaya Annals'. *Journal of the Malaysian Branch of the Royal Asiatic Society* 25, no. 2 (February 1952).

Burton, S. 'History with a Bottom Line'. *Time*, 12 July 1993.

Chang Hai Ding. 'The Early Shipping Conference System of Singapore, 1897–1911'. *Journal of Southeast Asian History* 10, no. 1 (1969).

Cheng Lim Keak. 'Pang Trade Specialisation in Singapore'. *Review of Asian Studies* 8 (December 1978).

Cheng U Wen. 'Opium in the Straits Settlements'. *Journal of Southeast Asian History* 2, no. 1 (1961).

Colless, Brian. 'The Early Western Ports of the Malay Peninsula'. *The Journal of Tropical Geography* 29 (December 1969).

Crane, TO. 'Remarks on the Cultivation of Cotton in Singapore'. *The Journal of the Indian Archipelago and Eastern Asia* 5, series 1 (1853).

De Josselin de Jong, P. E. 'Who's who in the Malay Annals Part I'. *Journal of the Malaysian Branch of the Royal Asiatic Society* 34, no. 2 (1973). Reprint, *Singapore 150 Years* (Singapore: Times Books International, 1982), 150th anniversary of the founding of Singapore commemorative book.

Ee, Joyce. 'Chinese Migration to Singapore, 1896–1941'. *Journal of Southeast Asian History* 2 (1961).

Firmstone, HW. 'Chinese Names of Streets and Places in Singapore and the Malay Peninsula'. *Journal of the Straits Branch of the Royal Asiatic Society* 42 (February 1905).

Freedman, Maurice. 'Colonial Law and Chinese Society'. *The Journal of the Royal Anthropological Institute of Great Britain and Ireland* 80 (1950).

____. 'Immigrants and Associations: Chinese in Nineteenth-Century Singapore'. *Comparative Studies in Society and History* 3 (1960–61).

____. 'Overseas Chinese Associations: A Comment'. *Comparative Studies in Society and History* 3 (1960–61).

Gibson-Hill, CA. 'Tongkang and Lighter Matters'. *Journal of the Malayan Branch of the Royal Asiatic Society* 25, no. 1 (1952).

____. 'The Orang Laut of Singapore River and the Sampan Panjang'. *Journal of the Malayan Branch of the Royal Asiatic Society* 25, no. 1 (1952).

____. 'The Master Attendants (Harbour Masters) at Singapore, 1819–67'. *Journal of the Malayan Branch of the Royal Asiatic Society* 33, no. 1 (1960).

____. 'Singapore: Notes on the History of the Old Straits, 1580–1850'. *Journal of the Malayan Branch of the Royal Asiatic Society* 27, no. 1 (1954).

____. 'The Date of Munshi Abdullah's First Visit to Singapore'. *Journal of the Malaysian Branch of the Royal Asiatic Society* 28, no. 1 (March 1955).

____. 'The Singapore Chronicle'. *Journal of the Malaysian Branch of the Royal Asiatic Society* 26, no. 1 (July 1953).

Hanitsch, R. 'Letters of Nathaniel Wallich 1822'. *Journal of the Straits Branch of the Royal Asiatic Society*, no. 65 (December 1913).

Haughton, HT. 'Notes on Names of Places in the Island of Singapore and its Vicinity'. *Journal of the Straits Branch of the Royal Asiatic Society*, no. 20 (1889).

——. 'The Landing of Raffles in Singapore. By an Eye Witness'. *Journal of the Straits Branch of the Royal Asiatic Society*, no. 10 (December 1882).

——. 'Native Names of Streets in Singapore'. *Journal of the Straits Branch of the Royal Asiatic Society*, no. 23 (June 1891).

Hexter, JH. 'Fernand Braudel, The Annales, and the Mediterranean'. *Journal of Modern History* 44, no. 1 (1972).

Hill, AH. 'The Founding of Singapore Described by, Munshi Abdullah'. *Journal of the Malayan Branch of the Royal Asiatic Society* 28, no. 3 (1955).

Hodder, B. 'Racial Groupings in Singapore'. *The Malayan Journal of Tropical Geography* 1 (October 1953).

Hough, GG. 'Notes on the Educational Policy of Sir Stamford Raffles'. *Journal of the Malaysian Branch of the Royal Asiatic Society* 11, no. 2 (December 1953).

Hsu, Yun-Tsiao. 'Singapore in the Remote Past'. *Journal of the Malaysian Branch of the Royal Asiatic Society* 45, no. 1 (January 1973).

Jackson, James C. 'Chinese Agricultural Pioneering in Singapore and Johor 1800–1917'. *Journal of the Malayan Branch of the Royal Asiatic Society* 38, no. 1 (1965).

Kernial Singh Sandhu. 'Some Aspects of Indian Settlement in Singapore, 1819–1969'. *Journal of Southeast Asian History* 10, no. 2 (1969).

Kong, Lily and Brenda Yeoh. 'Urban Conservation in Singapore: A Survey of State Policies and Popular Attitudes'. *Urban Studies* 31, no. 2 (1994).

Lew, Alan. 'English Speaking Tourists and the Attractions of Singapore'. *Singapore Journal of Tropical Geography* 8, no. 1 (1987).

Lian Kwen Fee. 'In Search of a History of Singapore'. *Southeast Asian Journal of Social Science* 20, no. 1 (1992).

Linehan, W. 'The Kings of 14th Century Singapore'. *Journal of the Malayan Branch of the Royal Asiatic Society* 20, no. 2 (December 1947).

Little, R. 'On the Habitual Use of Opium in Singapore'. *The Journal of the Indian Archipelago and Eastern Asia* 2, series 1 (1848).

Logan, JR. 'Manufacture of Pearl Sago in Singapore by Chinese'. *Journal of the Indian Archipelago and Eastern Asia* 3, series 1 (1849).

Mak Lau Fong and Him M Lai. 'Occupational Structures of Chinese Immigrants in Early Malaya and North America'. *Southeast Asian Journal of Social Science* 20, no. 1 (1992).

Maxwell, WE. 'The Founding of Singapore'. *Journal of the Straits Branch of the Royal Asiatic Society*, no. 4 (1973). Reprint, *Singapore 150 Years* (Singapore: Times Books International, 1982), 150th anniversary of the founding of Singapore commemorative book.

Miller, HE. 'Letter from Col. Nahuijs, 1824'. *Journal of the Malaysian Branch of the Royal Asiatic Society* 19, no. 2 (October 1941).

Murphey, Rhoads. 'Traditionalism and Colonialism: Changing Urban Roles in Asia'. *Journal of Asian Studies* 29, no. 1 (1969).

Neville, R. 'The Areal Distribution of Population in Singapore'. *The Journal of Tropical Geography* 20 (June 1965).

Ng Siew Yoong. 'The Chinese Protectorate in Singapore'. *Journal of Southeast Asian History* 2, no. 1 (1961).

Ooi Giok Ling. 'Harmonising Environment and Development: Ideological and Other Considerations'. *Southeast Asian Journal of Social Science* 20, no. 1 (1992).

Pearson, HF. 'Singapore from the Sea'. *Journal of the Malayan Branch of the Royal Asiatic Society* 26, no. 1 (1953).

——. 'Lt. Jackson's Plan of Singapore'. *Journal of the Malayan Branch of the Royal Asiatic Society* 26, no. 1 (1953).

Pearson, MN. 'Littoral Society: The Case for the Coast'. *The Great Circle* 7, no. 1 (1985).

Pit Kuan Wah. 'Chinese Coolie Immigrants in Nineteenth Century Singapore'. *Review of Asian Studies* 14 (June 1984).

Raffles, TS. 'The Founding of Singapore'. *Journal of the Straits Branch of the Royal Asiatic Society* 2 (1878).

Read, WH. 'The Landing of Raffles in Singapore'. *Journal of the Straits Branch of the Royal Asiatic Society*, no. 12 (1883).

Reid, Anthony. 'The Structure of Cities in Southeast Asia; Fifteenth to Seventeenth Century'. *Journal of Southeast Asian Studies* 11, no. 2 (1980).

Saw Swee-Hock. 'Population Trends in Singapore, 1819–1967'. *Journal of Southeast Asian History* 10, no. 1 (1969).

Savage, Victor. 'Singapore's Garden City: Reality, Symbol, Ideal'. *Solidarity* 131–32 (July–December 1991).

Siah U Chin. 'The Chinese in Singapore: General Sketch of the Numbers, Tribes, and Vocations of the Chinese in Singapore'. *Journal of the Indian Archipelago and Eastern Asia* 2 (1848).

Sim Loo Lee. 'Urban Conservation Policy and the Preservation of Historical and Cultural Heritage'. *Cities* 13, no. 6 (1996).

Skeat, WW and HN Ridley. 'The Orang Laut of Singapore'. *Journal of the Straits Branch of the Royal Asiatic Society*, no. 33 (January 1900).

Sowell, Thomas. 'How Civilizations Advance'. *Dialogue*, no. 95 (January 1992).

Tamanoi, Mariko Asano. 'Songs as Weapons: The Culture and History of Komori (Nursemaids) in Modern Japan'. *The Journal of Asian Studies* 50, no. 4 (November 1991).

Tan Kee Soon. 'An Index to the Chinese Names of Streets and Places in Singapore'. *Journal of the Straits Branch of the Royal Asiatic Society*, no. 46 (December 1906).

Teo, Peggy and Shirlena Huang. 'Tourism and Heritage Conservation in Singapore'. *Annals of Tourism Research* 22, no. 3 (1995).

Teo, Peggy and Brenda Yeoh. 'Remaking Local Heritage for Tourism'. *Annals of Tourism Research* 24, no. 1 (1997).

Topley, Marjorie. 'The Emergence and Social Function of Chinese Religious Associations in Singapore'. *Comparative Studies in Society and History* 3 (1960–61).

Tregonning, KG. 'The Origin of the Straits Steamship Company in 1890'. *Journal of the Malayan Branch of the Royal Asiatic Society* 38, no. 2 (1965).

Trevor-Roper, HR. 'Fernand Braudel and the Monde Braudellien'. *Journal of Modern History* 44, no. 1 (1972).

Trimmer, GW. 'The Port of Singapore'. *British Malaya* (March 1936).

Trocki, CA. 'The Origins of the Kangchu System 1740–1860'. *Journal of the Malaysian Branch of the Royal Asiatic Society* 49, no. 2 (1976).

Turnbull, M. 'Bibliography of Writings on British Malaya, 1786–1867'. *Journal of the Malayan Branch of the Royal Asiatic Society* 33, no. 3 (1960).

____. 'The European Mercantile Community in Singapore'. *Journal of Southeast Asian History* 10, no. 1 (1969).

Van Stein, Callenfels. 'The Founder of Malacca'. *Journal of the Malayan Branch of the Royal Asiatic Society* 15, no. 2 (September 1937).

Wang, T.P. 'Chinese Towkay and Worker Strikes in the Straits Settlements (1857–1900) With Special Reference to Singapore'. *Review of Southeast Asian Studies* 11 (1981).

Warren, James. 'Prostitution and the Politics of Venereal Disease, 1870–1898'. *Journal of Southeast Asian Studies* 21, no. 2 (September 1990).

——. 'The Ah Ku and Karayuki-San of Singapore — Their Lives: Sources, Method and a Historian's Representation'. *Southeast Asian Journal of Social Science* 20, no. 1 (1992).

Weigend, Guido G. 'Ports: "Their Hinterlands and Forelands"'. *The Geographical Review* 42, no. 4 (1952).

——. 'Some Elements in the Study of Port Geography'. *The Geographical Review* 48 (1958).

——. 'River Ports and Outports: Matadi and Banana'. *The Geographical Review* 44, no. 3 (1954).

Wheatley, Paul. 'Land Use in the Vicinity of Singapore in the Eighteen-Thirties'. *The Malaysian Journal of Tropical Geography* 2 (March 1954).

Wikkramatileke, R. 'Focus on Singapore'. *The Journal of Tropical Geography* 20 (June 1965).

Wilkinson, R.J. 'Old Singapore'. *Journal of the Malaysian Branch of the Royal Asiatic Society* 13, no. 1 (March 1935).

Williams, Lea. 'Chinese Leadership in Early British Singapore'. *Asian Studies*, 2, no. 2 (1964).

Winstedt, R.O. 'Tumasek or Old Singapore'. *Journal of the Malayan Branch of the Royal Asiatic Society* 13, no. 2 (October 1935).

——. 'Gold Ornaments Dug up at Fort Canning, Singapore'. *Journal of the Malayan Branch of the Royal Asiatic Society* 6, no. 4 (November 1928).

Wong Lin Ken. 'The Trade of Singapore, 1819–69'. *Journal of the Malayan Branch of the Royal Asiatic Society* 33, no. 4 (December 1960).

——. 'Singapore its Growth as an Entrepot Port, 1819–1994'. *Journal of Southeast Asian Studies* 9, no. 1 (1978).

Yeoh, Brenda and Shirlena Huang. 'The Conservation-redevelopment Dilemma in Singapore: The Case of the Kampong Glam Historic District'. *Cities* 13, no. 6 (1996).

Yeoh, Brenda and Lily Kong. 'Reading Landscape Meanings: State Construction and Lived Experiences in Singapore's Chinatown'. *Habitat* 18, no. 4 (1994).

——. 'The Notion of Place in the Construction of History, Nostalgia and Heritage in Singapore'. *Singapore Journal of Tropical Geography* 17, no. 1 (June 1996).

Yen Ching-hwang. 'Ch'ing's Sale of Honours and the Chinese Leadership in Singapore and Malaya (1877–1912)'. *Journal of Southeast Asian Studies* 1, no. 2 (1970).

——. 'Early Chinese Clan Organisations in Singapore and Malaya, 1819–1911'. *Journal of Southeast Asian Studies* 12, no. 1 (1981).

Yong Ching Fatt. 'A Preliminary Study of Chinese Leadership in Singapore, 1900–1941'. *Journal of Southeast Asian History* 9, no. 2 (1968).

——. 'Pang, Pang Organizations and Leadership in the Chinese Community of Singapore During the 1930s'. *Journal of the South Seas Society* 32, Parts 1 and 2 (1977).

Books

Adas, Micheal. *Machines as the Measure of Man: Science, Technology, and Ideologies of Western Dominance* (Ithaca: Cornell University Press, 1989).

Arasaratnam, S. *Indians in Malaysia and Singapore* (Great Britain: Oxford University Press, 1970).

Baker, Hugh DR. *Chinese Family and Kinship* (London: Macmillan Press, 1979).

Basu, Dilip (ed.), *The Rise and Growth of the Colonial Port Cities in Asia* (Lanham: University Press of America, 1985).

Begbie, PJ. *The Malayan Peninsula.* Reprint, Oxford in Asia Historical Reprints (Kuala Lumpur: Oxford University Press, 1967).

Bennett, George. *Wanderings in New South Wales, Batavia, Pedir Coast, Singapore, and China: Being the Journal of a Naturalist in those Countries, during 1832, 1833 and 1834.* Vols. 1 and 2 (London: R Bentley, 1834).

Berry, Linda. *Singapore River a Living Legacy* (Singapore: Eastern Universities Press, 1982).

Bickmore, Albert. *Travels in the East Indian Archipelago* (London: J Murray, 1868).

Bird, James. *Seaport Gateways of Australia* (Great Britain: Oxford University Press, 1968).

Bogaars, George. *The Tanjong Pagar Dock Company 1864–1905.* Memoirs of the Raffles Museum, no. 3, Singapore, December 1956.

Braudel, Fernand. *The Mediterranean and the Mediterranean World in the Age of Philip II.* Vols. 1 and 2 (London: Collins, 1974).

Broeze, Frank (ed.), *Brides of the Sea: Port Cities of Asia from the 16th–20th Centuries* (Honolulu: University of Hawaii Press, 1989).

— (ed.), *Gateways of Asia: Port Cities of Asia in the 13th–20th Centuries* (New York: Kegan Paul International, 1997).

Buckley, CB. *An Anecdotal History of Old Times in Singapore 1819–1867* (Singapore: Oxford University Press, 1902), Reprint 1984.

Burke, Peter (ed.), *New Perspectives on Historical Writing* (England: Polity Press, 1991).

Bury, JB. *The Idea of Progress an Inquiry into its Growth and Origin* (New York: Dover Publications Inc., 1955).

Campbell, Persia Crawford. *Chinese Coolie Emigration to Countries Within the British Empire* (Great Britain: Frank Cass & Co Ltd, 1971).

Cameron, John. *Our Tropical Possessions in Malayan India.* Oxford in Asia Historical Reprints (Kuala Lumpur: Oxford University Press, 1865), Reprint 1965.

Castells, M. 'Four Asian Tigers with a Dragon Head: A Pacific Rim'. In R Appelbaum and J Henderson (eds), *State and Development in the Asian Pacific Rim* (Newbury Park: Sage, 1992).

____. *The Urban Question a Marxist Approach* (Great Britain: Edward Arnold, 1977).

Chen Mong Hock. *The Early Chinese Newspapers of Singapore 1881–1912* (Singapore: University of Malaya Press, 1967).

Ch'en Jerome and Nicholas Tarling (eds.), *Studies in the Social History of China and South-East Asia* (Great Britain: Cambridge University Press, 1970).

Cheng Lim-Keak. *Social Change and the Chinese in Singapore* (Singapore: Singapore University Press, 1985).

Chew, Ernest and Edwin Lee (ed), *A History of Singapore* (Singapore: Oxford University Press, 1991).

Chia Lin Sien, *et al. The Coastal Environmental Profile of Singapore.* Technical Publications Series 3. Association of Southeast Asian Nations/United States Coastal Resources Management Project. Manila, 1988.

Chia Lin Sien and Chou Loke Ming (eds). *Urban Coastal Area Management: The Experience of Singapore.* Conference Proceedings 7. Association of Southeast Asian Nations/United States Coastal Resources Management Project, 1991.

Chiang Hai Ding. 'Sino-British Mercantile Relations in Singapore's Entrepot Trade 1870–1915'. In, Jerome Ch'en and Nicholas Tarling, eds. *Studies in the Social History of China and Southeast Asia* (Cambridge: Cambridge University Press, 1970).

——. *A History of Straits Settlements Foreign Trade 1870–1915*. Memoirs of the National Museum, no. 6, Singapore, 1978.

Cipolla, Carlo. *European Culture and Overseas Expansion* (Great Britain: Pelican Books, 1970).

Clutterbuck, R. *Riot and Revolution in Singapore and Malaya, 1945–1963* (London: Faber and Faber, 1973).

Coffin, Charles Carleton. *Our New Way Around the World* (London: Sampson Low, Son and Marston, 1869).

Crawfurd, John. *History of the Indian Archipelago: Containing an Account of the Manners, Arts, Languages, Religions, Institutions, and Commerce of its Inhabitants*. 3 vols. (Edinburgh: Constable and Hurst, 1820).

——. *Crawfurd's Descriptive Dictionary of the Indian Islands and Adjacent Countries* (London: Bradbury and Evans, 1856).

Cunyngham-Brown, Sjovald. *The Traders: A Story of Britain's Southeast Asian Commercial Adventure* (Great Britain: Newman Neame, 1971).

D'Aranjo, BE. *The Stranger's Guide to Singapore with Maps* (Singapore: Siragoon Press, 1890).

Davidson, GF. *Trade and Travel in the Far East or Recollections of Twenty-one Years Passed in Java, Singapore, Australia, and China* (London: Madden and Malcolm, 1846).

Davis, Donald. *Old Singapore* (Singapore: Donald Moore, 1954).

Dixon, Alec. *Singapore Patrol* (London: George G Harrap & Co Ltd, 1935).

Earl, George Windsor. *The Eastern Seas or Voyages and Adventures in the Indian Archipelago, in 1832–33–34* (London: Wm H Allen and Co. 1837).

Eastman, Llyod. *Family Field and Ancestors* (New York: Oxford University Press, 1988).

Edwards, Norman. *The Singapore House and Residential Life 1819–1939* (Singapore: Oxford University Press, 1990).

Edwards, Norman and Peter Keys. *Singapore: A Guide to Buildings, Streets, Places* (Singapore: Times Books International, 1988).

Emerson, Rupert. *Malaysia a Study in Direct and Indirect Rule* (Kuala Lumpur: University of Malaya Press, 1970).

Evers, Hans-Dieter and Korff Rüdiger. *Southeast Asian Urbanism The Meaning and Power of Social Space* (New York: St Martins' Press Inc, 2002).

Firbank, LT. *A History of Fort Canning*. Stamped University of Singapore Library, February 1963. National University of Singapore.

Forbes, DK. *Asian Metropolis: Urbanisation and the Southeast Asian City* (Melbourne: Oxford University Press, 1996).

Freedman, Maurice. *Chinese Family and Marriage in Singapore* (London: HMSO, 1957).

——. *Chinese Lineage and Society; Fukien and Kwangtung* (London: Athlone, 1966).

——. *The Study of Chinese Society. Essays by Maurice Freedman* (Stanford: Stanford University Press, 1979).

Fujimoto, Helen. *The South Indian Muslim Community and the Evolution of the Jawi Peranakan in Penang up to 1948*. ILCAA (Tokyo: Gaikokugo Daigaku, 1988).

Gamba, C. *The Origins of Trade Unionism in Malaya: A Study of Colonial Labour Unrest* (Singapore: D Moore for Eastern Universities Press, 1962).

Gamer, Robert. *The Politics of Urban Development in Singapore* (Ithaca: Cornell University Press, 1972).

Gibson-Hill, CA. *Singapore Old Strait and New Harbour 1300–1870.* Memoirs of the Raffles Museum, no. 3, Singapore, December 1956.

Ginzburg, Carlo. *The Cheese and the Worms: The Cosmos of a Sixteenth-Century Miller.* Trans. by John and Anne Tedeschi (London: Routledge & Kegan Paul, 1980).

Gondiarov, Ivan. *The Voyage of the Frigate Pallada.* Ed. and trans. by NW Wilson (London: The Folio Society, 1965).

Greenberg, Micheal. *British Trade and the Opening of China 1800–42* (Great Britain: Cambridge University Press, 1969).

Grew, JC. *Sort and Travel in the Far East* (London: Constable & Company, 1910).

Hall, Kenneth. *Explorations in Early Southeast Asian History.* Ann Arbor, Centre for South and Southeast Asian Studies (Ann Arbor: University of Michigan, 1976).

Hamilton, Alexander. *A New Account of the East Indies.* Vols. 1 and 2. Reprint 1727 (England: The Argonaut Press, 1930).

Hancock, TH. *Coleman's Singapore.* Monograph No. 15 (Kuala Lumpur: The Malaysian Branch of the Royal Asiatic Society in association with Pelanduk Publications, 1986).

Heraud, John A. *Voyages and Memoirs of a Midshipman* (London: James Fraser, 1837). Based on the logs of a midshipman, Mr William Robinson.

Hervey, Harry. *When Strange Gods Call Pages Out of the East* (New York: The Century Company, 1924).

Hon, Joan. *Tidal Fortunes, a Story of Change: The Singapore River and Kallang Basin* (Singapore: Landmark Books, n.d.).

Hornaday, William T. *Two Years in the Jungle: the Experiences of a Hunter and Naturalist* (London: Keagan Paul, Trench & Co, 1885).

Ileto, Reynaldo. *Pasyon and Revolution: Popular Movements in the Philippines, 1840–1910* (Manila: Ateneo de Manila University Press, 1979).

Jackson, RN. *Immigrant Labour and the Development of Malaya* (Malaya: Government Printer, 1961).

____. *Pickering Protector of Chinese* (Kuala Lumpur: Oxford University Press, 1965).

Josey, Alex. *Trade Unionism in Malaya* (Singapore: D. Moore, 1958).

Kapur, Basant (ed.). *Singapore Studies: Critical Surveys of the Humanities and Social Sciences* (Singapore: Singapore University Press, 1986).

Kathirithamby-Wells, J and Villiers, John (ed.). *The Southeast Asian Port and Polity: Rise and Demise* (Singapore: Singapore University Press, 1990).

Kernial Singh Sandhu. *Indians in Malaya Immigration and Settlement 1786–1957* (London: Cambridge University Press, 1969).

____ *et al.* (eds.). *Management of Success the Moulding of Modern Singapore* (Singapore: Institute of Southeast Asian Studies, 1989).

Lee Poh Ping. *Chinese Society in Nineteenth Century Singapore* (Kuala Lumpur: Oxford University Press, 1978).

Lee Ting Hui. *The Communist Organization in Singapore: Its Techniques of Manpower Mobilization and Management, 1948–66.* Field Report Series No. 12 (Singapore: Institute of Southeast Asian Studies, August 1976).

Le Roy Ladurie, Emmanuel. *Montaillou: Cathars and Catholics in a French Village 1294–1324.* Trans. Barbara Bray (London: Scolar, 1978).

Lilley, S. *Men, Machines and History the Story of Tools and Machines in Relation to Social Progress* (Great Britain: Lawrence & Wishart, 1965).

Lim William. *Asian New Urbanism and Other Papers* (Singapore: Select Books, 1998).

Lowenthal, David. *The Past is a Foreign Country* (Great Britain: Cambridge University Press, 1990).

Ludvig, Verner Helms. *Pioneering in the Far East* (London: WH Allen & Co, 1882).

Luscombe, FM. *Singapore 1890–1930* (Singapore: CA Ribeiro and Co, 1930).

Makepeace, Walter, *et al. One Hundred Years of Singapore*, Vols. I and II (London: John Murray, 1921).

Mak Lau Fong. *The Sociology of Secret Societies. A Study of Chinese Secret Societies in Singapore and Peninsular Malaysia* (Kuala Lumpur: Oxford University Press, 1981).

McGee, TG. 'Beach-heads and Enclaves: The Urban Debate and Urbanisation Process in South-East Asia Since 1945'. In YM Yeung and CP Lo (eds.), *Changing Southeast Asian Cities: Readings in Urbanisation* (Singapore: Oxford University Press, 1972).

McNair, JF and WD Bayliss. *Prisoners their Own Warders* (Westminster: A Constable, 1899).

Mills, Lennox. *British Rule in Eastern Asia a Study of Contemporary Government and Economic Development in British Malaya and Hong Kong* (New York: Russell & Russell, 1970).

Minchin, James. *No Man is an Island a Portrait of Singapore's Lee Kuan Yew* (Australia: Allen and Unwin, 1990).

Moor, JH. *Notices of the Indian Archipelago and Adjacent Countries.* Reprint 1837 (Great Britain: Frank Cass & Co Ltd, 1968).

Mulliner, K and Lian The-Mulliner. *Historical Dictionary of Singapore* (London: The Scarecrow Press Inc, 1991).

Mundy, Captain Rodney RN. *Narrative of Events in Borneo and Celebes Down to the Occupation of Labuan: From the Journals of James Brooke, Esq. Together with a Narrative of the Operations of H.M.S Iris.* Vols. 1 and 2 (London: John Murray, 1848).

Murfett, Malcolm, *et al. Between Two Oceans: A Military History of Singapore From First Settlement to Final British Withdrawal* (Singapore: Oxford University Press, 1999).

Mydin, Iskander. *Pioneers of the Streets* (Singapore: Art, Antiques and Antiquities, 1989).

Netto, George. *Indians in Malaya Historical Facts and Figures* (Singapore: Published by author, 1961).

Newbold, TJ. *British Settlements in the Straits of Malacca.* Vols. I and II. Reprint (Singapore: Oxford University Press, 1971).

Ooi Jin Bee and Chiang Hai Ding (eds.). *Modern Singapore* (Singapore: University of Singapore Press, 1969).

Pacey, Arnold. *Technology in World Civilisation: A Thousand-Year History* (Oxford: Basil Blackwell, 1990).

——. *The Maze of Ingenuity Ideas and Idealism in the Development of Technology* (London: Lane, 1974).

Pan, Lynn. *Sons of the Yellow Emperor the Story of the Overseas Chinese* (Great Britain: Mandarin, 1991).

Pearson, HF. *Stories of Old Singapore* (London: University of London Press, 1953).

——. *People of Early Singapore* (London: University of London Press, 1955).

Pelras, Christian. *The Bugis* (Oxford: Blackwell Publishers, 1996).

Perry M, L Kong and B Yeoh. *Singapore a Developmental City State* (England: John Wiley & Sons, 1997).

Phipps, J. *A Practical Treatise on the China and Eastern Trade: Comprising the Commerce of Great Britain and India, Particularly Bengal and Singapore, with China and the Eastern Seas* (Calcutta: Sold by Thacker, 1835).

Pridmore, F. *Coins and Coinage of the Straits Settlements and British Malaya, 1786–1951*. Memoirs of the Raffles Museum, no. 2. Singapore, June 1955.

Raffles, Sophia (Lady). *Memoir of the Life and Public Services of Sir Thomas Stamford Raffles*. Reprint, Oxford in Asia Hardback Reprints (Singapore: Oxford University Press, 1991).

Raja-Singam, S Durai. *Malayan Street Names: What They Mean and Who They Commemorate* (Ipoh: Mercantile Press, 1939).

Rathbourne, B. Ambrose. *Camping and Tramping in the Malaya Fifteen Years, Pioneering in the Native States of the Malay Peninsula* (London: Swan Sonnenschein & Co, 1898).

Reid, Anthony. *Southeast Asia in the Age of Commerce 1450–1680* (New Haven: Yale University Press, 1988).

Rennie, JSM. *Musings of JMSR mostly Malayan* (Singapore: Malaya Publishing House, 1933).

Robson, JHM. *People in a Native State* (Singapore: The Singapore and Straits Printing Office, 1894).

Rodan, G. *The Political Economy of Singapore's Industrialisation: National State and International Capital* (Hong Kong: Macmillan Press, 1989).

Salim, Agus. *Kisah Raja Raja Melayu Singapura* (Kuala Lumpur: Dewan Bahasa dan Pustaka, 1969).

Schama, Simon. *Landscape and Memory* (London: Fontana Press, 1995).

Scott, James. *The Moral Economy of the Peasant Rebellion and Subsistence in Southeast Asia* (New Haven and London: Yale University Press, 1979).

Sharpley, R. *Tourism, Tourists and Society* (Huntingdon: ELM Publications, 1994).

Sherry, Norman. *Conrad's Eastern World* (London: Cambridge University Press, 1966).

Siddique, Sharon and Nirmala Shotam. *Singapore's Little India Past, Present and Future* (Singapore: Institute of Southeast Asian Studies, 1982).

Song Ong Siang. *One Hundred Years, History of the Chinese in Singapore* (London: John Murray, 1923).

Spence, Jonathan *The Death of Woman Wang* (Harmondsworth, England: Penguin, 1979).

——. *The Gate of Heavenly Peace: The Chinese and their Revolution, 1895–1980* (New York: Viking Press, 1981).

——. *Emperor of China; Self Portrait of Kàng-hsi* (London: Cape, 1974).

Spengler, Oswald. *The Decline of the West* (Great Britain: George Allen & Unwin, 1971).

Stainer, RF. *A Short Geography of the Malay Peninsula* (Singapore: The American Mission Press, 1901).

Steinberg, David. *In Search of Southeast Asia* (Honolulu: University of Hawaii Press, 1987).

Stenson, MR. *Industrial Conflict in Malaya: Prelude to the Communist Revolt* (London: Oxford University Press, 1970).

Sullivan, Margaret. *'Can Survive, La' Cottage Industries in High-rise Singapore* (Singapore: Graham Brash, 1985).

Ta Chen. *Emigrant Communities in South China:A Study of Overseas Migration and its Influence on Standards of Living and Social Change.* English version edited by Bruno Lasker (New York: AMS Press, 1978).

Tan, Sumiko. *Streets of Old Chinatown Singapore* (Singapore: Page Media Pte Ltd, 1990).

Tamney, Joseph. *The Struggle over Singapore's Soul:Western Modernisation and Asian Culture* (New York: Walter de Gruyter, 1996).

Tarling, Nicholas. *Anglo-Dutch Rivalry in the Malay World, 1780–1824* (Brisbane: University of Queensland Press, 1962).

——. *British Policy in the Malay Peninsula and Archipelago 1824–1871.* Reprint, Oxford in Asia Paperbacks (Kuala Lumpur: Oxford University Press, 1969).

——. *Imperial Britain in Southeast Asia* (Kuala Lumpur and New York: Oxford University Press, 1975).

Theroux, Paul. *Saint Jack* (England: Penguin Books, 1976).

Thompson, V. *Labor Problems in Southeast Asia* (New Haven: Yale University Press, 1947).

Tosh, John. *The Pursuit of History: Aims, Methods and New Directions in the Study of Modern History* (England: Longman, 1998).

Tregonning, KG. *Home Port Singapore:A History of the Straits Steamship Company Limited 1890–1965* (Singapore: Oxford University Press, 1967).

Trocki, C. *The Temenggongs of Johor, 1784–1885.* PhD Thesis, Cornell University, 1975.

——. *Prince of Pirates: The Temenggongs and the Development of Johor and Singapore, 1784–1885* (Singapore: Singapore University Press, 1979).

——. *Opium and Empire Chinese Society in Colonial Singapore, 1800–1910* (Ithaca: Cornell University Press, 1990).

Turnbull, CM. *The Straits Settlements 1826–67: Indian Presidency to Crown Colony* (London: Athlone Press, 1972).

——. *A History of Singapore 1819–1988* (Singapore: Oxford University Press, 1989).

Vaughan, JD. *The Manners and Customs of the Chinese of the Straits Settlements.* Reprint 1879, Oxford in Asia Paperbacks (Kuala Lumpur: Oxford University Press, 1977).

Warren, James. *Rickshaw Coolie: A People's History of Singapore 1880–1940* (Singapore: Oxford University Press, 1986).

——. *At the Edge of Southeast Asian History* (Manila: New Day Publishers, 1987).

——. *Ah Ku and Karayuki-San: Prostitution in Singapore 1870–1940* (Singapore: Oxford University Press, 1993).

Wheatley, Paul. *The Golden Khersonese* (Kuala Lumpur: University of Malaya Press, 1961).

——. *The Kings of the Mountain: An Indian Contribution to Statecraft in Southeast Asia* (Kuala Lumpur: University of Malaya, 1980).

Wise, Micheal (ed.). *Traveller's Tales of Old Singapore* (Singapore: Times Books International, 1985).

Wolters, Oliver. *Early Indonesian Commerce: A Study of the Origins of Srivijaya* (Ithaca: Cornell University Press, 1967).

Wurtzburg, CE. *Raffles of the Eastern Isles.* Edited for publication by C Witting (Singapore: Oxford University Press, 1990).

Yen Ching-hwang. *A Social History of the Chinese in Singapore and Malaya 1800–1911* (Singapore: Oxford University Press, 1986).

Yeoh, Brenda. *Municipal Sanitary Surveillance, Asian Resistance and the Control of the Urban Environment in Singapore.* Research Paper No. 47. School of Geography, Oxford University, 1991.

____. *Contesting Space: Power Relations and the Urban Built Environment in Colonial Singapore* (Kuala Lumpur: Oxford University Press, 1996).

Yvan, Dr., physician to the scientific mission sent by France to China. In, James Blackwood, *Six Months among the Malays and a Year in China* (London: Paternoster Row, 1855).

Index